the Battle of Silence

BY THE SAME AUTHOR

The Silence of the Sea
Three Short Novels
You Shall Know Them
The Insurgents
Sylva
Paths of Love
Quota
The Battle of Silence

the Battle of Silence

VERCORS

Translated from the French by Rita Barisse

HOLT, RINEHART AND WINSTON
NEW YORK   CHICAGO   SAN FRANCISCO

To my sons
To Rita

CONTENTS

PART ONE

PRELUDE
TO A METAMORPHOSIS

In memory of Jean Prévost

I

When the Nazis occupied France after the defeat of 1940, French writers had two alternatives: collaboration or silence. It was to provide them with a means of expression without the enemy's knowledge that the *Editions de Minuit*—the Midnight Press—was founded. At the time, Jean Guéhenno, the essayist, wrote in his diary: 'This is a great honour. By attaching so much importance to our thoughts, a tyrannous power forces us to recognize just how singular and outrageous they are. We had not dared to believe we were so interesting . . . '

'This is a great honour,' was my first thought, too, when I was pressed last year, with friendly insistence, to note down my recollections of those days when we lived under cover. It would never have occurred to me to do so: I had not dared to believe I was so interesting. I had never, like Saint-Simon, consorted with the Great nor had I been subjected, like Châteaubriand, to violent changes of fortune, and their giant shadows were too overwhelming to invite comparison. What had I to tell that was worth the telling? Oh, I admit that the founding of a clandestine press under the nose of the Gestapo, the printing, publishing and distribution, after *The Silence of the Sea*, of some forty other titles, making over twenty-five volumes in all, was something of a *tour de force*. And, certainly, it produced quite a stir inside and outside France. But how could this story of what was basically a spiritual adventure, which unfolded in the midst of the dangers faced by some, the camps and prisons endured by others, the merciless death meted out to still others, without—so far as I was concerned—any of the thousand thrills that go to the making of an epic—how could so unremarkable a tale grip anyone's interest? I was assured very kindly that it would (though I never felt quite convinced). Anyhow, the reader is forewarned: throughout this enterprise, while all around me countless underground companions—writers and intellectuals—were jailed, deported, shot, murdered; while death robbed us of Saint-Pol Roux and Saint-Exupéry, of Benjamin Crémieux and Jean Prévost, of Louis Mandin, Jacques Decour, Max Jacob, Robert Desnos,

Pierre Unik, Marc Bloch and many others whose names are less well known or whom I have forgotten; while other friends, like Jean Paulhan, Gabriel Audisio, Jean Cassou (later to be left for dead by the Nazis on a pavement in Toulouse) spent time in prison or led the hunted lives of outlaws; having to change house, town, province at a moment's notice, 'running in circles round the prison-yard inside the frontiers', as it says in the poignant Complaint of the Clandestine Resister, or even took refuge for a while like Paul Eluard in a lunatic asylum; throughout that time I slept in my bed every night and returned from 'work' in Paris each week to join my family in our country home. Nothing in particular happened to me. There is nothing that I can boast about. I did not, like my friend Emmanuel d'Astier, have to hide in a goods-wagon beneath a pile of shoes, and then, rowed out to sea, leap from a little boat on to a submarine; nor, like Pierre Villon, did I work myself to a shred with walking by day and writing by night, and then have to knock down a member of the Milice on watch outside my flat in a house surrounded by the Gestapo; then hurriedly knot bed-sheets into a rope, only to have the rope tear and pitch me from the third floor into the yard, from which I was transported into a cellar by a panic-stricken fellow-tenant; to persuade him, despite his terror, to notify a couple of doctor friends by dropping into their letter-box a plan scribbled on a small volume of the Editions de Minuit to help them find me; and, returning to consciousness and finding one of the two friends holding my hand to mutter at last: 'You see what the Resistance can make of an intellectual . . . ' The Resistance never made anything of the sort of me. I have no such memories to record, and I can only offer mine as they come back to me now, in their unglamorous sequence.

Let me make myself clear: I am not trying to minimise anything. The perils that surrounded me were just as menacing as those that surrounded them; but the heavy hand of adversity never struck me, nor even brushed my cheek. Whether the rest is worth recording is, I repeat, something I cannot judge. Be that as it may, and what-ever others may think of these pages, I shall not regret having written them. When one's memory begins to fade, when whole slabs of the past, like a brittle cliff eroded by time and tide, crumble and fall into the depth of oblivion, the moment has come to piece together what is left, for later will be too late. I have never managed to keep a diary, and under the Occupation it would have been out of the question anyhow, except for recording meaningless trivia. So there is no other source for my recollections of that period than the dark well in which they slumber, and when the bucket is hauled up one must be content with what one finds in it. In the course of three hundred pages I have hauled up the bucket many times. Such a method, however, means that a tale remembered after a quarter of a century cannot claim the accuracy of a historical record. Gaps, errors, chronological confusions must be expected. If they exist, may I be forgiven: I have done my best. And anyway, I am not writing History. I shall only try to relive, and make others relive, a momentous experience—for me perhaps the most momentous of all: the experience of an individual caught up in the whirlwind of a vast cataclysm who, together with a few friends, attempted at the risk of their lives to save something that mattered to them more than life.

Thus narrowed down to my own person and a handful of others, the story that follows (which begins with a metamorphosis) bears some resemblance—with all due allowances—to the famous stroll of Fabrice at Waterloo. What Stendhal's hero uncomprehendingly perceives of the battle bears no relation to the immensity of the conflict. The events I witnessed and took part in during four years of running the clandestine Editions de Minuit bear no relation to the vast resistance movement of French intellectuals, whose many facets gleamed in the thick of the gigantic battle that shook the earth twenty-five years ago. But if Fabrice's fragmentary view of Waterloo, or Bezukhov's of Austerlitz, have added a new and essential dimension to accounts of battles—narrower no doubt, but also more 'human' than that of the historian's epic panorama— perhaps some sort of equivalent can be found in this plain report of a simple soldier of letters, caught up in the mighty stream of a phantom army.

*   *   *

Before the war I once wrote to the great novelist Roger Martin du Gard, who was very much my senior, to thank him for the friendship he had so generously extended to the young artist and engraver I then was—a friendship, I told him, which I used to dream of as one dreams of becoming an emperor. By way of an answer, he sent me his *African Confidences*, with a sentence from the book as a dedication: 'These things, you see, come about quite naturally.' He meant that if you dream of gaining the friendship of a man you admire, it implies that you are willing to make the effort to rise to his level, and that friendship can then spring up and burgeon 'quite naturally'. But if I had formerly thought of it as a mirage, a hopeless aspiration, it was precisely because I had serious doubts that I should ever be able to reach those heights; and what astounded me was that he already considered it 'quite natural' to treat me as an equal.

Similarly, before the war of 1939, I should have been very much surprised if anyone had predicted that I would participate in it in any capacity other than that of obscure cannon-fodder, that I should play in it 'quite naturally' an 'historic' role, however small. In those days, under my real name of Jean Bruller, I was an artist, living in the country, ambitious as regards his art but not as regards his life, and rather frightened of the world and its trappings; one who, while doing his duty as a voter with a socially progressive outlook and even attending occasional meetings or demonstrations, would never have thought it possible or desirable to intervene actively. Not that he looked down on public affairs—on the contrary: but it did not seem to him that one had the right to become involved with them unless one was prepared to give them all one's time and thought. Or unless one happened to be one of those exceptional figures—a Rubens or a Victor Hugo—who were able to take both art and politics in their stride. I saw this done at first hand by such writers as Jules Romains and Jean-Richard Bloch who were also kind enough to consider me their friend—and through them I was able to keep more personally in touch with the march of History.

Not that those writers were always exempt from delusions and errors of judgment. Romains wrote to me from Geneva that Pierre Laval had assured him of his unshakeable determination—outward appearances notwithstanding—to put a stop to Mussolini's war in Abyssinia; Jean-Richard Bloch, who edited *Ce Soir*, informed me in 1938 of a great republican opposition movement that was taking shape in Nazi Germany. . . . For in spite of their sharp intelligence, they often deceived themselves—or were deceived. But isn't everyone at times a self-deceiver? And this ability to give oneself to one's art and at the same time act so as to influence, at least to some degree, the destiny of man, seemed to me utterly outside my scope.

Once indeed, in 1935, I had become a contributor to a political weekly called *Vendredi*, founded after the attempted Fascist *coup* of February 6, 1935, by André Chamson, Jean Guéhenno, André Gide and others to help promote the birth of a popular and democratic front. For a few months I published in it a series of caustic cartoons on topical questions, but I soon had to give up: my initial verve was spent. The necessity of sticking to topical problems, up-to-the-minute events, was diametrically opposed to my personal vision, the inner inspiration that guided my pencil. I became winded trying to keep pace with the topical and ephemeral, when I had always striven, through humour and satire, to reach through to the permanent, timeless problems of Man confronted with his condition on earth. So despite my wholehearted support for its fight, I soon ceased drawing for *Vendredi* and returned to working alone. I did so without blinding myself to the future: Hitler was sharpening his sword in Spain, and our turn would soon come. I drew as one writes one's last will and testament. And though there was no conscious intention on my part, it was not sheer accident, perhaps, that my last album of drawings before war broke out was called *Silences*, that I chose shortly after to illustrate one of Edgar Allen Poe's poems entitled *Silence*, and that the word 'silence' figured once more in the title of my first piece of clandestine writing. It was as if, with this word, I had meant to strike the three taps to signal the rise of the curtain on the long tragedy which France, gagged, was to live through, in effect, in silence.

Besides, had I not predicted the exact date of the German invasion, and been only a week out? And that as far back as 1935? In the album I composed that year and published in 1936 the following prophecy occurs: '*On May 12, 1940, during the defence of Bapaume, the nth infantry battalion was wiped out.*' In actual fact the German offensive started on May 10th and overran Bapaume on the 18th: so I think my prediction, made five years before, may be considered reasonably accurate . . . Crystal-gazing? Second sight? Sheer coincidence? The truth is less stupendous, but more instructive, perhaps.

The album, entitled *Visions rassurantes de la Guerre* ('War as a

Reassuring Prospect') depicted a variety of persons taking a rosy view of the coming war, from which they hoped to gain some advantage. Among them was a staff colonel who had invented a special shorthand for his daily reports and was dying to test it in the field. Meanwhile he toyed with the example I have quoted, without the slightest thought for the bloodshed it implied, just for the pleasure of transcribing it into four small symbols occupying less than a centimetre . . . All right, but how explain the uncanny accuracy of my fictitious example? Well, I had reasoned, even a junior staff officer with a minimum of intelligence must surely calculate, in 1935, that Hitler would need another four or five years to have an army ready to wage war on us; that the offensive would, as usual, be launched during the first fine weather—late April or early May; that it would obviously strike at the Belgian frontier left uncovered by the Maginot Line; that we, being on the defensive, were bound to suffer reverses in the early days; and that the town of Bapaume would therefore soon find itself threatened. For a staff officer such reasoning seemed to me self-evident. But I must have overestimated the acumen of our military leaders, since at that very time and place, so easily predictable, the enemy none the less took them by surprise. . . .

I have told this anecdote to show that, though I was unwilling to be personally involved in political activity, I was not unfamiliar with politics and could make an informed guess. This being said, I must admit my gift for prophecy went no further. In fact, it was no better than the general average, beginning with our statesmen. More often than not, events confounded rather than confirmed my forecasts or analyses. Candidly speaking, it remains my private conviction that on many occasions the events were wrong!

*   *   *

During the First World War, I was still a boy, and I believed, of course, all that was said. How could I have doubted that all the Right was on one side and all the Wrong on the other? The *Boche* was the embodiment of evil, and I hated him with serenity.

He was the Hun who destroyed cathedrals and chopped off hands of little children. Since then, millions of little children have gone up in the smoke of incinerators or served as guinea-pigs for

Nazi doctors' experiments *in vivo*; compared to that, a few severed hands would have represented quite a modest atrocity—even supposing they were not the invention of newspapermen in a frenzy of patriotism. But in those days, this seemed to me the height of ferocity. I believed every word of it, and I was not the only one. So much so that, years later, André Gide could still tell in his *Diary* a short but touching story which happened in Flanders when occupied by the Kaiser's soldiery. A Prussian officer walks into a baker's shop to buy some bread, and sees a young French mother coming in with a baby in her arms. Injured in some stupid accident, the baby's mutilated arm sticks up with a blood-soaked bandage wrapped round it. The officer blenches at the sight, his eyes wide with the mute question: 'Is it true then, what they say of us?' And the woman, confronted with this speechless distress, cannot refrain from shaking her head, slowly and silently. This wordless dialogue, in which two human beings, two adversaries, express the highest sentiments of dignity and truth, was something I was to remember years later when the Germans once again were occupying France. I wondered which of the two, the Frenchwoman or the officer, had touched me more. But I also wondered what officer of Hitler's army would still have blenched with shame at a severed hand.

Towards the end of hostilities, in 1918, I was almost a young man, and by then I had learnt a lot about the real facts of that war. We were often visited at home by a young infantry officer, who, because of his extreme youth, got sent to all the toughest spots—Verdun, Craonne, Chemin des Dames. Afterwards he would be sent on leave to recuperate for the next time. He told us the unvarnished truth, exposing the eye-wash that was fed to the public. And so the war was gradually debunked in my youthful eyes. His name was Pierre Fort. His father had been *chef de cabinet* to President Combes. He was five years older than I, more or less secretly engaged to my sister—my father had insisted on the engagement being unofficial until the end of the war—and covered with medals. The awe and admiration with which I looked up to him may be imagined. I certainly owe him many of the convictions I acquired in my adolescence, first and foremost a hatred that has never abated: the hatred of war.

For he told us what the war was really like. The ribbons on his chest were proof of his valour under fire, so he could afford to give us the facts. Most of these were appalling: filth, blood, unspeakable suffering and needless massacres for which he blamed the army chiefs' incompetence, their 'bull-headed stupidity'. It is Clemenceau, I believe, who is credited with the famous quip in a critical military situation: 'Thank God the other side have generals too.' Our young officer was not far from sharing this view, and he looked with a sort of brotherly pity on the enemy soldier, the poor devil on the other side of the barbed wire who, like himself, was enduring senseless martyrdom and death in the icy mud for interests that were not their own.

In the years after the armistice, I became ever more convinced that the nations had been tricked into that terrible war which had hurled against one another men who were made to get on well. I grew to like the German people as brothers who had been led astray and who were being wronged by French public opinion. Having cared to know nothing but their vices, I now began to acquaint myself with their virtues, through the books of Romain Rolland and Edmond Vermeil. And it appeared to me that their virtues were complementary to ours. This deepened my conviction that Franco-German friendship was bound to bear the finest fruit. Besides, it would make any future war in Europe impossible. Throughout the 'twenties, for over a decade, these sentiments dominated my political thinking.

Everything tended to strengthen them. The old and the new Germany, become democratic at last, joined peaceful hands over the heads of Bismarck and Wilhelm II. From Handel to Beethoven, she had taught the world music, now with *The Three Lights, Caligari, Nosferatu*, she burst into the international cinema, opening up new horizons. Later, with *Kameradschaft*, it was again a German film which proclaimed the workers' solidarity across all frontiers. Two symbolic scenes highlighted its message. In the only gallery left intact by a pit explosion, which the German miners ought to have been able to use to rescue their French comrades buried in the coalfield that stretches all the way from the Rhineland to Lorraine, a sinister black iron grating bars the way. In a surge of brotherhood that disdains all frontiers, they dynamite the grille of discord and, after superhuman efforts, save the French from certain death. Tears and kisses, beanos and bonfires. And then the last scene shows officials, accompanied by the military, inaugurating the freshly-erected, padlocked grating and saluting from either side of it with chilly ceremony. The success of this film had been considerable, in France no less than in Germany. And it was not the only one of its kind. The same public which, in its hundreds of thousands, read German anti-war novels like *All Quiet on the Western Front* or *Four of the Infantry*, or the French *Under Fire* and *Lives of the Martyrs*, shared the same sentiment as they sat in the darkened halls: Never again! These war films, French or German, had a tone so similar in their common condemnation of war that I sometimes get them mixed up in retrospect and no longer remember if a certain memorable scene was part of *Verdun* or of *All Quiet*.

The resounding success of such works in France, above all among the youth, showed me that I was not alone in my abhorrence of war, nor in wishing, waiting and longing for a rapprochement between our two peoples. And anything that put an obstacle in its way was criminal in my eyes. Criminal the occupation of the Ruhr after four years of peace, for the purpose of mulcting a destitute Germany. Criminal the extreme reluctance of France to return the Saar which she obviously could not hold on to against the wish of its population. On the contrary, I was sure that every aid, encouragement and support should have been given to the young and still fragile Weimar Republic, so as to help her get the better of her adversaries.

For a new party had promptly sprung to life there, spouting vengeance and violence. It impudently called itself '*Rassenpartei*'—racist party—and though, in its early days, with its 2% at the polls, it had seemed a harmless anachronism, it gradually assumed more formidable proportions, playing on the rising unemployment, the widespread poverty and all the sequels of the Versailles Treaty, when more equitable arrangements would surely have restrained its growth. Would a less miserable Germany have listened as eagerly to the demons in her midst? I suspect not, in spite of the depth of ignominy to which the entire nation sank at Hitler's prompting, in spite of the distressing change which so many atrocities have brought about in my own feelings towards Germany—of which I am still not cured.

Yes, even today, when a new upsurge of neo-Nazi nationalism

can be perceived among the German people, even today I remain convinced that at the time their enthusiasm for Stresemann and his policy of rapprochement with France, and the enormous success of the books and films which all defended the same ideas, was quite genuine in 1925 and only asked to be given a chance. Among so much other evidence, I need only recall my meeting with that German at Montana-sur-Sierre, in the Swiss mountains, where I had gone ski-ing. We were both staying in the same hotel. I used to meet him on the snow-fields dressed in a hunting-jacket, riding-breeches and puttees: the ski-slopes in those days had not yet become fun-fairs with their own uniform fashions. Every ski-run in the mountains was still an adventure. The man was a good skier. With his square head and close-cropped hair shaved above the ears and nape, he looked the very image of the Prussian officer. Actually, he was a lawyer from Hanover, but he had been in the war as a lieutenant in the reserve. He came up to me on the track one day to say how glad he was to talk to a Frenchman. He considered, as I did, that the war he had been forced to fight in had been an unpardonable crime. Many of the words I put into the mouth of my von Ebrennac in *The Silence of the Sea*—his love for France, his longing to see our two countries unite and complement each other—I heard him express. And so did my brother-in-law who later joined me there, and who was regarded by the German, both of them having fought at Verdun, not as a former enemy, but as a comrade-in-arms and fellow-sufferer.

Some years later I was to run into him by accident as, lonely and dejected, he sat on a café terrace on the Boulevard Saint-Michel. He had just left Nazi Germany and was emigrating to America. He was full of shame for what was happening in his country, and of horror for what was going to happen in Europe. Between Germany and himself he was putting the whole width of the Atlantic Ocean.

I have never forgotten that man and his blighted hopes, the same hopes that all his friends had cherished too, as he told us only two or three years earlier—the hope of a Europe in which Germany and France would have merged in a common destiny. Now he was almost alone: those same friends had cast him out and made common cause with Hitler.

For me this was proof that these hopes could only have been

fulfilled if the victor had stopped humiliating Germany by treating her as a defeated power after a war of which the German people had been no more guilty than ours. I am certain that had Germany been less confined to a ghetto where she was left to moral rot and ruin, she would not have yielded to the Nazi delirium; with a little more clear-sightedness the world would have been spared the Second World War. But so long as Germany was still a democracy, none of the men who governed France, together or by turns, with Poincaré at their head, could be relied on to dare break with this boneheaded policy of victory. None, with a single exception: Aristide Briand. But by then it was too late.

In retrospect, and with hindsight, Briand's efforts seem to me extraordinarily pathetic. He was old and tired, with too many enemies and too little time ahead to have a chance to win through. Never, perhaps, was an apostle so basely and constantly reviled every morning. There is poignancy in his cry, shortly before his death, when he was already a sick man: 'Must one die, then, to be believed?' I imagine he departed with a very sombre view of the future in his mind. I can't help feeling a melancholy tenderness for the memory of this man, as one does for anyone who has lived through an ineffectual Passion.

I watched the Weimar Republic, lonely and defeated, reel under the deadly blows of Adolf Hitler, whom the old Field-Marshal Hindenburg had called to the Reich's chancellery. The Germans dote on strong men: the day before, the Nazis had obtained only half the votes cast by the electorate; the day after, they practically had the lot. The concentration camps, no sooner created, began to fill with Jews, Communists, ordinary democrats, while Hitler, tearing up the treaties, immediately set about resurrecting a powerful army, whose purpose he did not even bother to conceal: it was to wrest from Germany's neighbours, by force or by threat, the 'Lebensraum' he claimed. Austria, then Bohemia, then Poland, were first to yield, and we were forewarned that our turn would come. But, brandishing alternately the sword and the olive-branch, he promised to be lenient if we left his hands free. There were those who were gulled by his promises and encouraged Hitler to have a go at Russia in the hope of thus killing two birds with one stone. As if, once Europe and Russia had been defeated, the ambitions of an omnipotent Hitler would have spared us out of gratitude . . . .

What outraged me most was that those who were now begging for
the friendship of Nazi Germany's dictator were so often those who
had frustrated Briand's efforts a few years earlier and refused to
show friendship to the Weimar Republic.

I was never one of those gullible pocket-Machiavellis. I had
not the slightest doubt that if France allowed Hitler to rearm and
carry out his ominous plans, she would pay for her inaction with
her liberty and even, perhaps, with her very existence. But this
posed a terrible problem for my conscience: the problem of a pre-
ventive war.

For I continued to repudiate the use of war as a political exped-
ient. Before resorting to violence, all the possibilities of a diplomatic settlement must first be exhausted. And even after that,
every possible chance must be conserved of a change for the better—
a popular uprising, a revolt in the German Army, a break-up in the
Nazi party through internal strife, such as had already occurred
during the Night of the Long Knives, when Hitler murdered his
closest associates after his narrow escape from being overthrown
by them. The first shot fired would put an end to all those possibilities and irremediably let loose an endless slaughter.

Even when, by sheer bluff, the Führer's troops, still few in number, reoccupied the left bank of the Rhine and a sharp reaction by
the French Army would have made him retreat and perhaps lose
face, I was still among those who declared: 'Not a shot! . . . ' I
knew I was wrong. But I also knew that it would be several years
yet before Hitler had the necessary military supremacy to carry
out his warlike plans; and so many things, I thought, could still
happen during those years . . .

Throughout the various stages of Hitler's rise, the pacifist ranks
reacted with a sort of 'graduated response'. There were those who,
as far back as 1933 when the Nazis perpetrated their first crimes,
had the courage to break with their pacifist past, convinced that
one could not buy peace at the victims' expense. I was not one of
them, and today I bow contritely (as I soon did then) to their
unavailing foresight. Some others abandoned their convictions
three years later, while I still hesitated to follow their example
in spite of this last opportunity Hitler gave us to avoid a much
vaster conflagration by limited violence. Others, again, bade
good-bye to their beliefs only at the outbreak of war in Spain.

They were the most numerous, I believe. The overthrow of the Spanish Republic by the tanks and planes of Fascist Italy and Nazi Germany, sent to Franco's rescue, was for many Frenchmen a traumatic shock which has left its mark on them even today; they cannot forgive themselves for the fact that a Socialist France stood by while a friendly Republic was strangled on her doorstep, and Hitler and his accomplice Mussolini tried out in Spain the new armaments that were to pulverise ours. There were those whose convictions remained unshaken even by the long agony of the Spanish people, and who abandoned them only after the Anschluss, the capture of Austria by the Third Reich; or after the humiliation of Munich; or the invasion of Bohemia; or that of Poland; and finally there were those who, like Louis Lecoin or the writer Jean Giono, staunchly maintained their pacifism to the end, preferring even surrender and slavery to acceptance of war, and let themselves be jailed for saying so.

At what stage do I place my own conversion? Though the Spanish civil war dealt me the decisive blow, it wasn't so much a sudden collapse of my pacifist beliefs as a gradual crumbling which had been hastened by the fall of Austria and Albania. By the time of Munich, all had been said. I had admitted, with hopeless certainty, that against Hitler war was the only resort. And I honestly prepared myself for it.

But if I am to admit the whole truth, I must add that by then I had undergone in Prague, on the eve of Munich, such a powerful experience that I should have been unable to hold out longer without betraying the sentiments I held most dear.

II

THAT year, on the advice of Jules Romains, I joined the French Centre of the International PEN Club. (Though I was a graphic artist, I was admitted because some of my albums contained substantial commentaries which were kindly held to deserve the name of literature.) It was my first step into the realm of letters. The PEN at that time represented, by and large, what the League for the Rights of Man represents on a political level; its charter defended not only freedom of thought and speech, but also world peace, the equality of all nations and races, in short, everything then being flouted by the retrograde fanaticism of the master of the Third Reich. Every year the PEN Club congress was held in a different country. The previous year in Jugoslavia the German Centre which had rallied to Hitler and persecuted the democratic and Jewish writers in its own ranks, had been expelled from the International federation and had promptly been replaced by a Centre of German émigré writers, including Thomas and Heinrich Mann, Stefan Zweig, Feuchtwanger, Remarque, and many others. Jules Romains, the PEN's International President, and Benjamin Crémieux, Secretary General of the French Centre, had been the prime movers in this rejoinder to the Nazi tyrants.

The Ragusa congress had accepted the invitation of the Czechoslovaks for the following year. It would thus meet in Prague in June. This, in 1938, was a symbolic choice and not devoid of audacity. Hitler had in the meantime swallowed Austria, and everyone was now well aware, the Czechs better than any, who the next victim would be. Since the spring, Bohemia had been the scene of riots provoked by the German minority in the Sudetenland, clamouring to be reunited with the Great Reich. Prague that summer was the hottest city in Europe. Would our congress be able to meet there?

In May this still seemed far from certain. Hitler was exerting frantic pressure on the Benes government, threatening it with military action if it did not yield. Relying on his country's alliance, that with France in the first place, the President resisted with dogged courage. Nevertheless, it seemed that the crunch was coming when, at the last moment, the Führer retreated. It was his first climb-down, and all Europe hung out flags. Prague seemed crowned with a wreath of heroism. It was in this mood of rejoicing and relief that, on a June morning, we boarded the train (you did not travel by plane in those days) for the old city with the thousand spires.

I had never yet passed through Germany. When we stopped at the first German station after crossing the Rhine at the Kehl bridge, the first Teutonic face I saw—the station-master's—looked exactly like those in the Hansi albums that had delighted my childhood: the ruddy face with the potato-shaped nose, the fat neck above the apple-green uniform, the expression of jovial gravity beneath the red peaked cap with its gold braid. I was still gazing at this harmless, jolly mug of a face when I heard a voice behind me rap out: '*Pässe, bitte!*' I turned round, and had to restrain a shudder. In the open door stood two men in black uniform. One tall and slender, the other just as tall but stockier. Both of them handsome and fair-haired. The tall slender one was smiling, the stocky one, cold and close-mouthed, kept his face expressionless except for an affected, disdainful indifference. But both kept fixed upon me and my companions the inhuman stare of four blue eyes, as freezing as icicles. The first took our passports, the second stamped them, the momentary lowering of his eyelids making his baby-face look only more cruel. The first took our passports again and handed them to us, still with that smile on his lips under those bird-of-prey eyes. It was a terrifying smile. It seemed to me that if, instead of handing back our passports, the two had been told: 'Shoot those men!' they would have done so on the spot, still with the same smile.

When they had left the carriage, we all looked at one another. Words were superfluous, we had all had the same thought. Outside, as the train moved off, slowly gliding along the platform, the station-master's face seemed to recede into a sadly bygone past, to vanish there with the old Germany. I had the feeling that in one instant we had grasped the whole of this country.

For a whole day we rolled through Swabia and Franconia. I had not imagined the scenery so monotonous, so different from the French countryside. Nothing but austere grassland broken by sombre forests, almost entirely of black pines. There was something stern, insensitive about this landscape, a feeling of unbending harshness, almost of hostility towards man. Could man respond to it otherwise than by hardening himself, shedding all mellowing gentleness? Did not this explain many things, past and present? Amid this harsh, inclement nature, the cheerful villages with their roofs of old rounded tiles came as a surprise; houses hung with red swastika flags, boys and girls—it was a Sunday—marching in step along the roads bawling songs, here and there groups of small boys too, all this jollity took on, by contrast, an air of unwonted festivity. If Hitler had not beaten such a hasty retreat a month before at the prospect of a real conflagration, these antics would have put me in mind of cannibal tribes on the eve of battle, whipping themselves into a disquieting frenzy. And then, on the station platform of Bayreuth, buxom Valkyries offered the travellers sausages of such gigantic proportions that consuming them turned into a comedy act. And for the moment German bonhomie effaced other, more alarming impressions.

Arriving in Prague at ten at night, we found that there, too, the city was beflagged. As the taxi drove us to our hotel through streets and avenues ablaze with banners, I remembered that our hosts had made our congress coincide with the tenth *slet* of the Sokol movement, which is a great national Czech holiday. A holiday which this year was celebrated with particular brilliance, for the Sokols, who under Hapsburg domination had been a resistance movement camouflaged as a gymnasts' association, still symbolized, twenty years after, the love of a whole people for its independence. *Slets* took place only once every six years, and this one fell just a month after Hitler had yielded to a superior will for the first time—and it had been the will of the Czechs! Hence those banners of victory. 'But in that case . . . ' I thought, ensconced in my taxi, 'why, why are the German villages beflagged as well?'

If the magic of Romanticism does not leave your heart unmoved, discover Prague and you will fall in love at first sight. Her winding lanes make you expect to meet not so much the ghost of Kafka as of Werther, or E.T.A. Hoffmann's characters. And I should have been less startled to come face to face, at the foot of an eerie tower, with a frock-coated Devil come to bargain for my soul; or in the misty night, on the old bridge flanked by tortured statues, to pass a student clad in black velvet, gazing at the river with the lure of death in his eyes; or to hear rising, from beneath the jumble of moss-grown headstones in the former Jewish graveyard, the thousand-year-old lamentation of the chosen people; or to come across the Golem's wandering ghost under the looming black walls of the ancient synagogue, than to run all of a sudden, at the corner of a modern thoroughfare full of motor vehicles, into a man wearing a hussar's frogged cape thrown over his shoulder, with tasselled boots and a plumed cap, as if he had walked right out of one of Lehar's operettas! This incongruous ghost of the Napoleonic era was walking arm-in-arm with a girl in a short summer frock and holding a child by his other hand: in fact, he was one of the sixty thousand Sokols from Bohemia and Slovakia, who, in parade dress, was taking his family for a walk. Every minute we passed others on the pavements. Next day they were due to give a mass performance in sports clothes, in the monumental stadium, and would afterwards parade through the city in their full-dress uniforms. Frankly neither demonstration filled us with a thrill of anticipation.

In the meantime, there were thrills in store for us at the congress sessions. We had not expected them. There seemed no possibility of any false note among democratic writers of all nations when the times were so threatening. And indeed, one after the other, the resolutions were voted and carried unanimously, condemning all infringements of the major freedoms, the persecution of intellectuals, the banning and burning of books. The press in Nazi Germany called us 'a congress of gangsters'. A Yiddish writer proposed a motion condemning anti-Semitism. The voting was a foregone conclusion. Delegates on behalf of their respective countries mounted the platform to say a few words in support of the motion. Then came the turn of H. G. Wells, the Honorary President, representing Great Britain. The PEN Club worshipped him, both for his writings and his great age. During all the sessions he could be seen sitting on the tiered benches of the amphitheatre along with the *vulgum pecus*, from whom he kept his distance, though. I had often glanced at his impassive, wrinkled face, a little bloated with drink, like that of a whisky-soaked Indian Army colonel in reluctant retirement. The auditorium seemed turned to stone. Someone translated. In the name of freedom of opinion, Wells opposed the motion. It was the PEN's role, he said, to defend the liberty of all opinions, even of those we did not like, and consequently, he concluded, the liberty to be an anti-Semite. To vote against this right would run counter to the very foundations of our Charter.

Speakers followed one another on the platform to expose the sophistry of this argument at a time when the right to be an anti-Semite expressed itself in Germany by persecution, murder, concentration camps. Benjamin Crémieux, white-faced and bearded like a Talmudic rabbi, protested vehemently; Piérard, a Belgian Socialist deputy, couched his protest in more moderate terms, making a distinction between the abstract intellectualism of a Gobineau and rabid gangs of fanatics hunting down Jews like beasts. They were applauded. But Wells unhurriedly left his seat and, without further explanation, calmly announced from the platform, while his eyes roved over the audience with the ponderous gaze of a lion-tamer, that if the motion were adopted he would resign from the PEN.

Nobody was misled: this was the old lion's last revenge against a gathering which, two years earlier, had ousted him from the presidency in favour of a younger and more active member. For he was throwing us into an appalling, hopeless dilemma. His resignation would be acclaimed with delight by the Nazi press: the great H. G. Wells, ex-president of the PEN, repudiates his association of Jew-ridden gangsters! But if we threw out the motion to prevent his departure, they would be no less jubilant: even the PEN refuses to condemn anti-Semitism! We were flabbergasted. Jules Romains mounted the platform and addressed the meeting in his capacity of President. Deferentially and constantly referring to 'our dear great Wells' (he lost his temper only once, when he cried: 'We cannot condone crimes, after all!') he explained to him patiently that the Charter was no less outspoken in its condemnation of all racial discrimination. The freedom to be anti-Semitic ran counter to this quite explicit condemnation. No doubt there was a contradiction here. So, would our dear great Wells agree to draft a text which, while casting no aspersion on the freedom of opinion, would nevertheless condemn anti-Semitic discrimination? Judging his victory to be sufficiently great, the old lion agreed to take his place at the desk. We were all relieved, but I was indignant and even more troubled by disturbing thoughts. Could the highest principles be turned against themselves and used to justify infamies? Could freedom of opinion lead to supporting the Nazis against the Jews? And if so, mightn't peace, peace at any price, lead perhaps to condoning bloody massacres? That experience and those thoughts precipitated my change of mind. I discovered the ambiguity of abstract principles. I also discovered that a man's genius was no guarantee of his steadfastness, and that vanity can pave the way to frightful complicities. And I discovered that there was only oneself to rely on, both in weighing up principles and in watching their application. I discovered that to let your scruples keep you out of politics and rely on others to act was also a kind of political action, and the worst kind at that, since it meant leaving the field clear for men with no scruples at all. I may not have thought this out quite so clearly at the moment, while Wells Imperator was drafting his text up there surrounded by the apprehensive deference of the PEN Club dignitaries; but ideas have a way of burrowing a subterranean passage through the mind, and gradually managing to change it.

Two days later we were all gathered at the stadium, out of courtesy to our hosts and yawning in advance, like proper intellectuals, at the thought of a monster display of athletics. After a long wait, we suddenly caught our breath: thirty thousand girls in short cornflower-blue tunics were advancing with the same step, but not 'in step', a hundred abreast, with no interval, no leader. Thousands and thousands of honey-coloured legs glided in unison over flesh-coloured sand, with the exquisite suppleness, the slow pulsation of the incoming tide as it stealthily engulfs the beach. This was ancient Greece; we felt we had been transported to the stadium of Olympia. Those tunics alone! Can you imagine the dazzling shimmer of those thirty thousand blues? And of thirty thousand saffron-coloured wreaths on as many blonde heads of varying fairness? There was first, spread over the whole arena, a vast meadow of buttercups. A moment later, as thirty thousand backs bent over, the meadow gave way to the sea, peaceful at first, then rippling with wavelets, then heaving under a storm, and next instant transformed into a field of ripe corn gently swaying in the wind with thousands and thousands of girls' arms, purer than wheat . . . A Belgian poet next to me was weeping with emotion. And we thought, thinking of other stadiums in a near-by country, of other throngs, drilled and fanatical, half tribal, half conspiratorial, where a hundred thousand arms were outstretched in a violent, screaming summons to cruelty and death . . . .

A couple of days later, the entire population of Prague was massed on the pavements to applaud the sixty thousand Sokols marching past, in dress uniform, with banners flying. I roved on foot through the town which rang with one vast clamour. All over the city, the crowd and the Sokols were answering shout for shout, as if exulting together at being Czech, free and victorious. For they had intimidated Hitler. We had felt this pride in all our Czech hosts. Here, in the streets, it burst out in this explosion of joy, this exaltation, this mutual rapture. I shared their gladness, but mine was overcast with gloomy foreboding. For I was not at all sure, alas, that Hitler had said his last word. That he wasn't biding his time for a better occasion. The Czechs, in answer to such anxious thoughts, would say: 'Let him come, we're waiting for him!'— which was admirable but sent a shiver down my spine.

It was on the eve of our departure, I believe, that we decided at last to have a look at Prague's night-life. The evening had started inauspiciously: on someone's advice we had landed in a dreary, half-empty dance-hall which we left with all speed, as soon as we had downed our drinks. We were an all-French party of writers, some of us with our wives: Jules Romains, Luc Durtain, Claude Aveline, Benjamin Crémieux, myself, two or three others whom I forget. Determined not to be discouraged by this dismal flop, we hired three taxis and asked the drivers to choose some place where, in their opinion, we would find a gay, popular atmosphere. They put their heads together, and five minutes later stopped on Wenceslas Square in front of a big, brightly-lit hotel, with a gold-braided commissionaire at the door. We exchanged grimaces; it didn't look very promising. Still, now we were here . . . We walked down some steps and heard laughter and music coming from the basement. Halfway down our coats were taken; I caught a glimpse of a low, vaulted cellar which was bursting with people. There were a dozen of us, how on earth were we to find seats down there and stay together? 'One moment, please,' said the attendant, and ran downstairs two at a time before us. He returned with the head waiter, smiling broadly, who said in French: 'Just follow me, ladies and gentlemen.' The music had stopped. He led us to three adjoining tables, miraculously free. But it was evident that the people around

III

O<small>NCE</small> more we boarded the train to cross Germany on our way
home. In the compartment with us were the writer Pierre Loewel
and an eminent critic in charge of the literary page of an evening
paper, whom I shall call Flodobert, out of discretion for his later
development. He had been the only one among us who had been
unmoved by the splendours of the Sokol display in the stadium:
instinctively he detested all mass demonstrations and he had refused
to distinguish this pageant from those mass meetings where Hitler
and his slogans of hatred were acclaimed with a chorus of chanted
Sieg Heils. Anything that was in the least reminiscent of those
frenetic crowds irked and exasperated him. As the train ran alongside some huge factory buildings, his blond-whiskered, slightly
foppish profile of a latter day Rubempré turned to the window as
he exclaimed: 'I hope the Czech planes will blow all this to smithereens!' Poor Loewel's long, Jewish-intellectual face grew even longer
with apprehension, and he tried to make the other shut up, lest the
Germans in the corridor should overhear him and get tough with
us.

At Nuremberg, my wife and I left our companions to go sight-
seeing in the town. We were to take the next train a few hours later.
We were not disappointed by the ancient parts of the town, which
still retained the fragrant charm of Old Germany. Close to a big,
circular fountain flaunting its flamboyant wrought-iron lace stood
Albert Dürer's house, still intact. An ancient bridge looked as if
at any minute Marguerite and Faust might cross it, followed by the
Doctor's black poodle. From a seat in an inviting niche in the
parapet you could see a whole string of little, hump-back bridges,
ancient timbered houses toppling over each other higgledy-piggledy,
ivy-covered walls plunging into the sleepy river which, here and
there, flowed under an arch, narrowed into a canal, wound into
meandering bays, squeezed through tiny lock-gates. In the heart
of Nazi Germany, we savoured the quiet charm of this oasis, and
just opposite, a quaint eating-house with sloping roof and bottle-
glass windows invited us to refresh ourselves in the same congenial

atmosphere. We walked over to read the menu posted on the door. It wasn't the menu, but a notice reading: 'Dogs and Jews not admitted.'

At once the old quarter which we had found so appealing took on an inhuman, infamous, repulsive air. We returned to the modern part of the town, which at least was free of trumpery. We would lunch at the station buffet. At a table facing ours, some businessmen were gorging themselves as they talked. Two of them had big swastika badges in their lapels. Though continuing to talk, they listened to our French conversation and scarcely took their eyes off us: cold, piercing eyes like those of the men in black on our outward journey. I felt my heart contract as I thought of our Prague dancers. As we went on eating our tasteless *schnitzel*, an old man came in to sell what looked like sweepstake tickets. Everybody bought them. Having no use for them, I declined. The man insisted in an angry, indignant voice, explaining goodness knows what. The badge-wearers' stare became a fixed scowl. I realized that those tickets were something not to be declined—some national subscription no doubt. I persisted in my refusal: the risk was minimal, after all. Getting expelled or taken to a police-station. A deadly silence reigned for a few seconds, then one of the plain-clothes Nazis motioned as if to say: 'Leave them alone,' and the old fellow shambled off, still muttering.

But in the train we still retained the baleful impression of nazified Nuremberg. If the whole of the old Germany was already howling with her new masters, what hope was left? The answer was given us as we approached the Rhine and saw, with growing perplexity, our train overtaking an endless string of goods-wagons loaded with enormous pointed poles, a whole forest of them filing past us. 'What Roman siege? . . .' I wondered until, a little before Kehl, we saw that trenches had been dug over a vast area. The trenches passed between houses, through gardens, fields and orchards, their earth still fresh and obviously only recently dug. There were shelters, small forts, in front of them ran barbed-wire fencing, and still farther ahead were those long, brand-new poles stuck into the ground in staggered rows to make tank traps, their sharpened ends pointing towards the Rhine. None of this, I was certain, had been there a fortnight before when we had passed through on our outward journey. We were witnessing the birth of the Siegfried Line.

So the wolf-leader was getting ready! That is what I had called
Hitler ever since his howls, heard on the radio, had irresistibly put
me in mind of a nursery tale about a pack of wolves who adopt a
blacksmith as their leader. Every night the man joins the wolves in
the forest, urges them on and leads their attack on flocks and farm-
steads. Hitler had only retreated in May for lack of protection in
his rear. Once he had made sure of that—in a matter of months,
weeks perhaps—our Czech friends would have no choice but to
fight or surrender. And for France the moment of truth would have
arrived.

Back in Paris, I found an air of great serenity, as if the Führer's
retreat had cleared the sky once for all. No word yet in the newspapers about what I had seen being built beyond the Rhine. It
was a lovely summer, and I spent it with my family on Irus, a
diminutive island in the Gulf of Morbihan. We had been invited
there by Captain Diego Brosset—a son-in-law of General Mangin,
the famous First World War general—dashing, dynamic and a
wonderful friend whose brilliant mind and abundant vitality filled
me with envy and admiration. Five years later, promoted general
under de Gaulle, he was to be the liberator of Lyons, his native city.
At present, though, he was at Staff College, attending courses. I
told him of the work I had seen in progress beyond the Rhine which
had so alarmed me and which nobody this side seemed to know
about. Ought one not to warn the military circles?

'Oh,' he said, 'they know well enough.'

'What are they doing about it?'

'Nothing. They feel stupidly safe behind their Maginot Line.'

'But if Czechoslovakia is invaded, it's up to us to attack!'

He gestured helplessly and gave me a stricken look.

'They hide their heads in the sand,' he said, 'like that doddering
old fool of a field-marshal who usurped his fame in the first place.
They'll only move when they get kicked in the pants.'

I trembled for our Czech friends.

However, as the days went by in the halcyon Brittany summer
my anxiety abated. Hitler made no move; perhaps he was scared
of the Russians? The respite was short-lived: in less than six weeks
he resumed his vicious attacks on the Czechs and brandished the
threat of an ultimatum, which drew forth an energetic warning

from France, in accordance with her undertaking. The tension heightened. So much so that when, one afternoon, across the calm sea with its tangy iodine smell of seaweed, across the peaceful dunes on the far shore with their slopes billowing with broom, gorse and pines and dotted with white gables and slate roofs lit by the sun, I thought I heard the distant, faint but insistent tolling of the church-bell of Arradon on the mainland; then the answering echo of a more distant bell farther north, then another in the south, and one more from the east, all ringing unceasingly, I could not help think-ing: 'The tocsin . . . ' But our wives, in their bathing-costumes, were calmly having tea on the terrace; Diego, stripped to the waist, was forging a door-handle behind the house. And the fear of making myself ridiculous kept me at first from rousing the atten-tion of our easy-going islanders. I strained my ear: Bells . . . bells . . . bells . . . bells . . . called the bells, just as in Edgar Allen Poe's ballad. Peace . . . peace . . . answered the sea, and the blue sky, and the chattering sea-gulls, and the gently swelling sails of the *sinagots* . . . Then suddenly, coming also from invisible Arradon, the quavering voice of a bugle. So it wasn't a dream, and restraining myself no longer, I went to warn Diego. He cocked an ear, listened for a moment, then said: 'It's Sunday', and went back to his work.

And indeed, the bells fell silent, dusk descended over the sea and the motionless archipelago, we dined by candle-light, and I had little trouble in going to sleep. The next morning, however, I crossed to the mainland for news. No tocsin or war as yet, but the worst was feared. I could no longer bear being cooped up on this desert island, too wild and wonderful, too far from the world. I decided to advance the date of our return. Two days later we were on the road, but doing a leisurely twenty miles per hour, for my high-wheeled Ford had to tow a rickety, makeshift trailer with the old tub I had retinkered to do a little sailing in the gulf. At this snail's pace, I had time to see the newspaper headlines getting more disastrous from town to town. A broken axle held us up in Touraine for two days, and it looked as if it would be touch and go which of the two, the repairs or the war, would win the race against time. Chamberlain flew to Berchtesgaden and returned to London empty-handed. On reaching our village at last, I learned of Musso-lini's initiative and the subsequent meeting of the Big Four at Munich. Like everybody else in France, we sat glued to the radio, listening to Pierre Brossolette's sober, dispassionate commentary on the situation. I was torn between conflicting emotions, for it was plain that Hitler would not retreat and that sooner or later we would have to go to war with him. But a last inner twitch of weakness made me echo the Du Barry's craven plea on the scaffold: 'Just one more minute, Mr Executioner!' For Europe and for France, one more year's grace, one more month . . . Would I never get rid of the old Adam? Never conquer my hatred of war in face of the certitude of proven crimes? 'No more war!' to be sure—but at that price? For quite apart from this blackmail of total war, who could any longer ignore the persecutions, the horrors committed in Hitler's concentration camps? (Though as yet no one went as far as to imagine the reality, as discovered six years later.) I listened to the radio in this tortured frame of mind, sincerely hoping that the inevitably shameful compromise would fail, yet unable to refrain, surreptitiously, from wishing it to succeed . . . What followed is well-known: Hitler won all along the line. Czechoslavakia was left in the lurch and ordered to yield all. Stripped of the Sudeten mountains and her ramparts on the frontiers, she was left a defence-less prey, to be gobbled up by the wolf-leader whenever he felt like it. When she heard the announcement of the 'success' of the negotiations, my mother exclaimed: 'Children, we're saved!' a cry echoed by most Frenchmen. Though I too felt numbed by this 'craven relief', as Léon Blum called it, yet it left me clear-sighted enough to give the gloomy answer: 'Saved? Perhaps . . . But next year we'll all be in bondage.'

For I was horribly certain of the logical sequel. Munich was another Waterloo. Any doubts I might have had on that score would have been dispelled by Daladier's face, caught by the news-reel cameras on his return in an open car amid wild ovations: it looked stunned, incapable of producing a single smile. And a little later, his appearance on the balcony, opening his mouth as if about to shout to the acclaiming crowd below: 'You fools! Haven't you realized yet?' and then closing it again, discouraged, as he turned away and stepped back to melt from sight into the shadow of the window—the whole of this tragic dumbshow would have been enough to confirm my fears for the future inexorably in store for France. I was no longer certain that this would actually spell war: I feared worse than that. I thought that the French Republic had abdicated, capitulated in advance—probably with the blessing of Big Business, after the Great Scare they'd had with the Popular Front. The Front had proved a beast with blunted fangs and clipped claws, so they breathed again. But they had trembled, and now they felt they might get their revenge: if the French people were scared of war to the point of letting their best friends down and handing them over, they might still be sufficiently scared tomorrow to put up with *anything* rather than war—even a change of régime under some strong man approved, if not actually appointed, by Hitler . . . Oh, my Prague dancers! I felt overcome with shame as I recalled their singing, the love and trust they showed us, the sturdy young fellow's martial fist and his fervour displayed with such a proud smile . . . . What could he be thinking now? I imagined his pain, and his contempt for France, and perhaps also his pity for her, for he too must surely guess what was bound to happen to her, and that she would surrender, when her turn came, without a fight.

Hadn't the process already started? Hadn't Georges Bonnet, two months after Munich, signed a friendship pact with von Ribbentrop? What did Daladier think of that, he whose distracted face kept haunting my memory? I was soon to have occasion to find out. Jules Romains invited me to a dinner party he was giving for Daladier, with Georges Bonnet and some other celebrities: Paul Valéry and Paul Morand, the playwright François Porché and his actress-wife Simone, our future ambassador to Washington, Henri Bonnet and his wife, an exotic beauty, the Chief of Police, Langeron, and two or three less prominent guests among whom I was one.

Daladier at close quarters rather surprised me: the famous 'Bull of Vaucluse' looked small and frail, his face less full-blooded than blotched and purple, with candid, questioning eyes. Everything about him conveyed uncertainty, even shyness, ill-concealed under an assumed air of energy which he was unable to sustain. On the whole, he seemed likeable enough, but when you thought of what he was going to come up against, it made you shiver. I visualized him and poor Chamberlain facing those two fiends, Hitler and Mussolini. He was no match for them and had sold out against promises he well knew to be illusory. And now I realized that he was no match either for his foreign minister, Georges Bonnet. At this I was seized with fear, for I could read the latter's face like an open book— or rather like a tightly closed one. Rarely had crafty cunning struck me as ominously as in this long face with its big turnip nose and pale blue fish-eyes which never looked you in the face. Throughout dinner, during which he never once opened his mouth, he kept jerking his knee spasmodically so that it made his shoulders quiver. The 'Bull' bore the brunt of the conversation, and, when Valéry complimented him on the style of his speeches, he blushed like a demure young girl, flustered but none the less delighted by some over-bold flattery.

Over coffee, the great questions of the day were broached at last, and now Bonnet took the floor. He expounded his policy: to restore Franco-German friendship and, with its help, to discourage Soviet expansionism but also restrain Hitler from his bellicose plans by achieving a peaceful settlement of all problems by negotiation. I lacked sufficient presence of mind to ask him what the price would be. How could I have imagined that, in 1938, a minister of the French Republic would already have dared suggest to Ribbentrop that one way of ridding France of her Jews would be to despatch them to her overseas colonies? A project about which he kept mum, as might be guessed, and which we learned of only much later. I merely ventured to remind him of the Führer's proclaimed designs on Alsace-Lorraine. His eyes gazing into the distance, he answered that since Hitler had persuaded Mussolini, for the sake of peace, to stop clamouring for Nice, Corsica and Savoy, it was unlikely that he himself would claim our Eastern provinces. Ribbentrop had given him full assurances on this point. 'And you believe him?' I was on the point of asking, but shrank from such impertinence. 'Besides, we shan't be caught napping,' he added. 'We are also actively pursuing our talks with the Russians.' This left me speechless: so he was plotting with the Germans against the Russians, and with the Russians behind the Germans' back? Indeed, this kind of double-dealing went well with his sly face. But what on earth did he take his partners for? Babes in the wood, to whom it would never occur to turn the tables on France by negotiating behind her back, too?

I felt dejected as I left the party that night.

A few weeks later, I found a very different mood in the little flat which Jean-Richard Bloch occupied in the Square du Port-Royal. There I met Jean Guéhenno, with his shrewd, bespectacled beaver-face, Marcel Cachin, the veteran Communist, with the drooping moustache of a trusty old locksmith, Aragon in a salmon-coloured silk shirt, accompanied by a very beautiful woman whose name was Elsa Triolet. All of them, I found, shared my fears about the government's two-faced policy and the people's apathy, encouraged from above, in the face of the rising Nazi peril. I felt particularly close to Jean-Richard Bloch who, an ex-serviceman of the last war, had for long shared my own uncertainty about peace and war. Even as late as 1935, when sanctions against Mussolini and his Abyssinian war were being discussed at Geneva, he had published a leader in *L'Oeuvre* entitled 'NOT ONE CANNON-SHOT!' to which Romains had replied the next day, saying that this was the League of Nations' one chance, on the contrary, to establish its authority by courting the risk of a minor war in order to impose peace. What a strange reversal! Now it was Romains who seemingly approved Munich, while Jean-Richard was polishing his gun. Hitler did not take long to settle the issue between them. As was to be expected, in the first days of spring he trampled his agreement under foot, and the German army poured down the slopes of the Sudeten mountains, entered defenceless Prague without a fight, and occupied Czechoslovakia, which was transformed into the German protectorate of Bohemia-Moravia. France and Britain remained petrified, inert. What about the pact with Russia? It had been rendered inoperative, it was claimed, by the refusal of Colonel Beck's Poland to let anyone pass through her territory. Moreover, Poland turned Czechoslovakia's misfortune to account by lopping off a piece of it for herself. This shabby kick at the underdog outraged us, and there were many who declared indignantly that a new partition of Poland would be well-deserved. Imprudent thoughts! . . . . Mussolini, meanwhile, so as not to be behindhand, invaded Albania on Easter Sunday. Next day, in the letter-box, I found my call-up papers for an immediate active-service period of twenty-one days.

IV

I HAD been called to Embrun, near Briançon, close to the Italian
frontier, where I was to join the 15/9 Battalion of the Reserve. I
reported to the garrison commander, a lieutenant-colonel whose
name I've forgotten, but not his looks: wedged into his uniform
as if he wore a corset, his leather boots gleaming, he had a bony,
brick-coloured face, a protruding nose, and a skull as shiny as his
boots, surrounded by a halo of bright ginger hair. I learned later
that he was said to be a homosexual, but his haughty stiffness gave
no inkling of it. Right away he told me:

'Twenty-one days, of course, is just a manner of speaking. You're
here till the end of the international tension.'

I registered this without flinching but not without a somewhat
appalled emotion. Until the certain outbreak of war in a henceforth
unforseeable future, Europe was unlikely to see the end of international tension! What would become of my current album for
which the printer was waiting, what would become of my family,
dependent on my art? The pay I received as a reserve lieutenant in
peace-time would hardly cover my mess and hotel bills. 'But
supposing it lasts ten years?' I murmured. To which he replied:
'D'you mind?'

I had to smile as I admitted: 'Well, I do rather . . . ,' without
the slightest hope of being understood, for it was obvious that to
him the soldier's life was the most wonderful in the world and that
I ought to have been overjoyed at this unhoped-for stroke of luck.
And he did indeed give a shrug and observed that there was nothing
he could do about it, anyway: I was sharing the lot of all frontiers-
men. I suddenly realized how much, even in a democracy, we
were at the mercy of the powers that be, and liable at any moment to be sacrificed to their whims. The weeks seemed to me to
drag on endlessly. In spite of the colonel's lectures on political
strategy, in which he cheerfully assured us that we were already 'in
a state of war without casualties', I was daily more convinced that
France would knuckle under and suffer every indignity right up to
her final enslavement. In the officers' mess, where we were gorging

ourselves at every meal on tinned snails, which the chef prepared beautifully—unlike the rest of his confections—a fellow reserve officer, Captain Vernet, bet me that the war, contrary to my expectations, would break out within a week. A very young doctor already twice removed from his newly-set-up practice in civilian life by these partial mobilizations, hoped to God that I would lose: let's get it over with, once for all! A few days later we were sent back home. I had won my wretched wager, and this confirmed my fears that France would do anything rather than fight.

During the months preceding the summer, I began building a boat of my own invention during my moments of leisure—a sort of half-deck canoe with a flattened stern for more convenient tacking when under sail. The new boat would spare me the trouble —supposing we still had a chance to go on holiday—of towing a cumbersome craft behind my Ford, since this one could be carried on the roof of the car. I should thus be able to do a little sailing and still hurry back at the double in the event of a new mobilization. I called the boat *Paludes* in memory of André Gide's story of that name and so as to be able to say, like its principal character: 'I don't care a damn for the rest, I'm busy with *Paludes*.' And it was a fact that while I planed, sawed and hammered, my mind was more at ease.

When August came, I transported my boat to Morgat in Brittany, where we were to join a group of friends. We spent a few weeks of somewhat forced gaiety, for we were all conscious of dancing on a volcano. We sailed and fished and wallowed in Breton *crêpes* and lobsters; I even cooked a mackerel *bourride*, as prepared by the fishermen of Sète, for twenty-four persons, a bold enterprise this, for I had never before attempted to cook one for more than four or six. And the huge quantity complicated the task of slowly adding the cooking-stock to the *ailloli*—garlic mayonnaise—without curdling it, until a savoury basinful of creamy sauce resulted. At every awakening we strenuously hoped for another day's peace; every night we congratulated ourselves on having enjoyed it. And yet, when the dreaded event came, it took us by surprise: we had not expected it in the explosive form of the German-Soviet pact. (I remembered Georges Bonnet, and his crafty double-dealing: he must be laughing on the other side of his face now, hoist with his own petard . . .) Hitler would give no more quarter: he would now be able to swallow Poland, and after Poland our turn would come. Now the choice was clear: war tomorrow or slavery ever after.

Our party broke up in consternation, though unsurprised. I remember the farewell of one of our group, a man getting on for fifty but the most smartly dressed among us, with a white silk cravat; he gave me a sad smile: 'To think I probably won't see him again . . . .' thus expressing, somewhat crudely, his conviction that war was imminent and that I might well be killed. (In fact, by an irony of fate, it was he who was killed a week later in a car accident on the Place de la Concorde.) Indeed, no further Munich could be imagined nor a durable peace, unless a political upheaval in France produced a Fascist dictatorship.

'You don't seriously believe that, do you?' anxiously asked Yvonne Paraf, an old friend of mine, a few days later. Her name will crop up more than once in these pages. We had known each other since we were children. I had even been in love with her for a time in my young days, before my feelings had turned into a more solid and enduring friendship. We were walking at low tide over the rocky beach at Plougrescant, where I had stopped off on our way back.

'Don't seriously believe what?' I asked. 'In war?'

'Why, no! In a Fascist putsch?'

'That depends. If France doesn't mobilize within the next forty-eight hours—she's been havering about too long already—it means she is ready to give Hitler *carte blanche*. And to make a deal with him, she'll call in one of our Fascist types—Doriot, Déat, or worse.'

'You're a cheerful soul . . . Do you remember how we argued when Hitler occupied the Rhineland? No war at any price, you said in those days.'

'Yes, you were right then. And objectively I was wrong, seeing where it's got us. And yet, if we had the choice over again? With another five years of peace before us? Would I really think any differently? After all, people get assassinated—look at Doumer, Barthou, Alexander of Serbia—so why not Hitler?'

'Tyrants don't get murdered these days.'

On the rocks of Plougrescant, sunset burnished the wet kelp which squelched with a damp pop as our feet squashed its blisters. We knew that this last seashore walk with its tang of salt and iodine would live on in our memories as the end of an epoch, that of the years between the wars which had coincided with the springtime of our lives. We were both getting on for forty, so, whatever happened, *finita la commedia*. Tonight, as in a theatre, the curtain sank on our youth just as the sun was now sinking before our eyes below the watery horizon. In silence we watched its last gleam, which entered my heart with poignant sweetness.

And indeed, at dawn next morning, as we were driving away from Plougrescant in the old Ford, with *Paludes* on the roof, the posters were up on all the walls: Mobilization. A great many age-groups were called up simultaneously. So France meant business; that was good; but it also meant war. And that was such an enormous event that it seemed to me out of all proportion to what a man can feel about it; and indeed, faced with the imminent catastrophe, I was filled with a sort of bovine indifference. In no time I found myself back at Embrun, with Captain Vernet and a young subaltern by the name of Mattéi, just out of the military academy of Saint-Cyr— a small, squarish fellow who seemed very shy. This time there was no more question of a duty period of twenty-one days, nor even of 'international tension'. At any moment now the invasion of Poland was expected, followed immediately by France's entry into the war. Oddly enough, Vernet no longer believed in it: with striking optimism, slapping the leather-belt which strained round his fat, college-bursar's paunch, he now bet me that Hitler wouldn't dare. The next day the German Army invaded the Polish Corridor.

And now a strange thing could be seen: the right-wing press, all those patriotic, nationalist, sabre-rattling die-hard papers, were making common cause with both fascists and last-ditch pacifists in a clamour for peace. 'Die for Danzig?' protested the Fascist Marcel Déat in the daily paper *L'Oeuvre*, while the pacifist Jean Giono called on the farmers to desert: 'Better to live on your knees than die on your feet.' He was put in jail. Jailed too were the Communists, held to be responsible for the Soviet-German pact and hence suspected of being in sympathy with Hitler. Their party was banned. In fact, the pact had thrown their rank and file into wild disarray, and the ban brought them rallying back to their outlawed party.

Then came the declarations of war, first by Britain and eight hours later by France. This delay left me with a bad taste in my mouth: didn't it seem like a hint of French reluctance to follow her ally? As for us at Embrun, only a few miles as the crow flies from the frontier of Lombardy, Italy's entry into the war was what we were waiting for. But nothing happened; Mussolini made no move. Was he keeping himself in reserve to play the honest broker once again? Vernet was convinced of it, while I was again beset by fears. Suppose France had declared a bogus war? Suppose she was merely pretending, as a face-saving device, to fulfil her obligations towards Poland, but with a secret intention to negotiate? Was this the means devised by Bonnet and Daladier to keep the Republic alive without really opening hostilities? The fact that Mussolini had so far abstained lent credence to such theories and implied the existence of some secret agreement. And as if no threat need be feared from beyond the Alps, the troops covering that frontier were withdrawn and transferred instead to the banks of the river Isère, near Romans. Nothing moved on any other frontier, either; the front itself was quiet except for a few forays by isolated reconnaissance squads, although our forces there were said to outnumber the Germans by six to one. Hitler meanwhile was left to devastate Poland. Furthermore, our inactivity, which troubled me increasingly, produced among our troops a lazy scepticism and the comforting thought that things would turn out all right without any actual scrapping. The colonel's speeches to the men had an ambiguous ring: though he appealed to their patriotism, he never so much as mentioned Hitler and his régime, as if the war, in his eyes, were merely an opportunity to display military virtues. It was my task, afterwards, to fill in the gaps for my machine-gunners who were left puzzled by the colonel's words, but I don't know if I sounded convincing. My horror of violence, a legacy of my former pacifism, must have seeped through my words at times, and though I explained with deep conviction what we were fighting for, I wonder whether I was as good at stirring up martial spirits which had gone somewhat quiescent.

One piece of news appalled me: the appointment of Jean Giraudoux as chief of the Information Service. He had taken up his quarters at the Hôtel Continental, where all the bedrooms had been converted into offices. Everyone knows what Information means in wartime: the official distribution of eye-wash. I could not conceive a worse self-betrayal for a writer. To my mind, a writer took up the pen as a monk takes the cowl: to take the vow of truth. To write to order was necessarily to fail in this foremost duty. That on top of this the renegade should be called Giraudoux cut me to the quick. During the First World War at least, the eye-wash merchants were named Bordeaux, Barrès, Marcel Hutin. But Giraudoux! It smarted as if I myself were compromised, together with all who loved him. And when that all-too-famous poster blossomed out on every wall, proclaiming: 'We shall win because we are the strongest!' I felt affronted, not so much by this stupid piece of bravado, like that of a frightened child whistling in the dark, which left us more alarmed than reassured about our real strength, but because it instantly debased the essence of our fight, reducing the war to a mere rivalry between two competing powers, the justice (or injustice) of their respective causes being much of a muchness.

* * *

We had left Embrun for Romans, a small garrison town famous for its shoes, not far from Valence and the Rhône. In the train that arrived from Briançon towards three in the morning, our small detachment joined up with the bulk of the battalion, among whom were a dozen officers we did not know. A bunch of men thrown together in a coherent group will very quickly develop an *esprit de corps*, hostile to all outsiders, and our little trio of officers was received with immediate distrust by our fellow-passengers in the blacked-out train. We got separated from one another, and for the rest of the night, alone with strangers in the compartment, I felt a complete non-person. True, I was offered a cigarette now and then, caught a glimpse of faces in the glow of a match; but nobody spoke to me as I was not familiar with the topics of common interest to the officers from Briançon. What is more, I was the only Parisian, since the 15/9 Battalion of the Alpine Infantry was primarily recruited among men from mountain regions. Real contact only occurred in the morning, when the first ray of sunshine came through the windows. It was followed by another from the doorway leading to the corridor when the radiant face of a lieutenant, his amused smile beaming with a universal friendship that embraced all our group, appeared for a moment in the half-open door. In a voice enlivened with a hint of a Cévenol accent, he announced gaily that breakfast was served. Before passing on to tell the glad news in the next compartment, he gave a little wink of connivance to the 'new boy'—myself—and it was as if a door had sprung open: at once I felt welcomed, integrated. The cordial, cheerful visitant seemed, moreover, to have unloosed the tongues around me. I found myself conversing with the man opposite, who had the sturdy face of a Savoyard surmounted by a rebellious crop of black curly hair; I learned his name at last—Battail—and also that of the radiant lieutenant, Jean Chazal, a young magistrate from Thiers, at present in charge of the officers' mess.

Coffee, not very strong but boiling hot, was poured into our mess-tins, and while we were drinking it a murmur rose in the corridors: 'The Vercors . . . the Vercors . . . ' I knew it by name, and liked the sound of it for its suggestion of noble grandeur, but up to now I had only vaguely located this mighty mountain massif at the foot of the Alps. I stepped into the corridor and was surprised at the respectful awe, bordering on veneration, with which my mountaineer companions appeared to regard this natural fortress with its stern ramparts. Soon I was in the grip of the same feeling— perhaps it was catching—but the indomitable majesty of this enormous ship rising straight from the plain did indeed exercise a growing fascination. Slowly the train passed along its foot, as if intent on allowing me time to absorb this imposing vision, which would, I knew, be unforgettable. Yet how could I have guessed the place the Vercors was to occupy in my life?

The battalion was quartered near Romans, in a small village with roofs of Roman tiles, surmounted by an ancient Byzantine-Roman-esque church of ochre-coloured stone. Behind it rose two sugar-loaf hills which looked like the twin humps of a verdant camel. The village went by the—to French ears—uneuphonious name of Mours-Saint-Eusèbe.

Here we enjoyed the mellow charm of a prolonged summer. Men under arms are like children on holiday. They are no longer responsible for their lives, which are looked after by a motherly Army. By the sole virtue of having donned a uniform they are fulfilling their duty to society. From the youngest lieutenant right up to the battalion C.O.—a big paper-mill owner in private life— a sort of infantilism took hold of us all. Most of the time not spent in duties, mail distribution and letter-writing, we lived in a state of carefree unconcern which tallied with the 'phoney war' whose outcome was beyond our ken. Once again in Poland's history, it could be said that 'order reigned in Warsaw'; the martyred country had been divided up between the Germans and the Russians, whose armies stood face to face. From then on, all was quiet in Europe.

The important thing was how to kill time—for want of an enemy. Mealtimes were the highlights of our days, and Chazal was in charge of them. He would open these proceedings conscientiously, with an unfailing smile and the ritual formula: 'Good appetite, gentlemen, and may the last mouthful choke you, but only in order of rank and in the interests of promotion.' The rest of the day we played *pétanque*—the traditional French game of bowls. Battail, the big Savoyard, was the champion player, together with the little Corsican subaltern, whose shyness had vanished as if by magic to make way for a sardonic aggressiveness. Every day he would challenge his senior, who took a poor view of being beaten by this little pip-squeak. Part of Battail's charm consisted in his vast capacity for indignation at any kind of injustice, whether to him or anyone else. He would turn just as white with rage, calling all the bystanders to witness in speechless protest, at what we learned about the French internment camps where the Spanish Republicans or German political refugees were left to moulder, as he would at the malicious pebble that had driven his bowl off course and made it land miles from the jack. One night, after being invited to a neighbouring mess of balloon-crew officers, he returned possessed of a secret that impressed us all. We were having dessert, and there was a dish of walnuts on the dinner-table. He picked up a dozen nuts and proceeded to bombard the windows with them as hard as he could. Not a single pane shattered: what cracked was the nuts! We all followed suit—with the same result. He was almost chaired in triumph. This exploit rankled with Mattéi, who promptly bet him that he, Mattéi, *would* break a window. As usual, Battail accepted the bet, and at the first shy, the glass burst into splinters. The little Corsican had espied a pane with a crack in it!

So the days passed, since the only alternative to a good laugh was a good cry. At night, in the room I occupied in an old house which, with its vine-grown pergola and stone staircase, seemed to come out of an operetta and smelled fragrantly of cinnamon and woodsmoke, I would fret and fume to see France sinking ever more deeply into a careless apathy which made me fear a rude awakening.

No such fear was felt in the mess. Some of my fellow-officers had obtained copies of my *Visions rassurantes de la Guerre* for me to autograph for them. They laid bets on my prediction about May 12, 1940. We were now in October. It was widely held that in seven months either real fighting would have broken out long before and we'd be in it, or else it would all have been settled. The latter course seemed to them more likely, and I feared they might be right. 'In that case,' I said, 'we'll have Doriot or the *Cagoule*.'[1] But this met with general scepticism. Chazal took my arm and, smiling no longer, told me of his own anxieties, which were much the same as mine. What should we do if France let herself be dominated by Hitler? He was thinking of what Jules Romains, who hailed from the Velay mountains like himself, had conjectured in one of the volumes of his *Men of Good Will*: he had imagined that in the course of some interminable future war, masses of deserters might form organized bands on a medieval pattern, entrench themselves in caves or in the depths of forests, and spend years there living as outlaws. A prophetic vision? So Chazal was inclined to believe; and he could very well see himself, if he were prevented from pronouncing judgments within the framework of law and honour, taking to the mountains with other recalcitrants like himself. We had no idea that he had just invented in his own mind the Resistance movement and the *maquis* . . . .

[1]Clandestine French Fascist organization in the inter-war years.

V

Yvonne Paraf wrote: 'When shall we two meet in Plougrescant
again?' And I wrote back: 'Never. Our bodies may some day be
there again, but it won't be you and it won't be me. All our youth
was spent between two wars, as if between two walls. After what is
going to happen now we can have no idea of what we shall be like
on the other side of the wall, even supposing we are still alive.' But
the last thing that would have occurred to me at the time was that
I would have changed profession and turned into a writer, although
I already knew that I should never draw again the way I used to
draw. 'Perhaps as with the Breughels,' I wrote to Yvonne, 'people
will later refer to a Bruller the Elder and a Bruller the Younger . . . .'

The fact was that during the past months my ideas had undergone some kind of revolution. Ever since the distant day in my
youth when, at the corner of Rue Bonaparte and Rue du Four, at
the end of a deliberation on the purpose of the human race, I had
suddenly said to myself (as so many others have said before and after
me): 'In a world devoid of any *raison d'être*, nothing is any use and
nothing matters,' that nihilism had, if not actually impregnated, at
least inspired most of my creative work. Throughout the thirties
and in all the one hundred and sixty prints I had published up to
the war under the general title of *The Dance of the Living*, I had
satirized man's futile agitation on the surface of a planet lost amid
vast galaxies; I had stigmatized his ludicrous careerism, his wanton
malice, his idiotic snobbery. Often, though, I had thought to myself
that if nothing was any use, it was just as ridiculous to draw and,
even more, to worry about the success of my drawings. I answered,
with Pascal, that I was in the boat with the rest of mankind, and
since one had to fill one's life somehow and even make a living, I
might as well fill it with humour. At other times, again, I had said
to myself that if nothing mattered, then war and peace didn't
matter either, and to worry about them was therefore pointless. My
answer was that in an absurd universe, suffering was the most
absurd and thus the most odious thing of all, and that war, for the
suffering it caused, consequently stood condemned as the ultimate

absurdity. But for some time already I had had to admit that I never stopped contradicting myself, for in this meaningless World I was nevertheless ready to suffer and die to preserve an ideal as meaningless as itself, and if necessary by means of war—the height of immorality! Thus floundering in contradictions, I said to myself that some day I should have to find the clue to the puzzle, and whatever the clue might be, it would certainly no longer fit in with my previous inspiration. If my *Dance of the Living* had a later sequel, the desperate sarcasm which had constituted its black humour in the days of Bruller the Elder would be missing. But apart from this certainty, I hadn't the slightest inkling of what the future prints of Bruller the Younger might be like.

At Mours-Saint-Eusèbe some other truths began to dawn on me as well. We were given a good deal of battle-training to develop our fighting qualities. During one of these exercises, at some distance from the village, when I was ordered to protect the battalion's retreat with my machine-guns, Major Verney gave me specific orders: 'You will withdraw only at the last moment.' Having chosen suitable emplacements for my guns to ensure accurate cross-fire, I waited for the attack from the opposite side, and thereafter we fired away desultorily for over an hour before we found ourselves outflanked. If we stayed put, we risked being encircled and put out of action. But what if, by withdrawing too soon, I put the rest of the battalion in jeopardy? What did Verney mean with his 'last moment'? How was I to judge that it had come? That I couldn't hold out for one, or ten, or forty minutes more? While I was thus shilly-shallying, the circle closed around us. Attacked from all sides, we had to smash our way out with practice-grenades, and I virtually lost my mules as well as my machine-guns.

That is how I discovered that in the heat of action I was not a leader but a drivelling intellectual. A leader would have recognized the famous 'last moment' without getting bogged down in impotent reasoning; he would have relied on circumstances to prompt an almost instinctive judgment. But I could have reached a decision only in the midst of cataclysm, when I could see my men and guns being blown to pieces all around me. Wouldn't I, in action, be a positive cataclysm myself for the boys under my command? I thought of Hamlet, wavering as to whether the ghost he had seen was actually his father or the Devil, able to bring himself to slay the

royal murderer only in the cataclysm of buttonless foils and poisoned weapons swapped in fury, after his indecision had already
caused the needless deaths of Polonius and Ophelia, of Guilden-
stern, Rosencrantz, Laertes, the Queen—and himself. Neither
Hamlet nor I were cut out for such action, and this kept worrying
me.

Autumn was advancing, but not the war. The front was perfectly
quiet. We passed our time playing *pétanque* and making fun of one
another: of the M.O., who was chalking up an impressive score of
feminine conquests in Romans with his deceptive appearance of a
T.B. case on the point of death; of the youngest lieutenant who was
sighing for the pretty postmistress; of the three elderly captains,
who seemed to have walked out of a famous series of pre-war
cartoons, *Les Pieds Nickelés*—the Layabouts—and whose names even
stressed the likeness: Brochenin, Coup-la-Fronde and Dumollard.[1]
They were veterans of the Great War, bemedalled down to their
bellies, but a bit flabby with wine and fat, and I was worried how
they would manage against the steely-eyed athletic young SS. men
whom I had seen on the Kehl Bridge.

In mid-November we learned that the battalion was due to leave
Romans for an unknown destination. The rumour spread that we
were being sent to Rumania to attack the Germans from the rear,
far from the Siegfried Line; or else to Asia Minor to relieve the
Finns from Russian pressure. . . . Actually, we found ourselves one
rainy morning, after an endless journey towards nowhere, in the
plain of Rheims, billeted in a soulless village bang in the middle of
beetroot fields. Another pretty name: Poilcourt (lit.: Short Pelt).
A narrow, muddy brook passed through it, flanked by sickly bushes,
and called La Retourne. Orders from high up were to dig trenches
all along the outskirts of the village. I never grasped what they were
supposed to be for. But I wasn't given much time to worry about it:
a week or so after our arrival, marching back from exercises under
a drizzle that turned the road into a slushy mess of squashed
beetroot, I turned round, heavily laden, to see whether the mules
were following, and felt myself dragged off balance by the haversack on my back; my foot slipped and, as I was trying to right
myself with the other foot, I heard a dull crack beneath me. Even
before the first twinge of pain, I knew I had broken my leg. On a

[1]The names of the originals were: Ribouldingue, Croquignol and Filochard.

straight road in flat country, this was a vexing thing to happen to an officer of a ski unit . . . I had to be evacuated and, an hour later, found myself at the military hospital of Rethel. I was in great pain, but had to wait several hours before someone attended to me. The chief medico was a cheerful old-stager, a laryngologist in civilian life, who felt as if he too were on holiday and declared himself delighted at this opportunity of reducing a fracture, his first chance of doing so since his junior hospital days. He was obviously enjoying himself. My own enjoyment was rather less, for makeshift male nurses were stretching my leg in all directions and I sweated with the effort to keep myself from yelling, while he manufactured such a tight plaster cast that someone had to come and slit it open during the night to relieve my swelling leg.

The Rethel hospital transferred me to the one in Rheims. This time I fell into the hands of a kidney specialist. He declared the fracture inexpertly reduced and took a keen pleasure in rebreaking it without an anaesthetic, pulling my leg all over the place once again, and then encasing it in a plaster cast 'of a new type', as he said. The result was—and still is—a foot with a Chaplinesque tendency to turn outward and a shortened leg, which fortunately did not make me limp too badly, the hip being more or less able to compensate for the shortening, except in moments of fatigue. In the meantime, in my hospital bed, I was making various discoveries. My neighbour was a staff captain who was getting over an attack of nephritis, and whose sceptical detachment on the conduct of the war bordered on black humour. His division was in line along the unfortified Belgian frontier, to the west of the Maginot Line. (In fact, more or less covering Bapaume . . .) The troops, he told me, spent their time digging trenches, whereupon there would be a change of generals, the new one would countermand everything, and the men would proceed to fill up the trenches and dig new ones elsewhere. My amazement made him chuckle. That's nothing, he said. Against the tank units which, in defiance of official doctrine, had proved such a shattering striking-force in Poland, we possessed no efficient armament other than the old 75 cannon, which was useless in a war of movement. With wry humour he pretended to reassure me with the information that the manufacture of more effective weapons was under consideration and that, anyhow, according to the same official doctrine inspired by Pétain, the Ardennes forest was impenetrable by armoured divisions. But how long would it take, I enquired, to supply the front-line units with sufficient anti-tank guns? Twelve to eighteen months, he said, and we both prayed that Hitler would be considerate enough to bide his time till then. . . .

After leaving hospital I spent my convalescence with my family at Villiers-sur-Morin. It was a dry, fine winter. The press was vociferously slamming the Russians and supporting the Finns, without asking themselves any awkward questions about whether Field-Marshal Mannerheim's Finland might not be planning some military pact with Germany. I went back to my interrupted album, which dealt with human foibles, the sort of mild madness we are all prone to. (It was never published, having been destroyed by fire some years later.) I found out that Colonel Humbert was stationed in the neighbourhood, only a few miles away; he had been my captain fifteen years earlier at the Officers' Training School of Coëtquidan. Moreover, he was the brother of my friend Paulette, a very gifted illustrator. General Headquarters were in fact situated in our area, between the two rivers, the Grand Morin and the Petit Morin. Humbert ran the Personnel Section from an office at Jouarre. This was a piece of luck. I asked him for an appointment, he invited me to lunch with him, and I expounded my problems.

My broken leg had solved the major one which had worried me: that of the machine-gun officer who had misgivings about his ability, in a crisis, to take decisions with the necessary promptness. I had been warned that I should limp for some time, and there was no question meanwhile of sending me back to a marching unit. So far so good. But on the other hand, I told him, the prospect of being relegated to some office 'funk-hole' while all my friends in the battalion were under fire would be quite intolerable. Couldn't I get posted to the artillery? Or else to one of the Geographical branches, the Divisional Topography Section, where you work at the front in liaison with the combat units?

Humbert feared that a transfer to artillery would be difficult, since changes of corps were suspended in wartime. But he would see to it that I got transferred to Topography; that was a promise. We began chatting, and I asked him how he thought the war would evolve, in the light of his information. He told me that they were looking for a battlefield: there wasn't room for one on the front any more, what with the Maginot and Siegfried Lines facing each other . . . And where could they find a battlefield? Well, on the beaches of Northern Germany, for instance, a sea-borne landing perhaps. This, I thought, might have been feasible in the days of carbines, but in 1940 it seemed to me a complete anachronism. How could one hope to effect a landing under the overwhelming firing-power of modern weapons? What about the lesson of Verdun?

This seemed to me just as fanciful as what I heard on another occasion from Captain Mangin, the general's son and Diego Brosset's brother-in-law. Impregnable fortifications? he cried. That was disregarding the invention of new weapons of as yet unknown power. Had he already got wind of atomic research, of heavy water taken to safety (or so it was fondly hoped) in Norway? I knew nothing of all this: sea-borne landings and mysterious weapons both seemed to me figments of the imagination. It is clear that there was a lot about our century I had not yet grasped.

* * *

At the end of my convalescence, in April, I went back to Romans to join the base unit of the 15/9. And there a surprising series of coincidences occurred—lucky or unlucky according to how you look at them—without which I would not now be writing these lines.

On my arrival at Romans, my first concern was to look up the sergeant in charge of entering arrivals and departures. I knew him well and asked him to put me down, against all rules, as being there 'in transit'. The idea of rotting at base did not appeal to me. My battalion was in the Haute-Marne, more or less at rest. Why shouldn't I join them and, in the company of Chazal and Battail, wait there for my transfer to the Geographical Section at Montmorency? But no sooner had the sergeant obligingly put my name down than the Colonel walked in as if he had been eavesdropping. He recognized me and enquired to what duties I had been assigned. I risked everything and confessed my plan. 'On two sticks?' he cried. 'I don't want to see you brought back here on a stretcher!' That finished it. Had I succeeded, I should have reached the battalion just as they began to retreat and I should never have been able to keep up with them. . . .

Instead, I was directed to the despatching unit and put to work fitting the men out before sending them back to active service. Routine work but depressing, for whenever I asked for new footwear from the Quartermaster, who was as stumpy and fat as *Père Ubu* and just as stupidly pig-headed, he would raise his arms towards heaven and swear that he had none. At Romans, centre of the shoemaking industry? It hardly seemed likely; all the same, I had to see the men leave with old patched boots which made their feet ache and would fall to pieces in six weeks. It was sickening.

Nor was I any happier in the mess, where a bunch of reserve officers—with two or three exceptions—were concerned with one thing only: to get overlooked. This was understandable in the case of the old Major, a businessman from Montélimar and a provincial councillor of the Gard. A stick-in-the-mud of the Radical Party, he had the long heavy jowl of a Marseilles actor, and a liquid accent which sounded as though he had dipped each word in his soup. He ate like four men but dozed off for a few seconds after every mouthful, and was certainly no longer fit to fight. Fair enough too, at a pinch, for the two elderly regular captains, as happy as sand-boys to be back in uniform but not anxious for any more mud and blood. What I found unbearable was the cynical attitude of the lieutenants in their thirties, who laughingly proclaimed their fondness for their own skins. Back at the battalion, nobody had gone in for heroics, but neither had anyone made a parade of his cowardice. How I missed the friendly gaiety of our good, plain meals, with old walrus-moustached Barthola as treasurer and Jean Chazal in charge of the grub.

Battail went home on leave. He dropped me a line from Grenoble, which was an hour's train-ride from Romans. The following Sunday I hastened over to lunch with him in the primary school at La Tronche where he lived with his wife, who was also a teacher and had a delicate, sensitive face. It was mid-April. There were a few other guests at the luncheon and, over dessert, Battail fetched out my album about the war and made them all read the famous sentence. 'May 12 is coming closer,' he warned, 'coming closer!' And he laughed, and they all laughed with him, for the sunny spring day and the flowering trees seemed so far removed, despite the disturbing events in Norway, from any threat of violence. Nobody could believe it.

And then it was my turn to go to Paris for a week. I should be staying there till the evening of May 9th. I don't know why spring in Paris has always seemed to me so movingly gay. Here too, on the pavements or in the cobbled streets, under the flowering chestnut-trees, nothing recalled or foreshadowed the war. I dropped in at the War Ministry in the Rue de Grenelle to see about my transfer: if I could only get sent to Montmorency without having to pass through Romans again! An obliging lieutenant showed me my file, ready for signature. He would do his best to speed it up.

I went back for news on the morning of my departure. My file? Expected back any day. Tomorrow perhaps, or the day after . . . It was vexing and rather silly to have to go to Romans just to say hello and good-bye.

On my way out I dropped in on my brother-in-law, who had been assigned to the military vetting of news before its release to the Ministry of Information. The two offices were practically facing each other. I expected to find him in civvies like myself, but he was wearing a smart, brand-new captain's outfit. In him too, I noticed, the uniform had produced a pleased sense of rejuvenation. He seemed confident. While we were chatting, his aide entered. Casually he mentioned that troop movements had been reported in Hanover in the direction of the Netherlands; then he joined in our conversation. Pierre Fort seemed unperturbed by this news, so I did not worry either.

Outside, the May sunshine filtered down between the roofs, illuminating the street. Many women were already wearing summer frocks. I should be happy enough at Montmorency. I'd soon kiss Romans good-bye!

Still, there was nothing to do but take the train that evening. As usual, I didn't sleep much. In the pasty dawn, as the train pulled into Lyons, the station rang with the wail of sirens. An air-raid warning? Nobody seemed to pay much attention. Perhaps it was a practice-alarm. The train went on. An hour and a half later we reached Valence, where I had to change. Since there was quite a long wait for the local slow train, I walked out of the station to have a *café crème*. As I opened the door of the café, the sirens went off. Something was up, for sure! The waiter told me that this was the third warning, that the Germans had invaded Holland and that French troops had crossed into Belgium.

VI

MAY 10th! It was incredible! Was I gifted with second sight? And if so, what would happen at Bapaume in two days' time? As I sat in the crawling local train it suddenly occurred to me that my friends in the battalion would be asking themselves the same question. Unless . . . my heart missed a beat: 'The *n*th battalion was wiped out.' What if it were theirs?

A fortnight later this idea had developed into an obsession. Madame Battail kept 'phoning and 'phoning. She had had no news. Had I? Did we know where the battalion was? I reassured her as best I could with logical arguments that failed to set my own mind at rest. Actually, I had not been clairvoyant at all: the battalion was in a quite different sector. But that was something we discovered only much later.

During those early days, Giraudoux and his crowd lived up to their job as dispensers of soothing syrup: their news bulletins, full of detail, merely lacked any particulars that could have given us a clear idea of the situation. . . . In the mess, where everyone was convinced that the Germans had fallen headlong into the trap we had laid for them in the Flanders plain, optimism was rife. I should have liked to share it. But it did not seem to me that to declare Brussels an open city was an earnest of success. I was uneasy; this was too much like my childhood memories of the early days of the last war, in 1914. It had caught us unawares in Switzerland, and for a whole long month we had been unable to leave. In early September, full of trust in the official French news bulletins, we had taken a train for Paris when, on the platform at Lyons, we saw in the packed, wild-eyed crowd a friend of my father's, minus collar and tie, who asked us where we were going. 'To Paris?' he cried. 'But the Germans are there by now!' My father almost fainted: on the strength of the official communiqués, he thought they were still at Charleroi.

This time, even Giraudoux's talent would have been incapable of keeping such illusions alive for long. After a period during which we kept victoriously 'containing' pockets and breaches in our positions, he was obliged to announce the disintegration of General Corap's army. Cocking a snook at the opinion of Field-Marshal Pétain and the French High Command, the German armoured troops had passed unhindered through the Ardennes. Sedan proved to be a permanent symbol of French rout. Leopold II of the Belgians capitulated and was named 'the traitor-king' in an effort to preserve the prestige of General Blanchard, who had let himself be encircled like a novice. The wholesale retreat towards Dunkirk turned into an epic, but it was a sombre epic. The disaster was immeasurable. The French army was smashed to pieces, cut to shreds by the tanks, nailed to the ground by the enemy's Stukas. A hundred miles from the front dazed soldiers were still streaming back. There was no more mention in the press of Corap or even of Gamelin, the defeated C.-in-C. I was convinced that, disgraced by their own incompetence and responsible for their country's collapse, they had committed suicide. Today I can only wonder at my naïvety. Gamelin was very much alive and quite self-satisfied: he put the entire blame on his subordinates.

Weygand was recalled from his Middle East command. An unknown figure became Minister of Defence: a certain Colonel de Gaulle, who had been promoted general for the occasion. His photograph in the newspapers showed him wearing an unduly tall *képi* and gloves affectedly turned back. His long, disdainful face, with its small moustache, wore an air of aristocratic arrogance. Then the whole cabinet went to the Cathedral of Notre-Dame to pray to the Holy Virgin to save France. So that was the depth to which the Republic had sunk . . . What next? A pilgrimage to Lourdes? Were we reverting to childhood, sliding back five centuries? And here I was stuck in this damnable base, this dump, this sump, losing all hope of receiving my transfer. I didn't belong to the battalion any more, and where was it, anyhow? I badgered my colonel to give me some assignment where I could make myself useful; pointing to my limp, he answered that I was useful where I was, and I no longer knew what to do with myself.

By-passing the normal channels, I had sent off a spate of telegrams—but who knew if they were still being delivered?—to Colonel Humbert, to the War Office and to Montmorency, without getting any reply. And then, on June 12, the base at last received advice of my transfer. Three days earlier I might still have been able to get there, but now the hoped-for order was merely a bad joke: the whole of the Geographical Service, between the Marne up north and the Garonne down south, had evaporated; where could I look for them? At Bordeaux? Meanwhile, since I was now redundant at Romans, and since Italy had just declared war on us to be in at the kill, the Colonel sent me with a handful of officers on a mission: to prepare the withdrawal to the far side of the Rhône of the raw recruits who were still untrained and unarmed. An imperfectly covered truck trundled us through the rain to Saint-Etienne, where a dapper general in high spirits sent us off to the Velay, to a forlorn mountain hamlet by the name of Boën. The name made me jump, for it was also the title of a play by Jules Romains: *Boën, or Personal Possessions.* What rasping irony, at this moment when Paris was falling, a year after the French had sacrificed Prague so as not to imperil their own personal possessions . . . Where were they all now—Romains, Crémieux, Claude Aveline—who had been there on that memorable evening when we had been welcomed with little flags and hymns of victory?

Next day at dawn I was having breakfast in the restaurant of Boën's modest little hotel when the door opened and a man came in. It was Claude Aveline. We gazed at each other thunderstruck. Years later, after the war, a serious personal difference separated us, but at that time we were linked together by common memories and a common hatred of fascism in all its forms. He had been driving all through the night, convoying a niece who had been entrusted to his care from Brittany to Provence. He had been on the point of stopping for coffee at another café a little farther up the road but had changed his mind and walked into this one. . . . Wasn't it strange? In turn I related how I had missed by a minute being sent to my battalion, and by a day being posted to the Geographical Service, both now out of reach. How many coincidences had led up to this incredible encounter! And at Boën (or personal possessions)! As I made this remark, I never suspected that this was only the modest beginning of them.

I left him and spent two days preparing the billets for the new recruits, and we then climbed back into our truck. We had removed the tarpaulin, for the sun was shining. It was a Sunday. The tree-lined roads were filled with people taking a Sunday walk. Girls in flowered frocks were laughing, cars were dawdling slowly. Other cars, by contrast, sped past us, carrying mattresses and assorted household goods on their roofs, their drivers clutching the steering-wheels: they were the first units of the vast stampede which was called the exodus. The strollers watched them with amusement, unaware that in a week's time they themselves would be fleeing along those roads. So difficult is it for a human being to imagine panic or misfortune before the very minute when he himself is struck by them.

On reaching the base, we found out that we had been sent to Boën on a fool's errand: without waiting for our report, the recruits had been sent off to Charente. And where in Charente? To Bussac. Better and better: the Mayor of Bussac was Gustave Fort, my sister's father-in-law; and she herself had rented a house near there for the summer, where my sons had just joined her together with their mother and with mine. . . .

I was dumbfounded and furious. How many more dirty tricks was Providence going to play on me? Instead of this senseless waste of time at Romans, wouldn't I have been a lot better off there? Why the devil hadn't I been sent to escort the recruits to Bussac instead of traipsing round Boën like a fool? Once again I had missed my chance, probably by no more than an hour or two.

I thought I should have one more chance to get away from the damned place, though. The defeat was reaching its final stage. The Panzers were tearing along the roads, meeting with no resistance except on rare occasions. They were overtaking the retreating troops and the fleeing population—and both were being ruthlessly machine-gunned out of a sky as bare of clouds as of French fighter planes. In the depot, ragged soldiers, haggard and limp with fatigue, lay sleeping on the cobbled yard, packed like sardines. What had become of the Government? Nothing was known of its whereabouts since Paul Reynaud's voice, after a series of historic utterings, had fallen silent. It was said that Churchill and he had met somewhere south of the Loire. In Paris, the great surgeon Thierry de Martel had committed suicide as the Germans entered the city. And on this morning, June 16, the papers informed us that a government of generals had been formed under the presidency of the victor of Verdun. Did this mean a mass levy and a fight to the finish? Most people thought so. Less numerous were those of us who believed that such a galaxy of soldiers, including the most venerable, had been called to act, on the contrary, as official liquidators. Long hours passed as we waited to know which of us was right. But when at noon Pétain's quavering voice announced over the radio that 'we must cease the fight', we were all equally stunned. For all of us, up to that minute, had hoped deep down, like Paul Reynaud, for a miracle. . . . So now, after the Poles, the Norwegians, the Belgians and the Dutch, the French Army too was laying down its weapons. Hitler was victorious all along the line.

What would Britain do? All alone now, face to face with a Germany in complete control of the whole of Europe, would she not ask for quarter? The answer came the next day. From London, over the radio, General de Gaulle told the French that losing a battle did not mean losing a war, and that the war was going on. He appealed to all Frenchmen able to do so to join him and continue the fight. Wasn't that precisely my case? Without men and without a posting, there was nothing for me to do anywhere. Whether de Gaulle was politically on the right or even the extreme right no longer mattered: one must fight under his command. Besides, in my boundless innocence, I had no doubt that he had spoken with official backing, since it was as a Cabinet Minister that he had flown to London. I already saw myself getting on a ship at Bordeaux. I therefore went to see my Colonel to obtain his permission for my departure. He approved, saying he would have done the same at my age, and added that he would naturally have to obtain agreement from Divisional Headquarters. . . . He called up Valence. There was no doubt in his mind, any more than in mine, about the answer. He was, in consequence, as bewildered as I when he heard himself being asked at the other end whether he had gone out of his mind. Two days later de Gaulle had been dismissed from the service and sentenced to death *in absentia*.

This opened our eyes to certain facts. It was no longer a matter of negotiating a cease-fire 'as between soldiers and in honour'. This was a dishonourable attempt to quit at the expense of yesterday's ally. One word on the radio should have tipped us off. The sinister speech had been repeatedly broadcast throughout the day in each news bulletin. But it was no longer Pétain's voice one heard; it was that of an announcer. And the phrase was no longer the one he had used: 'We must cease to fight;' it had become: 'We must try to cease the fight.' This 'try to', inserted as an after-

thought, showed that the fight *might* be continued—which is what
de Gaulle was saying—but that the ending of it was to be a matter of
bargaining with the enemy. At whose expense? Why, at England's,
of course.

But it was also at the expense of the fighting men, as we know.
Duped and demoralised by Pétain's statement that we must lay
down our arms, the men no longer defended themselves and even
stopped retreating. In whole units they allowed themselves to be
disarmed, convinced that they would be left at liberty. They
promptly found themselves shipped off to Germany for the next
five years. Never had so few words cost so many men so dear.

As for me, I called myself every name under the sun for not
having decamped without a word to anyone: I no longer figured
on the roll, I was as free as air. What if I left now, in spite of the
Division's refusal? Events decided the matter for me: by-passing
Lyons, which had been declared an open city, the Germans were
tearing along the Rhône. In less than forty-eight hours they would
be on us. To decamp now would be tantamount to deserting in the
face of the enemy.

The depot was divided up into combat units. For my part, I was
allotted some thirty men returned from convalescence. The armoury
was opened up to distribute weapons; we were allowed one rifle for
three men, obsolete Lebels (apart from two old chassepots which
had doubtless escaped from some museum) and about a hundred
rounds of ammunition. For my own use I had been able to lay
hands on a regulation revolver with half a dozen bullets. The rest
armed themselves with cudgels. I began to think I had slandered
that wretched pachyderm of a quartermaster and that he had
no more boots in his store than machine-guns or modern rifles.
There was a persistent rumour that thousands of unused tanks and
planes had been found by the Germans in army car-parks and
airfields. All this negligence seemed to me the very pattern of the
defeat.

Towards 11 p.m. (by now the dull rumble of the armoured vehicles could be heard along the Rhône) an orderly came to wake me;
the Colonel was summoning all officers. In the dark streets I met
a strange throng of people—silent shadows making unhurriedly
for the upper part of the town. If the population had been
fleeing from the invader it would have been going in the opposite

direction, across the River Isère to the south. What was going on?

Things became no clearer when the Colonel informed us that orders from Divisional Headquarters were that we were to cross the Isère and dig in on the other side. We were to start at 4 a.m. in the first light of dawn, and use the rest of the night preparing to remove all the material from the depot.

At this point, a breathless major hurried in, apologized for being late and reported excitedly that the riverside dwellers were moving away from the Isère because the bridges were to be blown up in a quarter of an hour. The Colonel turned pale with consternation, grabbed the 'phone and called Valence. Yes, the bridges were to be destroyed. At midnight. But weren't our instructions to cross the river at dawn? Maybe, but the Engineers had received different orders. Muddle through the best way you can.

We dashed to the river; at the foot of the downstream bridge we found the engineer officer in charge of the operation. There was a violent altercation between our Colonel and him; the latter eventually gave way, and we were given an hour's grace in which to get our men and animals across the river. The rest was to be abandoned.

I tore back to my billet, a bit handicapped by my gammy leg. After assembling my men, I had only just time to cram my haversack as best I could. The rest of my things? Too many mules were required for evacuating the necessary supplies to allow me to think of my own stuff. I said good-bye to my field-trunk and left it there. But when a little later the disorderly procession began to cross the bridge, I found I had been a fool; all the mules were laden with field-trunks. . ·. . That was the only material saved from the enemy.

It was there, too, that I had the pleasure of seeing the fat Quartermaster hurriedly dump into the Isère, along with other things, two thousand brand-new pairs of boots, of which the local inhabitants tried to salvage a few for their own use.

The bridges were blown up before dawn. On the other bank, the town changes its name and is called Bourg-de-Péage. We watched a bleak dawn come dismally up over the nearby fields. We stood around waiting in the damp dew while each detachment, after an endless farrago, received its orders. The whole of our strength, amounting to two or three hundred men, barely half of them armed with rifles, was ordered to pin the enemy down on the Isère, along a 40-kilometre front between Saint-Nazaire and Châteauneuf. My group of convalescents, moreover, was relieved of its weapons in order to equip fitter men. I just managed to hold on to my revolver.

The Division sent us reinforcements amounting to battalion strength, plus a naval gun with a crew of four. This gun was placed in position opposite one of the wrecked bridges, on the shattered glass from nearby buildings. As for the rest of the battalion, since it was impossible to deploy so few men in a continuous line over the distance to be covered, they were set up as pockets of resistance every mile or so in the hope, no doubt, that the enemy would feel in honour bound not to cross the river at an undefended point.

The unarmed men, mine among them, were christened by the Division 'reserve units' and placed under the command of the gallant Major who used to fall asleep between courses. They were scattered over the hamlets in the rear, first around Chatuzange, a small village in the plain, and then—so as to be more conspicuous—on a hilltop crowned by the village of Marche, some thirty houses with old Roman tiles and a main street like a corkscrew. Behind it and all round, a great void. Not a ghost of artillery, of course, except the naval gun. And this was the extent of the firing power with which the High Command was preparing to withstand the onslaught of the German Army on the Isère.

VII

If the Mayor of Romans had not come to seek out the Colonel, should I have made the strange encounter which was to bring a poignant memory to mind and turn my thoughts, in the middle of defeat and catastrophe, in an unforeseen direction? To cease fire after the signing of the armistice with Germany, all we were waiting for was the armistice with Italy. How had the Mayor learned that, despite this, orders had been given to open fire instantly on the first enemy units that might turn up on the Isère? He came to beg the Colonel to stay his hand at least until the Germans started shooting. What purpose would be served by such a provocation, he asked, which would merely call down cruel retaliation on his town, and perhaps even its destruction? The Colonel sent someone with him to Valence to talk to the Division. The interview was a stormy one. In the heat of the argument, the accusation was made that the only reason for staging a token resistance which, given the disproportion of the forces engaged, could not even qualify as a last-ditch stand, was to obtain an additional star for some ambitious tunic. The Mayor was put under arrest, released by the Prefect, put back behind bars and threatened with being shot.

That evening the Colonel was very pale as he gave us a terse account of the whole affair. The order to fire at sight was confirmed. Back in the billets, I consulted the map. Whenever the Germans felt like it they could cross the Isère at L'Ecancière without firing a single shot; their armoured vehicles could bowl down the Departmental Road 125 between the Vercors and us, and in less than an hour all chance of retreat would be cut off. I sensed very little alarm at this prospect in the Mess. Being without arms, we should surrender with the honours of war; then, two days later, after the signing of the Italian armistice, there would be a cease-fire and everybody would be sent home. Such colossal illusions left me aghast. I was certain of just the opposite—that if we surrendered we should be prisoners for countless years. I am not ordinarily given to superstition, but who does not have fancies in moments of crisis? In a few days it would be June 24th, St John's Day—my patron saint.

What if this chain of bad luck which had kept me here despite all my efforts for the last three months, was to culminate in my being taken prisoner on that very day, like a fool? But I would refuse to give myself up, I decided. Somehow I would manage to head for the Vercors and there I would take to the *maquis* and anyone who liked could follow me.

The first thing to do was to get away from this idiotic hilltop where one spent one's time playing *pétanque* and waiting to be picked up by the Germans. I don't remember what pretext I used, one evening after dinner, to spread a Michelin map out before the eyes of our old Major. I showed him with my finger the trap we were in, behind the trunk road which cut off our retreat, whereas if we went and dug ourselves in three kilometres farther off, our unarmed invalids might yet be able to get away, withdraw to the banks of the Drôme. (I did not mention the Vercors mountains.) He listened to me, his eyes half closed, pulled a face and made no answer. I wondered whether he had already made up his mind: surrender with the honours of war and thus avoid a retreat which would be rendered painful by his varicose veins. I was mistaken. Next day, without any reference to our conversation, he announced in his soupy voice that he had persuaded the Colonel to send us to Peyrus, some distance away from the trunk road. We were to get moving that day.

And that's where the final coincidence occurred, the one that was—though of course I did not yet know it—to give all the previous ones a totally different meaning from what I had feared. Peyrus, though only at the foot of the Vercors range, has all the air of a mountain village, rising in terraces along a road which starts to climb in hairpin bends. This situation suited me down to the ground; we no longer ran the risk of being outflanked and would retain the chance right up to the last moment to take to the heights. I had been billeted in one of the last houses along that road, and was to sleep on the first floor; a refugee family from Lille already occupied the ground floor. Rain had fallen, but a genial summer sun was at last peeping through the clouds and inviting you to get warm again. Outside the house, on a folding canvas chair, sat a fat woman, her flabby flesh bulging all over; at her side sat a little girl of ten or twelve. Across the road, leaning against the wall, stood a young girl who smiled at us as we approached.

All that I saw of her at first glance were her eyes: black, lustrous, dewy, their beauty arrested my glance to the exclusion of the rest of her face, of which I noticed only the harmonious oval with its rather high cheek bones. The resemblance was so fantastic that I stood stock-still with amazement. And I saw myself, twenty years back, at Combloux, which was then still a little-known holiday resort in the Mont Blanc range. I had gone to join my parents there for the summer holidays. I had got down from the motor-coach. A girl was leaning against a tree, watching me, with a smile in her black, lustrous, dewy eyes. Actually, at the time, she had seemed to me scarcely more than a child, dressed in a sailor suit, her fragile shoulders hidden by her long jet-black hair. She was fifteen, the same age as Juliet. I was eighteen, the age of Romeo. I had a distinct preference for older girls, and if I was nevertheless struck by her beauty it was to my eyes the beauty of a child, a mere prom-ise of future loveliness. And indeed my fancy was soon a-flutter round a rather stupid blonde with an English-rose complexion, who was certainly at least nineteen. All the same, on the frequent occasions when the young people staying at the hotel were thrown together, a look from those dark, deep-glowing eyes—not quite black, rather the colour of ploughed earth after rain—would seem to probe me to a great depth, and I felt somewhat troubled. Her name was Stéphanie, and this old-fashioned name for such a young girl had a singular flavour.

One morning about noon I was returning to the hotel after a solitary walk in the nearby woods when I heard through the door of the smoking-room the sound of the piano. Someone was playing Chopin. I was about to go on, but the beauty of the music stopped me. It was the Etude in E major. I had not heard it before, and its gentle sadness, followed by such fury, such fierce rebellion and near-frenzy which consumes itself by its own violence, then fades into resignation and a melancholy reminiscent of its opening bars— all this vibrant harmony awoke a response in my young, romantic heart. Moreover, the Etude was played with a power and intensity, with a sense of pain, too, which apart from exceptional talent revealed an over-sensitive heart that had been wounded by life but which, with the strength and wisdom that come with the years, has learned to overcome all scars. And I wondered what virtuoso had arrived at the hotel, imagining some man in his prime. Already

I felt the onset of a shyness too great to permit me to approach him. How heavily youth weighs on one! I dared not even open the door, and stood listening in the corridor until the melody came to an end. As the last chord, the last vibration died away I managed to summon up the resolve to risk a quick look. The first thing that met my eyes, in front of the piano, was a luxuriant mane of hair. 'Blue hair, a tent of darkness spun . . . ' It cascaded over slender shoulders under a sailor collar. Stéphanie turned round. She saw me and smiled. Her mother and mine, seated a little way off, motioned me to come in.

I was dumbfounded. I was no longer conscious of her childish appearance, so greatly did her inner maturity seem to tower over mine. I asked her if she would play the piece for me again. She did so quite simply, without much urging. I was uplifted, transported, but when she finished all I could do was stammer some formal compliment. We talked; she questioned me about my musical tastes. I did not dare enquire about hers; I felt such a schoolboy before her. She asked me to play something in return. She chose an easy piece, to save me from losing face: the adagio of the Moon-light Sonata. I put as much feeling into it as I could. She listened, standing by the piano, her head a little to one side, with a secret smile, her deep eyes veiled beneath satiny, almost brown eyelids. When the last note died away, her forefinger gently brushed my hand, without a word. My honour was safe, and her eyes told me that this made her glad. The sound of the luncheon gong spared us from spoiling this silence by clumsy words.

During lunch I recovered my spirits a little. Across the tables, from afar, I admired a profile which might one day become the grave, stirring one of a tragic actress but which was now scarcely that of an adolescent. Surely I wasn't going to fall in love with a schoolgirl!

Nevertheless, from that day onward, she never sat down at the piano, even to practise, without my being there to listen. The presence of her mother, emphasising my pianist's youth, aroused contradictory feelings in me: it forced me to keep my distance and at the same time made me impatient. I yearned for a tête-à-tête but had no idea what I would have made of it. Besides, could so young a heart be awakened? Often, in groups of seven or eight, the young people went off to the woods to pick bilberries which we would bring back for the hotel cook to make into jam. We gathered few and talked much. Once I noticed that Stéphanie was not joining in the conversation. Lying on her stomach on the moss, a little apart, she was absently pulling up handfuls of grass, looking at me with unwavering eyes that glowed in the shade. I hardly dared meet that insistent gaze: it seemed to me that if my eyes fastened on hers they could never be torn away again. I had already had a number of youthful flirtations, but the sensation those eyes aroused in me I had never experienced before.

Shyness, reserve, and also the constant presence of a gay, laughing crowd, kept our emotions for a long time in the limbo of the unspoken, the unavowed. One evening, when some foolish, now-forgotten remark of mine must have hurt her, I saw her nervous hand crush the flowers she was holding—perhaps I had picked them for her—and, white-faced, she turned her eyes towards me. I felt sucked into two deep, dark wells, in which I read such pain, such total, naked self-bestowal that the memory of it, impervious to time, still makes me shiver forty years after.

That was the only declaration that passed between us. But on that day all was said. And thus, for a whole month, we loved one another in silence. Once, only once, when we were alone and she had read in my face, or in my attitude, or in something I had stammered out, the irresistible desire to open my heart or perhaps take her into my arms, she had stopped me with the murmur: 'No, Jean, we're too young.' A trembling little hand, stained with bilberries, was laid on mine. I rested my cheek on it for a long moment, and I heeded the warning. Our unspoken love later underwent all the ups and downs that love is prone to: happiness, misunderstandings, disappointments, reconciliations, and these, because they were always half-uttered and fraught with such extreme feeling, assumed an intensity, a suppressed violence that wrought havoc in our hearts. At times, we must have revealed such pitiful torment that even our parents, to enable us to patch things up, sent us out on errands together to Mégève, or to pick more bilberries in the woods. We would come back from these expeditions at peace, full of happiness, of a gentle ecstasy, without once breaking by a word or a gesture the discretion we had tacitly pledged one another. I suppose childhood alone is capable of such strength, such loftiness, such

purity of love. It lasted for four weeks. But in forty years it has never
quite died in my heart.

What happened in Paris after the end of the holidays? I never
knew, at least not with certainty; the tinge of regret, of remorse
which pervades my memories makes me think, however, that I
must bear some guilt: some trivial lie, the covering up of some
ridiculous but unpleasant weakness which was disproportionately
magnified by my failure to confess it and which she must have
found out (or someone helped her to find out)—and all this abandon,
this trust in me spoilt, lost for ever. Probably this is why I have ever
since felt a boundless loathing for even the most trivial lie. I didn't
stop seeing her—her parents liked me, and to this day I enjoy the
faithful friendship of her brothers—but she had drawn back; a
subtle barrier had slipped between us which she never again allowed
me to break down. Perhaps it was simply that distance and absence
had caused her to stop loving me? I would often have preferred to
think so. It would have made me feel less responsible for so bitter a
loss. There are feelings of such lofty nobility that one cannot
descend a single step, admit the slightest flaw, the smallest stain.
A silly fib, aggravated by boyish giddiness, the gambols of a playful
puppy—and though Stéphanie did not yet refuse to see me it was,
I believe, only because she was waiting: more mature than I, and
conscious of it, she may have been expecting with pathetic hope
some reform on my part, some sign of redemption. Alas! I did not
understand. How could I? Not yet twenty and hungry for life,
I still enjoyed flirting and gallivanting about. How I must have
disappointed her! She never let me see it, never deigned to show
her feelings. All the same, one other look she gave me still haunts
me; the look I caught, during some party or other, months—or
years?—later, when I suddenly turned round in the crowd. And
there, resting on me, was that fixed, ardent gaze, filled with
anguished questioning, like the look of a mother who watched over
her sick child sleeping. It was a matter of seconds; the next moment
her face assumed a 'party' smile so natural that I might easily have
doubted having caught that other, poignant flash. Ah! if I had been
older, more mature, perhaps I would have known at that moment
how to force her to speak out, to accuse me, perhaps to listen to
me . . . But I was a child, and with the blundering stupidity of
youth I merely conceived the bright idea of using the confession

that had betrayed her to try and rouse her jealousy. All I succeeded in doing was to get myself entangled with two or three girls in succession and finally to destroy myself, of course, in Stéphanie's eyes.

But it was a long, slow tearing apart, often concealed from me by my own thirst for life, so that time and again I thought I'd got over it and forgotten her; and then a word, a memory, a phrase of Chopin, the mere name of Combloux, a sprig of bilberries on a jam-jar label, and I would be choked with sorrow and regret. We still saw each other, at long intervals. Together we laughed at Jouvet at the Vieux-Colombier in Molière's *Médecin Malgré Lui*. For the space of an hour I could believe that nothing was lost; happiness seemed to spring afresh from our shared laughter. She leant her frail shoulder against my arm. How easy everything seemed, suddenly! But her mother was with us, I was tongue-tied, the opportunity passed, perhaps I let it pass; perhaps that day was the last time Stéphanie waited for a word from me, an impulse I had been unable to offer; it was the end and I did not see her again until much, much later—at her wedding.

Never again after that. The last sight of her I recall (except one fleeting glimpse as she came out of a concert) is that of her face under the bridal veil which she is tearing into fragments, according to custom, to present the filmy shreds to her friends. She is smiling. I reach out my hand in turn. I receive my shred, but do not succeed in catching her eye.

Behind me there is a confused hubbub of voices, music, clinking glasses. Ah, and afterwards . . .

> *Have another biscuit,*
> *A swell like you can risk it,*
> *Fill your glasses, drink your beer,*
> *And then get out of here!*
> *To hell with you! Go boil your head!*
> *I'm sick of you. My love is dead.*[1]

Dead in the abomination of Auschwitz. More than twenty years ago.

To call back that past rips open a wound in my heart—but where was I? Ah, yes, in Peyrus, walking listlessly towards the house

[1]Jacques Prévert.

where I was to stay. And being knocked backward by the perturbing eyes of an apparition. I felt suddenly flooded with purity. The memory of Stéphanie burst upon me in a great gush of freshness, of almost unbearable, crystal whiteness in the pestilential swamp all around me, as if to say 'Don't despair!' The girl smiled. I approached her . . . but when I got within a few steps of her the illusion began to pale, to vanish; the shining mirage gave way to a coarser reality. No, I no longer recognized in those black eyes the tender warmth, the clear, candid fervour of Stéphanie's look, there was only a commonplace flicker of sly curiosity, a sort of challenge emphasized by the provocative breasts encased in a tight, gaudy sweater, and the vulgar stance. I came crashing back to earth. Suddenly drained of feeling, I nodded a greeting, passed without a word, entered the house. Locked in my room, I strove to clear my mind of that girl and my disappointment, so as to refresh my soul with precious memories summoned from the depths. I could not. As if I were being pursued by some cruel, destructive demon, coincidence overleapt all bounds, all credibility. For up through the grimy floorboards from the room below came a sound so stupefying that I thought I must be the victim of a hallucination. But no, I was not raving. What I was hearing—those opening bars, sung in a crude, flashy voice as clumsy fingers tormented the keys of a tinny piano, were—believe it or not!—the sloppy words of an impious lyric-writer, set to that melody I held sacred, the melody of the poignant Etude in E major! When I recovered from my incredulous astonishment, rage gripped me. This was too much! Too much! I stuffed my fingers into my ears, but in midst of all this phoneyness, this monstrous trickery, I was no longer really surprised. On the contrary, sickened with disgust, I even thought: 'I might have known it!' as if I had indeed been expecting, with loathing, that nothing, not even this profanation, would be lacking from this vast hoax, this all-engulfing caricature. In its cacophony, the ridiculous ditty even out-parodied parody; in the depth of our disgrace it taunted me like a symbol, a jeering blasphemy, a wanton wreckage, the malevolent destruction of my most intimate consolation. In this vast cataclysm, everything turned to farce, became a rotten joke—this mockery of a return to the past and the mockery of a battle which a cynical general was pretending he was going to wage on the Isère, compelling me to pretend that I was holding my thirty unarmed convalescents in reserve as reinforcements. Parody! Parody! An hour earlier I had learned some news. The Germans were in Romans. One of their tanks had come patrolling along the riverside opposite Bourg-de-Péage; the naval gun on the other side of the wrecked bridge had opened fire as ordered and succeeded only in de-gutting a house on the bank, whereupon the tank, turning its gun-turret towards the aggressor, had blown the gun and its crew to smithereens. The nearest machine-guns had fired a few rounds in support, but not too many, so as not to exhaust their scanty ammunition. The tank hadn't even condescended to reply and, after a little stroll, had lumbered back into the town.

During the night I was awakened by the intermittent, distant but regular sound of gunfire. The Germans must be harassing our few positions on the banks of the Isère. I got up and dressed, certain that the Major's orderly would come any moment to fetch me. I waited in vain; nobody appeared. Unable to contain my impatience, I finally went out. In the village all was sleeping. The gun down there seemed to rumble slowly, boomingly, just to put on an act. I reproached myself for my excessive zeal. Hadn't Marshal Joffre on the eve of the Battle of the Marne given orders that he was not to be wakened on any pretext? Ought I to rouse the Major just for a few cannon-shots? But supposing the Germans crossed the Isère before dawn? And caught us napping in bed, as it was said they had already, on the Somme, caught a general at his dinner? I decided to stay awake, on my own, until morning. I settled down on the outskirts of the village, on a rock which overlooked the road from a reasonable height. As soon as dawn broke I should be able to survey the approaches over a fair distance. I dropped off several times, always to the sound of gunfire. In the first light of a greying sky, still twinkling with a few stars, I saw in the distance a vehicle approaching. It disappeared and reappeared round the numerous bends in the road. An enemy reconnaissance? There was no one between the Isère and us to stop it. I had loaded all my six bullets into my revolver. The car drew nearer. It came into sight. It was a Citroën, with the number-plate of the *département*, and on its roof a mattress and a pram.

I was vexed, but nevertheless relieved. I believed I thus saw the last car of the exodus pass by. Towards 6 a.m. the gun fell silent. Three hours later we were informed of the cease-fire; the armistice with Italy had been signed the previous night. The Germans had made no attempt to cross the Isère. Their merely routine firing had caused a few casualties. An erratic exchange of small-arms fire had caused a few more. Thereupon an Order of the Day congratulated the troops on their heroic resistance, thanks to which the advance of the German Army had been stopped. Those few shots were soon to be christened 'the victory on the Isère'. All officers and NCO's present in the front line were mentioned in Divisional despatches. Even an unlucky machine-gun lieutenant who had relieved his colleague an hour *after* the cease-fire got his medal like the rest; it wasn't his fault, was it, if like the carabinieri in Offenbach's operetta he had arrived after the event. The victorious general was awarded his fourth star.

In memory of Jean-Richard Bloch

I

I FELT utterly swamped in counterfeit, pastiche, mockery and indecency. A defeat, a lost battle, are the hazards of war. But this long-drawn-out rout was besmeared with ignominy. We learned some of its shameful, degrading circumstances—reserve officers of the upper and middle class deserting their men to flee with their wives, children and valuables in army cars. Perhaps they reasoned that in putting their duty as husbands and fathers before their duty as soldiers they were displaying time-honoured French virtues . . . .

The collapse of these virtues in the great national stampede seemed to be the outstanding feature of the débâcle. '*Travail, famille, patrie,*' intoned Field-Marshal Pétain, Chief of State, showing clearly what was in *his* mind: amid the general disaster, to save the bacon of the dishonoured bourgeoisie. A bourgeois myself and the son of bourgeois parents, I had never felt any loyalty to the class to which I belonged, but its disgrace smarted all the same. To think that military leaders in the hour of their country's misfortune should have thought only of their own promotion! 'What promotion can there be in a defeated country?' I wondered, but I was wrong and they were more perspicacious than I. In the free zone under Pétain there was more military flummery, more gold braid, parades, fanfares and oriflammes than in a victorious country. It was the circus rampant.

An army captain, previously wounded in a real battle, who witnessed our 'victory on the Isère', had come back from there so humiliated that he was positively unable to smile any more. He was called Cabanetos; and the name went well with his haughty air of a hidalgo embittered by his country's disgrace. He remained silent and permanently white with pent-up indignation during the endless days that preceded our demobilization. He had joined us at Besayes, the village to which we had moved after leaving Peyrus, because it was closer to Bourg-de-Péage; directly the Germans had left, the engineers had thrown a temporary bridge over the piers of the one they had previously wrecked. At Romans, the shopkeepers scarcely

concealed their regret at the Germans' departure; the occupying
forces, in the few days they were there, had spent lavishly. At first,
people had been terrified—of violence, of looting—and had cowered
in their back rooms behind closed iron shutters. And then a shop-
keeper's wife, less scared than the rest, had run down the street
announcing triumphantly: 'They're paying!' And she showed her
neighbours the *marks* exchangeable against French money. The
shops opened like flowers in the sun. The soldiers bought butter by
the quarter-pound and wolfed it down just as it was in its silver
wrapping, as if they were eating ice-creams. And people had a fine
time selling everything they had, quite unaware as yet that they
were letting themselves be swindled of their own free will by what
amounted to camouflaged looting.

The summer was just as tranquilly blue as the beautiful spring
of the débâcle had been. Besayes during that July was sweltering
under the sun. In other circumstances I might perhaps have liked
this village, which already had something of the charm of Provence.
But there were no Provençal planes, no trees of any kind. All around
a vast, flat expanse, like the Beauce, of maize, barley and oats.
We had nothing to do but wait, under that brassy sky, to be demobilized in some undistinguishable future, and I dragged my limbs in
fruitless despair.

In the mess, the mood was full of cheer; it was over and doné
with. Having dropped a tear or two over their country's misfortune,
those officers and gentlemen bore it bravely; the poor Northerners
would have a hell of a time no doubt, but they, the Southerners . . .
The débâcle, moreover, was not without its advantages: a whole
lot of stuff from the quartermaster's stores seemed not to belong to
anyone any more. It would have been silly to let it go to waste.
The Major himself, who owned a dress shop in Montélimar,
considered it his duty to prevent sacks of rice and flour from going
bad and had them transferred to his business premises. What was he
going to do with them? Suffering from acute uraemia, he was
increasingly prone to falling asleep between the courses, which a
diploma-holding army cook smothered under appalling fancy
sauces; these were generally much appreciated, but they made
my gorge rise. One day—I no longer remember the occasion—a
private who had come to deliver a letter found us all at table,
guzzling, laughing and joking, except for Cabanetos and me and

one other, a newcomer whose name I have forgotten, a die-hard monarchist who never spoke a word to anyone. 'Ain't you ashamed of yourselves?' cried the soldier, dumbfounded. 'I've been at Dunkirk! Disgraceful, that's what it is! Disgraceful!' he repeated. The lighthearted gathering fell silent with amazement. Although I attended this feasting only because I was obliged to, I felt included with the rest in the man's contempt. Through no fault of my own, I was among those who had not risked their skins. I did not foresee at that moment that there could be any possible redemption.

Nobody dared rebuke the private for insulting a whole group of officers. At my side, Cabanetos went even paler than usual, which deepened the red of the scar that ran from his brow to his chin and raised one eyebrow as if he were wearing a monocle, accentuating the expression of haughty disdain which never left his face. The monarchist officer had turned his big jutting nose in our direction and for the first time gave me a friendly look. It occurred to me all of a sudden that in the common plight certain minds might forget their differences and find themselves on the same side, perhaps, at the right moment.

It was during these horrible days that, in the scanty mail that reached me, I found an envelope on which the handwriting, the stamp and the postmark made such a surprising combination that for a while I kept turning it over and over, unable to bring myself to open it, as if it were a problem which must first be solved. The writing was that of my friend, Major Brosset, whose character and courage I deeply admired. It was dated May 10—May 10!—and came from the Panama Canal. . . .

It was a letter full of sombre irony: *I smile as I imagine your surprise. It's a grim smile. So while you, perhaps, will soon be fighting, I've turned my back on the scrap!* But during the whole of the winter, from his observation post in the Deuxième Bureau (Military Intelligence) in Lorraine, he had sounded the alarm without managing to get himself heard. Such obstinacy on both sides had rendered his job there untenable, and since he spoke Spanish he had been shipped off to Colombia *to teach the Colombians the things the French Army doesn't want to know!*

After all, he ended up, *it's better this way. If, as I hope, by the time I return the enemy is still hesitating to invade us, maybe facts will have been faced at last, maybe France will at long last have roused herself from her*

*mortal slumber and I'll kiss the lips of the awakened Beauty. Let's hope so!
If not, if the enemy hasn't waited, things will happen that it will be better
not to have had a share in . . .*

To receive this letter in Besayes, after having seen what I had
seen thoughout those horrible, abject forty days . . . *things will happen
that it will be better not to have had a share in* . . . this letter written on
May 10th, in which everything was predicted with such relentless
foresight . . . left me even more stricken with hopeless rage.

And yet it was in Besayes, in that atmosphere of obscene idle-
ness under the scorching sun, that the opening bars of the rhapsody
which was to give meaning to my life rang softly out.

After the unbearable inactivity of standing by while France
was crumbling, the inactivity after the collapse was perhaps even
more intolerable. But what could I do? I couldn't bear the company
of the others. Sometimes I sought refuge with the local doctor, who
was married to a charming woman and whose hospitality was an
inestimable comfort. I shared their friendship with two very young
subalterns whose future, in this defeated country, filled us with
anxious pity, and with a soldier who came to practise the piano,
which he played very well. I too practised. I asked him to play the
Etude in E minor, and the music made us forget our pain for an
hour or so. Or else, our hosts took us in their car on expeditions into
the Vercors and I travelled as a tourist through this natural fortress
in which I had so recently been planning to hide as a *maquisard.*
On the terrain I found the places I had so often studied on the map,
which would have made practically impregnable strongholds. Then
we would scramble on foot to the treeless heights above the timber
line, where pastures covered the velvety green slopes. A crystal
silence reigned in the clear air, gently punctuated by the shrill
bells of cows grazing unseen on distant mountain flanks. My heart
felt like bursting. So such peace could still exist! Ah, that was where
one ought to live from now on, far from a world in which I foresaw
nothing but cowardice, baseness and treachery under the Nazi rod.
A leader-writer in the *Petit Dauphinois,* who a few days before had
been smacking his lips over the Teuton corpses which the Somme
was allegedly bearing on towards the sea, had now suddenly
discovered that it was perfidious Albion, our hereditary and Jew-
infested foe, which had burnt Joan of Arc. Reading this diatribe
over my shoulder, Cabanetos had laughed aloud for the first time,

a grating laugh which rasped our sore hearts. Yes, why not keep a
herd of cattle in the Vercors, or else—as my doctor friend advised—
plant apple-trees and be a market gardener, perhaps on Irus, that
little island in the gulf of Morbihan, and thus safeguard, if not my
freedom, at least my inner integrity? In any case, so long as the
Nazis ruled over a vassal France, I would do no more drawing
or etching; what sort of prints could I publish? How was I to know,
even, that I wouldn't be arrested immediately on my return, for
my anti-fascist drawings?

Battail had returned to Grenoble after the numberless difficulties
which the battalion had encountered during its retreat; half the
men had been captured, unable to keep up the pace. Mattéi had
collapsed exhausted in a ditch near Epernay; the battalion medico
too had fallen into the hands of the Germans—at an inn, because
he had been loth to leave some amorous business unfinished before
crossing the Loire at the very last minute, after which he had
somehow or other managed to escape and rejoin the battalion; the
indolent trio Brochenin, Coup-la-Fronde and Dumollard had
snapped out of their lethargy in action and galvanized their com-
panies into extricating themselves with hand-grenades from en-
circlement in a wood. Chazal, finding himself overtaken by Panzer
units every night and obliged each morning to get away from them,
had nevertheless managed to lead his company, in an orderly
retreat, right up to the edge of the Central Massif; and Battail
himself, evacuated to Moulin and taken prisoner in his hospital
bed, had yet made good his escape one night and had gone back to
his school-house at La Tronche.

Battail, then, and his wife, often came to see me and urged me
not to expose myself to the Nazi presence in the northern zone
but rather to settle down in Grenoble; I could stay for a while
with my family in their small house—it would be a tight fit, but who
cared? They had even told Arthaud, the owner of the big bookshop,
that I was in the neighbourhood, and he had cried: 'Bruller!
Why, he dips his brush in vitriol! We'll find work for him all right!'
I was genuinely moved. I did not say no, nor yes either; I had no
idea yet what I would do, but drawing, whether in the North or
the South, was out. Even in the so-called 'free zone' I knew quite
well that I should not be able to express freely all that was weighing
on my heart. If Arthaud thought otherwise, he was fooling himself.

When Verney, the C.O. of the battalion, succeeded in getting back
to his paper mill at Voiron he too dropped in on me, once, with
Battail. He strongly urged me to accept; Laval was a scoundrel,
but like his fellow-scoundrel Talleyrand he would manage to pull
France out of her predicament, and he was sure I would find more
freedom in the southern zone than I imagined. I would gladly have
believed them and shared their optimism, but I couldn't. When I
was alone again, pacing the dusty road under a scorching, steely
sun, I longed to be one of those ducklings who trooped past in
Indian file every day, yellow balls of fluff who never lost their
dignity even when they were sent sprawling by an over-large
pebble in their way, and who didn't care a hang about anything
happening in the world. I wanted to be like them, but how could
I escape reality? I would go back to the neat little room where I had
been billeted, throw myself into the arm-chair and spend hours
racking my thoughts, as one keeps pressing the sore gum of an aching
tooth.

It was unbearable. More and more often I called the past to my
rescue, the memory of that lost purity, the unsullied ghost of the
young girl of Combloux. And I was suddenly seized with the poignant desire to write to her. Not for the first time. Though my first
marriage was not without its good periods, it had been afflicted
from the start, despite our mutual affection, by the curse of in-
sincerity. I was struggling in an impalpable net woven of constant
dissimulation. And thus I learned, to my cost, the dull pain that
inhabits you when you can never be sure of anything, not even the
most trivial matter. Even quite recently, when I had waited in
vain in my hospital bed at Rheims for a visit from my unreliable
partner, and later when I was about to leave her on the eve of the
dramatic events of May 10, she had hurtfully made me doubt the
reality of her affection. In those moments of crisis I had often
recalled from the bottom of its well of innocence the guileless face
of my fifteen-year-old Stéphanie. That distant memory brought
balm to my mortified heart. I slaked my thirst at its remote purity.
Now that I myself was ensnared in the quicklime of perpetual
doubt, I understood too late how my own artifices, naïve though they
may have been, must have wrought havoc with the unsuspicious
frankness of a too trustful child. And this aroused afresh the
only half allayed torment of wondering whether I had lost her by

my fickleness or for the no less likely reason that her own heart had
been too young for constancy. At such moments I would feel once
again the imperious need for an answer, a certainty, and I would
promise myself that I would write and ask Stéphanie to see me again,
and force her at last to tell me the truth.

But I had never written. It was such ancient history! Besides,
in spite of my bitter feelings I was a very faithful husband, incapable
of dissimulation; moreover, wasn't there a risk of my reviving in
Stéphanie a feeling that she had been at pains to conquer? I knew
she was leading a quietly happy life between her sons and her
husband, the kindest of men. Never in all this time had she given
me the slightest sign. If she *had* loved me once, this was wisdom
itself; I owed it to myself as well as to her to show the same wisdom.
And if she hadn't, what was the point? But now, after that encounter
in Peyrus, the urge to pick up the threads again, to ask, to know at
last, assumed, in my abominable loneliness at Besayes, a strange
and almost irresistible force. Yet the same reasons, the same
scruples, still held me back.

I had to find some outlet. In compensation for what I could not
bring myself to do, I might find some small relief in doing it by
proxy, as it were. I would begin a fictional account of it, here and
now. It did not take me long to draft the outline. My hero (I would
call him Marc), pursued like me by memories of an unforgettable
purity, gnawed by regret and ceaseless questioning about the real
causes of an irreparable loss, decided—unlike me—before going
to the front and perhaps losing his life, to write to the girl he'd
lost—whom I would call Delphine. In his letter he begged her to
give him a straightforward answer: through whose fault, hers or his,
had he lost her? He received no reply, was sent into action, and a
few weeks later was wounded and seriously burned in his blazing
tank. He was evacuated to Carcassonne, which he reached only
after ten agonizing days in a furnace-hot hospital train, following a
devious route under the scorching sun and leaving behind it the
horrible stench of rotting flesh. In Carcassonne at last, Marc slowly
succumbed to his burns. His fellow-officers learned of it as, after the
armistice, they sat stricken round the mess-table where his chair
stood empty; and that is where they received a month-old letter,
addressed to him. On the envelope, Delphine's name and the postmark: she had replied by return! But what had she said? One of the

lieutenants, a close friend of Marc to whom he had opened his heart, turned the envelope over and over between his fingers. How was the promptness of this reply to be interpreted? It might equally be due to the chill frankness of indifference or to the agitation of a still-vulnerable heart. And what exactly had the dying man hoped to learn? That a fickle Delphine had been incapable of loving him for longer than a summer month? What a crushing disillusionment . . . Or that he had slowly driven her to despair by his flightiness, his frivolous lies? In that case, what a stab of remorse . . . Could either truth comfort his last days, would it not darken them either way? What should one wish for him? A bitter clarity instead of the floating dreams of uncertainty? Send him the letter with whatever dagger it may contain, or let him go to his death cradled in ignorance? Marc's confidant dared not decide by himself. He consulted the comrades of the dying man; through the whole of one night (which would occupy the bulk of the novel) he would slowly unfold to them the facts that had been confided to him, trying to make them recapture, with the sole fragrance of vanished things, a fleeting reality. Tormented, they argued this way and that as to the right thing to do with the envelope, closed upon its secret like the sheath upon a murderous blade. By morning, with torn hearts, all were agreed to burn the letter unopened.

For I knew very well that if I had written to Stéphanie and received an answer, either truth would have been equally cruel to me. I burned to know, yet feared to find out. But the writing of the first pages of my story brought me a strange solace; this being my first attempt at writing, I was still unfamiliar with the inner peace that comes from putting a confused ordeal down on paper. I became so engrossed in this work that the days began to pass too quickly. Finally, in early August, I was demobilized. I was one of the last. But like the rest of those who hailed from the Occupied Zone, this did not mean that we were on our way home. We had to wait for a train to take the demobilized men back up North.

I had returned to Romans, where I stayed in the same hotel as before. Miraculously, I found my field-trunk and my bicycle intact. I spent some of the worst days there. At first, for a fortnight, mail passed almost normally between one zone and the other. I received reassuring news from my family, and learned, by the way, that by spending the night at Boën I had escaped by the skin of my teeth: had I gone to Bussac with the new recruits to join my family there, I should now be a prisoner—for the Germans, on arrival, had released the recruits but detained the officers. In fact, the evil genius which had kept me chained to Romans despite all my efforts now turned out to have been motivated by the best, even if impenetrable, intentions. I was still unable to guess where this rather farcical chain of mishaps was leading me, when the evil genius popped up once more in threatening guise. In the last letter I had received from my mother, she had spoken of her worry at the number of German families who were arriving in the region day after day. What had they come for? Whereupon, one fine morning, all postal services between the zones was stopped. I tried to send a telegram; all communication was prohibited. A wall of silence. What were the Germans hatching behind it? Suppose it meant a transfer of populations? In Poland their first move had been to colonize the most productive land and expel its inhabitants to starve on the shores on the Baltic. Could it be that it was now the turn of the rich Charente soil? I imagined my family already being sent off to the sandy wastes of East Prussia while I had no way of finding out what was happening to them or of joining them. Cooped up at Romans, from which trains no longer left.

Then I was ordered to proceed to Montélimar, where a trainload of demobbed ex-servicemen was due to leave for Paris in two days' time; I did as I was told. The barracks were swarming like a sliced-off antheap. Here the issue of civilian clothing developed into a wild game of snatch: we were warned that at the demarcation line anyone found wearing uniform would be taken prisoner. In view of my lieutenant's rank I was put in charge of a carriage. I was to be responsible for the men, their conduct, and their papers. If the slightest thing were wrong, or a single man drunk, we were told, we should all be turned back. So it was up to me to see that everything was correct, an honour I would gladly have relinquished.

The crossing of the demarcation line was made at the railway station of Chalon-sur-Saône. We were welcomed there by huge flags that hung from the roof to the ground, two scarlet curtains with the sinister black spider on them. My chest contracted. Shouldn't I have listened to Battail? Was I flinging myself into the jaws of the wolf? Anyway, it was too late now.

Other trains were waiting, full of soldiers who, unlike us, were wearing not civvies but uniform with a white armband: they had been told that any soldier caught wearing civilian clothes would be shot out of hand . . . I had expected a meticulous scrutiny of passes and men. A fat gendarme in field-grey, wearing an official-looking chain with a steel disc dangling on his chest, perfunctorily checked my list with his without even calling the roll, and passed on to the next carriage. The whole train was cleared in less than an hour. As we moved out, a young German Apollo, stripped to the waist, stood in the sun drying himself after a shower. He waved an arm at us in a gesture of friendship, with a broad grin that revealed his sparkling teeth. A few arms waved back from the train-windows. Had it been some other war, this comradely behaviour might have touched me. But his eyes were steely-blue and I knew that if he had been ordered to do so he would have machine-gunned us or put a bullet through our necks with the same grin.

The convoy crawled along. In the corridor I started chatting with a man whose pock-marked face was alive with intelligence. He was a scenario-writer, married to a well-known actress. The defeat, to him, was like a slur on his masculinity. The first letter he had received from his wife had started with the words: 'My defeated darling . . . ' He had no more idea than I had what was going to become of him, repelled by the very idea of working for a Hitler-censored cinema. Both of us agreed that if we had had to lose a war it would have been better to do so in 1914; at least under Wilhelm II neither France nor Europe would have known the horrors that were now in store.

It was still dark when the train, by I don't know what detour, pulled in not to the Gare de Lyon but the Gare de l'Est. We had to wait for the end of the curfew on the utterly deserted platform, with no station staff in sight nor any other train except the one that had brought us. The absence of noise and bustle in the station (and presumably all around it) were like the silence of the grave. At daybreak we were allowed to leave. Outside, as far as the eye could see, not a car, not a bus, not a living being. I mounted my bicycle and raced down the boulevard to the Seine in a dream-like silence and solitude. I could have fancied myself transported into an old film by René Clair, *Paris qui dort* (Paris asleep) in which a mysterious ray, beamed from the top of the Eiffel Tower, had plunged the city into a coma. What a prophetic vision! Only today's mysterious beam stemmed from defeat and exodus.

As I approached our old flat close by the Luxembourg Gardens, where my mother had continued to live after my father's death ten years earlier, where every brick, every piece of furniture, every object was impregnated with thirty years of memories, another feeling took hold of me: astonishment. A strange feeling indeed: astonishment at finding everything in its place, the streets, the shops, the houses, the spires of Saint-Sulpice. As if, after this cataclysm, I had expected things to have got lost, demolished or else, I don't know, deformed. But no, everything was in its place, in the flat too, which stood empty and silent as if in a deep sleep from which even my presence did not arouse it. Or was it I who had changed? It seemed to me that I no longer belonged there. The things no longer spoke to me of the past, of my father, and I had the impression of being a stranger, a passing traveller. That morning in the silent flat, I experienced a stronger feeling of having lost it than when, years later, in the ruin of my household, I was to lose it for good.

I had hoped perhaps to find some news of my family there, but not a word. This did not exactly allay my fears. At the post-office they set my mind at rest somewhat. The mail? Yes, still very erratic. Telegraph? The demolished lines were not yet repaired. In front of the Senate, under the swastika which had replaced the tricolour, facing the sentry-boxes where grey-clad guards in jackboots and peaked caps, tommy-guns in hand, kept watch, a news-stand displayed mainly German papers and periodicals, *Signal*, *Stürmer*, *Völkischer Beobachter*, and a few French ones, among which a conspicuous newcomer *Le Pilori* (The Pillory) specialized in Jew-baiting. They hadn't lost any time! Had I then, during all these years, been unwittingly rubbing shoulders with so many would-be persecutors who had just been biding their time? Had this vermin been crawling about all the while under the soft armpits of France? I bought the old *Matin*, though I cherished no illusions; the tone was no less odious, but nothing seemed to confirm my apprehensions about a transfer of populations. None the less, my first concern was to go to the Gare d'Austerlitz and see if it was possible to travel to Saintonge. I found some stir there, mainly due to troop movements. A train—what luck!—was due to leave for Angoulême next morning. From there I could get a local slow train which was still running between the two Charente departments. I could be at Saintes by the evening. I booked a seat.

Relieved at this immediate prospect, I turned my thoughts to finding out which of my friends might possibly not be absent from the deserted capital. Back at the flat in the Rue Servandoni, I made a series of telephone calls, without much hope, and heard indeed as I had expected: No answer. No answer. No answer. One more attempt, and at the other end someone at last lifted the receiver; I heard a voice I recognized, and found it almost as surprising there as the spires of Saint-Sulpice. It was the voice of Pierre de Lescure.

Among my circle of friends, Pierre de Lescure occupied a curious place. Although my senior by fifteen years, he was not my oldest friend. Nor yet my most intimate one. But for reasons which I will presently explain, we were linked by the firm bonds of a great mutual trust. The fact that in the whole of Paris he alone answered my call was like a sudden beacon in a fog, the hope of a compass at sea.

I hurried round to his place. And curiously enough, being back in his small study, wildly untidy as ever, the chairs cluttered with books, the walls with art-prints, and finding the portraits of Emily Brontë, Keats, Katherine Mansfield in their usual places—this put me back on my feet more effectively than the Rue Servandoni had done. The smile on his full lips was unchanged, at once warm and aloof, as if the man behind the smile were always careful to keep his distance, fearful of surrendering too much of himself.

After our first exchange of joyful greetings, he made me relate my tribulations. Then he told me of his flight from Paris, how they had stormed the last train to leave the Gare d'Austerlitz, which had then been halted at St Pierre-des-Corps, outside Tours, where all the bridges over the Loire had been blown up; how the passengers had been transferred to a goods train made up of flat wagons, which had crawled at a snail's pace to Montluçon—not empty but loaded from end to end with those enormous spools on which tarred cables are wound. Hundreds of empty, useless spools. In the midst of a routed army, submerged under a deluge of war material, this futile train load was one more sinister absurdity. What was even more surprising, the crowd of fugitives settled down among the spools and made themselves comfortable. From one gigantic reel to the next they would exchange visits as if they were all in a holiday camp. Clans rapidly formed, with their rivalries, malicious gossip, adulterous love-affairs, family scenes. Whenever the train stopped for a few hours in the bare country, people went off to pilfer the abandoned farmhouses, coming back with sundry loot—a wash-copper, a bread-trough, a frying-pan, a decrepit arm-chair. The space between the enormous spools became ever more limited, promiscuity sparked off stormy rows. In three days on that train, Lescure said, he had learned more about human nature than in ten years of urban isolation.

The future? An open question. France and Frenchmen could scarcely fall any lower than they now were. When you reach the bottom of an abyss, you can only scramble up again. It would be a long, slow climb. But one must never abandon hope.

Perhaps. I was not so sure. During the thirty-eight years of my life, it had never once occurred to me that France might not necessarily be eternal, that she might one day disappear in the graveyard of history. And yet history had seen many a motherland be wiped from the map and die with its national culture. France herself had come into being by wiping out Occitania with its refined civilization, its poets, its mellow tongue, the *langue d'oc*. Hitler might well create his Europe by wiping France and the French from the map. So ran my gloomy meditations next day, as my train travelled through Sologne, Berry, Poitou, Angoumois, and in my heart the names of the towns and villages we passed already tolled like a knell, like a roll-call of the dead . . . Artenay, Cheverny, Ardentes, Ravel, L'Eparcelet . . .

> *Orléans, Beaugency,*
> *Notre-Dame de Cléry,*
> *Vendôme! Vendôme!*[1]

I rebelled. No! This could not be. It would not be. The train was almost empty. In the next compartment were two young German sailors. As we reached Angoulême and I was about to get out, they stopped me in the corridor and asked if this were Bordeaux. I told them it was, and saw them grab their bags and bundles and hurriedly alight. Afterwards I reproached myself for having misled them. They looked decent enough.

[1]Charles d'Orléans

II

And now what? For a week I had been back with my family, in the summery calm of Montcharente, a stately hilltop mansion, pervaded by the scent of a giant magnolia that flowered all the year round. The view over the valley, where the river meandered among the meadows, made the heart swell. *Mon Dieu, mon Dieu, la vie est là, simple et tranquille. . . .*[1] There was no food-rationing as yet; at Saintes, the near-by market town, everything could be found as before, one might believe that life would go on and pick up the threads as if nothing had happened. The Germans behaved well, everywhere. No violence, no looting. On the contrary, affable, helpful, paying cash on the nail, attentive and playful with the children, compassionate towards the refugees whom they sometimes even helped to find lodgings and move their furniture. Jews? Communists? Never a question asked. So these were the abominable creatures we had been told about? Brutes? Torturers? Propaganda! We had been deceived!

My mother told me that at Saintes the population had given the victors a hearty welcome, the girls waving their handkerchiefs and scarves at the athletic young men on motor-cycles, handsome as gods, with laughter in their eyes. Oh, had it been any other war, how glad I would have been to welcome this harmony, to believe in this reconciliation! Alas, in my eyes this attitude on the part of the French revealed only cowardice or blindness, and I could not make up my mind which was worse. Cowards, after the first fright had passed, might pull themselves together, wake up. Whereas the blind might well not open their eyes until it was too late.

And what about me? What was I going to do? How nice and restful it would have been to give my countrymen up as hopeless and wrap myself in slumber in this tranquil province, the cradle of the Fort family, where they had so many friends and where I could doubtless quite easily find means of leading a secluded life without luxury but without compromise. I had a small nest-

[1]Verlaine. (Oh God, oh God, life is out there, so simple and calm. . .)

egg, not much but enough to give me time to feel my feet. Moreover, a reply from the Mayor of my village in Brie had informed me
that the Germans were occupying my house. For a week or two I
toyed with this soothing idea; it was the reaction, I suppose, from
the many blows I had sustained. It was also the last flicker of my
former philosophy: to let the stupid human ants devour and destroy
one another, to keep out of their idiotic quarrels, to stand apart
and lead the frugal, detached life of a sage, with no great needs but
also without snares or cruelty. There were times when I wondered
whether the curious chain of coincidences which had detained me
at Romans without giving me the opportunity to fire a single shot,
whether this obstinacy of fate had not been a way of forcing me to
remain faithful in spite of myself to my non-violent principles . . . I
recalled, not without irony, the shocked surprise I had felt, perched
on my rock on the outskirts of Peyrus, watching myself—as one
sometimes does, from the outside—grip my revolver at the approach
of the black motor-car and instead of keeping quiet, preparing to
fire away like any one of those million foolish ants. I scolded myself,
told myself: 'Don't be an ass!' but all the time I knew that if it
were an enemy car I should not have heeded, I should have fired
at it. The memory of that incident subsequently inspired one of my
short stories[1], but in it the hero fires and is killed, whereas I still
had six bullets in the chamber of my revolver.

Similarly, in Montcharente, I was dwelling on the vision of a
monastic life in some quiet place in this region when a second letter
from the Mayor of my village in Brie informed me that if we returned our house would immediately be restored to us. I knew at
once that we had to go back. I did not try to explain to myself the
sudden haste that gripped me. I was content to obey it. The difficulty was to get home in the old Ford in which my wife, anticipating
the exodus, had driven down with the children; having only just
passed her driving test and being still scared of the gears, she had
driven all the way in second. Despite this shock treatment and its
ten-year life-span, the Ford had survived and seemed to me still in
running order. However, we had to have petrol coupons as well as
an *Ausweis* permitting us to travel. I had to go to the Kommandantur
to apply for them. Bruller is an Alsatian name (it means, roughly,
'roarer'). I had to submit to quite a lengthy interrogation, but I

[1] *'Le Démenti'* (The Denial), in *Les Yeux et la lumière*.

emerged unscathed with my petrol coupons and my pass, even though I was fuming with suppressed humiliation.

More than once the Ford almost stalled on the pot-holed roads, in the traffic jams at the bridges where we queued for hours amid dust and petrol-fumes to get across the makeshift structures. But each time it consented to move on again, like a poor old hack in its shafts. It held out to the last—but finally gave up the ghost just before the gate, ten yards from home. We had to push her bodily into the barn which served as a garage, to wait there till the end of the war.

It was the middle of the afternoon. The weather was wonderful all that summer. The long, low house with its Virginia creeper looked tidy and empty. But everything in it indicated the recent presence of the occupants. A pair of army boots sprawled in the vast kitchen. There was a pile of dirty crockery, and on the table the remains of an unspeakable cheese, unlike any cheese known to man either in looks or smell—something like a piece of yellow soap that had gone bad with a stench of decomposing crabs. I still wonder what *ersatz* had gone into its composition. The neglected garden was nothing but a wilderness of nettles, with broken glass and empty bottles glinting amid hundreds of yards of insulated wire in a wild tangle. But as if to point the contrast, the so-called 'reception rooms' were in impeccable order. As evidence of extra-special care, the carpets had been turned over to keep them clean. I kept a death-mask of Pascal in a cupboard; it had been taken out and set in a place of honour in the centre of the mantelpiece. (Perhaps they had mistaken it for Napoleon?) Above the mantelpiece in our bedroom, on the other hand, had been placed a photograph, flanked by green plants. It showed a woman's breasts with a hand beneath one of them, as delicately modelled as a Praxiteles sculpture. It had been given me long ago by the photographer—a friend—and must have been ferreted out of goodness knows which drawer. This proved that there had been a thorough search, but as I was able to ascertain later, nothing had been stolen.

After our first survey we returned to the garden, at a loss to know what to do next. Should we go to the Town Hall? To the Kommandantur? A fellow in grey-green appeared at the gate, spotted us, turned and ran down the road. Ten minutes later a powerful armoured car, of the phaeton type, turned into the drive. A young officer stepped out. He was not particularly handsome and he was not blue-eyed, but he had a pleasant look on his chubby, rather Latin face which wore a broad smile. He walked towards us.

'Hello!' he said, and bowed. 'Madame . . . ' Then to me in good French: 'You're Mr . . . ?'

'Bruller.'

'That's right. Have you any children?'

'Two boys.'

'So there are four of you?'

'Yes.'

'You're an officer?'

'Lieutenant in the reserve.'

'Wounded?'

'No.'

'But that stick?'

'An accident.'

He kept smiling.

'You have demobilized, yes?'

'Do you wish to see my papers?'

'Oh no! No need: you are a French officer! You naturally wish to reoccupy your home?'

'Naturally.'

'I found it extremely pleasant. It's a delightful place, it has a soul. I compliment you. And I shall regret. In twenty minutes it will be yours.'

He hadn't stopped smiling, despite my cold face and curt answers. He motioned to the two soldiers who had followed him, saluted us and walked away as he had come. And indeed, twenty minutes later two enormous field-trunks stood piled on a hand barrow, the soldiers saluted us in their turn and left us to ourselves.

It felt strange to be at home again, in a house that was unchanged and intact, as if we had come back from holidays. The feeling didn't last. After previous homecomings I had gone straight back to work. This time I was unemployed. Voluntarily, to be sure, but quite determined. What were we going to live on? I had no idea. And soon I was back in the same mood I had experienced at Besayes, under the dismal glare of the August sun which shone all too crudely on the flabby unconcern of an inert populace. In the village street farther down, the shopkeepers smiled at the soldiers, chatted with those who knew a few words of French. My neighbours—the wife a little Flemish woman with coiled auburn tresses, gossipy and prying, her husband a painter with greying hair and a delicate sensitive face, a fine though modest artist with whom I'd always got on well—had practically adopted as a *filleul de guerre* a young German to whom they'd given the run of their house. So I no longer went there. This pained my painter friend, who did not understand that my former desire for Franco-German friendship was, unlike his, unable to surmount my injured patriotism; twenty-five years hence, in a united Europe, who would remember these outmoded sentiments? Against his arguments I cited the Nazi terror, racist policy, concentration camps. He replied: 'Propaganda! We were scared stiff when they first arrived, and look at them now! In a pacified Europe, humaneness will come out on top, you'll see. We must help them.' Confronted with such wishful thinking I felt floored. And I was appalled.

There were other grounds for consternation. Writers, and among them some whom I held in great respect, were hastily turning their coats, as if afraid of missing the bus. H. R. Lenormand, the dramatist, author of well-known plays like *Les Ratés* and *Simoun*, confessed with a repulsive pen his self-disgust at having raised his fist with the Popular Front in 1936, and thanked heaven and Hitler for having opened his eyes. One of our companions on that trip to Prague, our dear Luc Durtain, who could never talk of that occasion without tears in his eyes, publicly rallied to Pétain and called on his compatriots to get a better grasp of the new thinking.

In contrast, a letter from Jean-Richard Bloch, from La Mérigote near Poitiers, showed that he was anxious to know if I had emerged from the adventure free and alive; and when I replied that I had but was feeling pretty desperate at the sombre prospect before us, a second letter sought to allay my pessimism, vowed that all was not lost and that after this fit of understandable lethargy following such a traumatic shock there was every reason to put one's hope in the French people. Temporarily the battle was halted but it would be resumed some day, and victoriously. Besides, the first signs of an awakening were already perceptible. He recounted some anecdotes— market-women, for example, asking some soldiers who were buying tomatoes from them: 'Now then, are you or aren't you going to invade England?' and the poor privates sadly answered: 'Glug-

glug!' (for the rumour had spread that several attempts had ended dramatically in blazing oil poured on the sea). Paul Valéry had written to tell him that on the dunes of the north coast the corpses washed in by the waves were *floating upright* by reason of the weight of their waterlogged boots. Many people were beginning to think that England might hold out. A woman in a shop, sensing the growing impatience of the German officer in the queue behind her, had called out: 'Serve this gentleman first, he's expected in London!' And then there was the Soviet Union . . . It came as a happy surprise to me that my first encouragement came from a Communist, in spite of the pact with Hitler.

Friends were slowly trickling back to Paris. At Yvonne Paraf's place I found her friend—and later husband—Léon Motchane, who at that time was both a businessman and a mathematician, and who is today the director of the Institute of Higher Scientific Studies. He was the same age as the century, had been born in St Petersburg (he never called it Leningrad), had taken part in the Revolution as a young student, then emigrated, not being a Bolshevik, and had finally become French. He had a long, rather fleshy face and never seemed to take a tragic view of things, poised half way between confidence and scepticism. He was running a firm of chemical products and also owned, somewhere in Guinea, a banana plantation, about the future prospects of which he felt uncertain.

I talked to him about the idea that had been suggested to me, of planting selected apple trees. It appealed to him, and for a few months we seriously studied its possibilities. For this purpose I even undertook some trips to the Creuse and Nivernais regions, where I sometimes met odd people—I remember in particular a former nobleman who had gone back to the land, with a weatherbeaten skin but the airs of an aristocrat, leading the life of a medieval peasant: he lunched in his kitchen on bread soup in a big wooden bowl, and tilled his field by loosing on it a dozen ravenous hogs which ploughed it up with their snouts, having been kept off all other food for this purpose. Motchane had obtained assurances from his banana-customers in the Halles that they would purchase our future supplies if they were of top quality. We even had soil analyses made. Happily I did not discover the ideal situation for the hermitage I was dreaming of, so this ambitious project petered out and I remained available.

One day in September, on the Boulevard Montparnasse, I came to the bookshop 'Les Nourritures Terrestres' which had been the main distributor of my albums before the war. I saw with surprise that, after having been closed for a long time—for good I had feared, since its owner Jacques Goldschmidt was Jewish—it was now open again. Goldschmidt himself was there, surrounded by his books and some of his friends, among whom I was glad to find the excellent poet Robert Ganzo. The time had not yet come, though it soon would, when Jewish shops would be compelled to put a notice in their window saying JEWISH CONCERN, but Goldschmidt was privately amusing himself with a dangerous game: he had prepared a poster with these words which he kept inside the shop on his desk. Many German officers were keen on modern art books (in Germany they were banned as 'degenerate art'). He would let them come in, look around and make their choice and then, as they paid at the desk, they would read the notice and he relished their confusion.

While I was there an officer did in fact walk in. He skimmed through several monographs and had a parcel made of two or three of them. Without paying attention to the notice, he was already holding out a banknote when Goldschmidt pushed the poster under his nose. There was a silence, then the officer turned his hands palms upward in a helpless gesture. 'Oh . . . I am so sorry.' And he looked sorry too. He kept repeating: 'Really, ter-rib-ly sorry . . .' But he did not move. He was obviously wavering. We could not tell (and perhaps neither could he) what mortified him most: the idea of having to forgo the books or the odious law that forced him to do so, and at the same time to insult the smiling man in front of him. Had he been alone it is possible that he would have disregarded the notice and said he didn't care. But there were three or four of us watching him in silence. He finally bowed to Goldschmidt, then to us with lowered eyes, and walked out looking very miserable. I was moved by a curious feeling, half way between laughter and pity. If the fellow wasn't a Nazi, what a coward he must have felt! He had not been able to look us in the face. Robert Ganzo said to me: 'They're washed up!' 'Who?' 'The Jerries.' He grinned at my astonishment. 'Sure they are,' he said. 'Let them shake us as much as they like with their parades of tanks and machines, so what? They've now got to hold down the whole of Europe; they're

like the fellow in the story who shouts that he's captured a prisoner.
When he's told to bring him in, he says: "I can't, he won't let me
go!" '

This was not such a paradox, provided Europe didn't give in—
and the trouncing Mussolini and his *bravissimi* fascist troops had
just received from the tattered army of the Hellenes at the gates
of Greece (while Graziani was getting knocked about by the British
in Tripoli), a defeat so resounding that the Germans had had to
fly to the rescue of their ally, was no bad omen. It was the comic
relief in this huge Shakespearean tragedy. But the French? What
about their inertia? Their torpor?

I had looked up Jean-Richard Bloch in his Paris pied-à-terre
behind the Molière fountain, and his flat seemed to me even more
lifeless than mine in the Rue Servandoni. True, the shutters were
closed, for he was hiding rather than living there; his liberty was
more than precarious: to be Jewish, communist and the former
editor of the progressive evening paper *Ce Soir* was a bit much for
one man. Repression had already begun to strike his family. One
of his sons was in prison; his 84-year-old mother was soon to be
deported to Germany. Later his daughter was to be sentenced to
death and beheaded. His son-in-law, taken to Châteaubriant as a
hostage, escaped, was recaptured and finally shot. He had a pre-
monition of these misfortunes, but none the less he was brimming
over with optimism. 'Can't you see the Parisians?' he asked. 'You
talk of their flabbiness, their inertia. But they've already emerged
from it, they're rubbing their eyes. Just watch them when they meet
a German officer in the street. They pass by without a glance,
straight as a ramrod, they blot him from the landscape, he doesn't
exist. Oh no! The Germans are already getting jittery, the tension
grows. Like tautening a fiddle-string,' he ended, slowly turning his
tightly-clenched fingers as if twisting the key of a fiddle.

At the time this was still, perhaps, wishful thinking, for this
tension 'like tautening a fiddle-string' was barely discernible to me.
More than once I saw a passer-by, when asked the way by a soldier,
show it him most affably. But maybe he was sending him in the
wrong direction, as I had done with my sailors? It may also be that
two big posters, which remained for a long time on the walls of
France, had helped to make people think.

The first showed a soldier of the Wehrmacht, with a forage cap

—no longer a helmet—on his head, holding a small child in his arms. Soldier and child were smiling at each other, and the caption read: 'Abandoned populations, trust the German soldier!' The poster had begun to blossom right after the exodus in all the villages of the fleeing country. The French have a perceptive ear. 'So!' they said to themselves. 'So this correct behaviour, this amiability is *organized*, is it? The German Army has been *ordered* to be friendly? In Poland, their orders were to lay waste, burn and slaughter; here, they're supposed to be smiling and helpful. What for? What's the idea? And for how long?' And they began to be suspicious.

This clumsiness and total ignorance of psychology were often to have an excellent, sometimes even unhoped-for effect on the French people. Following the tragic affair of Mers-el-Kébir when, after Pétain refused to move the French fleet out of reach of the occupying Germans, Churchill—fearing that it might be used as a bargaining counter with Hitler—had the fleet bombarded and partly sent to the bottom, a traditional Anglophobia had flared up again in the heart of many a Frenchman. Fanned by Pétain, Laval, their government and the entire press, this threatened to spread and ramify, and who knows if Vichy, having no further reason to fear public opinion on this point, might not have yielded to its natural inclination and made common cause with Hitler against the ancient rival, as they almost did at a later date? Fortunately, the French people saw their walls being plastered with one poster too many: it showed a wounded sailor, half-drowning in a blood-stained sea, shouting vengeance as he held aloft a tattered tricolour flag. A touching spectacle. Unfortunately, his cap was adorned not with the traditional red pompon of the French Navy but with the twin black ribbons that dangle on the napes of German sailors . . . and immediately upon the appearance of this poster, which could conceal neither its origin nor the intentions of the Occupying Power with regard to the French Navy, Mers-el-Kébir was recognized for what it was—a serious defeat which infuriated Hitler. Churchill was forgiven. History, in this case perhaps, hung by a pompon. . . .

Encounters such as those with Ganzo and Jean-Richard Bloch shored up my confidence in my fellow-countrymen, but others tended to shake it. Certain people who had been militant socialists when I had last seen them now talked 'common sense' (as they called it), or else claimed that beyond the hideous events of one day we ought to learn to distinguish the future and 'apprehend its visage' (according to the expression of a writer whom I had previously admired greatly). Even among my close familiars, sudden differences of opinion came to light which pained me. At each encounter with a pre-war friend a nagging doubt insinuated itself: 'What is he thinking now? Can we remain friends?' There were some glad surprises. One day a couple of my acquaintances, having learned by chance that I was on a visit to a friend in the same street, went there, rang the bell and asked to see me. They were Francette Mangin (Jacqueline Brosset's sister) and her husband Jacques Lecompte-Boinet (whose name will often crop up again). In the gamut of my relationships, they represented the traditional upper bourgeoisie of a certain standing, whose political bias was to the right or the extreme right.

'We have come up here,' they said, 'to ask you a straightforward question.'

'Well?'

'Are you for or against Pétain?'

I remarked that in the present circumstances they could hardly put a more straightforward one, nor one indeed that might be more fraught with danger for the person addressed . . . We all laughed at this and then I openly expressed my feelings which were so contrary to the Franco-German rapprochement they had heard me advocate before.

'You see!' said Jacques, turning to his wife. 'And you?' I asked. They both smiled. 'You see, they're pretty divided in our circle . . . . And we're very glad to hear what you say.' In fact, they had come to fortify their nonconformist views. I learned from them that General Mangin's two sons were in Morocco. Weygand, out there, seemed to be wavering . . . . And Diego, in Bogota? No news. 'Do you know that the Boches blew up my father's statue when they arrived?' Francette Mangin told me proudly. Our agreement on the main issue warmed our hearts.

III

I HAD naturally seen Pierre de Lescure again more than once. Unlike Jean-Richard Bloch, he was not expecting any miracle from the French people: having been dragged to the bottom of an abyss of abandonment by a corrupt ruling class, their reawakening could not be counted on for a long while. De Gaulle? Pierre had misgivings: 'A Maurassien!'[1] Moreover, there was no doubt he was a bit of a bungler: look at that rash, ill-prepared attempt to land at Dakar! But nothing infuriated him so much as any assumption of a possible double game by Pétain. If I had ever been tempted to give any credence to this fiction, his violence and certainty would have restrained me from falling into the trap, for he was convinced that behind the old Marshal there stood in full array the power of the Church and of Reaction, whose only concern was to drag France back, with Germany's help, to the days of Louis XVIII.

In his view, the only hope resided in England. Her doggedness in the face of adversity had proved its strength throughout the centuries. Undaunted by the blitz, angered by the destruction of Coventry, cheering Churchill who promised her nothing but blood, toil, tears and sweat, she stood firm as a rock and would continue to do so. And we must help her.

Saying this, he stared at me with his small piercing eyes in which there hovered the glimmer of a smile though his face was grave, as if he was amused beforehand by the effect his words would produce. 'Help her?' I said, 'but how?' According to his own words, we were disarmed, washed up, all passion spent. 'I'm referring to myself,' he said. 'And to you too,' he added, 'if you're ready.' This was a pure formula, for he had not the slightest doubt what my reply would be. On certain points he knew me as well as himself.

He had turned up in my life at the outset of my career, in 1926. I was just back from Tunis where I had spent the last six months of my military service. Determined to devote myself to drawing, I had abandoned all idea of turning my engineer's diploma to

[1] A supporter of the extreme right-wing doctrinaire Charles Maurras.

practical use and for the last few months had been earning a living in advertising. My designs gave satisfaction, and this presented a serious danger: that of being swallowed up. The spate of orders left me no time to draw for myself. I had not thrown up engineering just to get submerged in advertising and if I was going to fight clear of it I should have to do something reckless.

I decided to have a shot at publishing a series of humorous drawings which I had done as an amateur some years before, to see if I could make a little money to give me time to look around. But I was too scared of being snubbed to risk showing my work to a publisher. Working in advertising had taught me the ropes of typography, photogravure, printing, in short all that was needed to go in for publishing myself. I decided to call on a few booksellers and get advance subscriptions which would enable me to publish the volume at my own expense. And after that, we'd see.

The album was entitled *Twenty-one Practical Recipes for Violent Death* (or as the American version later had it, *Twenty-one Delightful Ways of Committing Suicide*). The person originally responsible for it was my old friend Yvonne Paraf whom I have already mentioned. We had happened to spend our holidays together at Saint-Cergues. Not quite by accident. It was at a time when Stéphanie was keeping her distance; she was in Combloux again; I had written asking her to find me a room, anything to doss down in, so that I could be near her. It was a way of sounding her out. She answered that she had not found anything. I ought to have taken no notice, gone to Combloux all the same, and slept in a barn if necessary. But I was young enough still to be touchy, hesitant, and I minded the rebuff. Yvonne, when I met her with friends, had cried: 'Why not come to Saint-Cergues?' We had flirted mildly at one time, and I took up her suggestion. She enjoyed being liked, and I appreciated her wit and her intelligence; I wanted to forget Stéphanie, perhaps to get my own back. In short, I courted Yvonne, she let me, and I got hoist with my own petard. I was riding for a fall. One evening, feeling qualms at having led me on, she confessed that it had been merely coquetry on her part. The effect of this setback, as can be imagined, was to kindle my feelings and reinforce my ardour to such an extent that it actually lasted several seasons. But after permitting myself a night of sleepless sorrow I began to fear that my love-sick sighs would soon make me unbearable in the eyes of my charmer, and as I didn't want to expose myself to the irony of which she was far from unsparing, I decided to fall back on humour; in this way we would remain friends and my pride would be safe-guarded. On rainy days we often played a game which we called *les petits points*[1] (though some give it a grosser name . . .). Once, as Yvonne gnawed her pencil, hesitating before the criss-crossed paper, pondering her next move as seriously as if it were a game of chess, I doodled in one corner of the sheet an unrequited lover on the point of blowing his brains out. When my turn came to ponder and play, she drew a man, straight as a ramrod, falling head first into a smoke-billowing stove. I drew a man who, like Poil de Carotte, was drowning himself with his head in a bucket of water. She drew a man throwing himself from a fifth floor window. I drew a man passing, flat as a pancake, between the cylinders of a rolling-press. We stopped there, but back in Paris shortly afterwards I picked up the idea again, carried the possible ways of committing suicide to twenty-one variations, wrote suitable instructions for each drawing, tied the lot together with a coloured ribbon inside a paper cover, and posted it to the heartless girl. When she showed the album to her friends they were highly amused and declared that it ought to be published. I didn't think much of this idea. Besides, I didn't know any publishers. And anyway, I was much too timid.

But two or three years later, after my military service, when I was caught up in advertising and a little cocky at the success I had in that line, I decided to try my luck. Someone recommended me to the Librairie Champion, on the Quai Malaquais. A buxom woman received me, seemed much entertained by the set of drawings, consulted her husband in the next room, and told me that if I published the album they would place an advance order for their own customers. This was encouraging, since a sizeable part of the printing cost would thus be covered. The woman advised me to go and see Simon Kra. Kra, after following all kinds of trade including that of a diabolo-performer in a circus, had become one of the great booksellers of Paris, with a shop opposite the church of the Trinité. He was a tall, gawky fellow, full of heavy insolence, with a pipe permanently jutting beneath his long, prominent nose. He leafed absent-mindedly through my dummy album, handed it back to

[1] A French version of noughts and crosses, consisting of filling up the squares with series of five pencil-marks.

me and advised me to go and sell nightcaps. A bit shaken, I hesitated to present myself at the third address, the Librairie Martin in
the Faubourg Saint-Honoré. However, taking my courage in both
hands, I went there and was received in an office by a big man with
a sulky, impatient expression. The title made him smile. He opened
the album, chuckled at the first drawing, burst out laughing at the
second. I had never seen a man laugh so much. He almost choked,
his eyes filled with tears, his belly shook, and at each new suicide he
laughed louder still. I walked out of his office with a fat order which
would practically cover the whole cost of the album. A few more
subscriptions and I should be able to go ahead.

But I was still worried: which of the two—the tall Kra or the
fat Martin—was the better judge? I felt in need of some sort of
divine arbitration, and as I passed, on my way home, the wide
display window of a bookshop in the Rue des Saints-Pères, I walked
in on the offchance and asked to see the manager.

I was shown up to the first floor. There I waited for a while in
the corridor. At last a door opened and a sickly-looking man with
narrow shoulders motioned me to come in. He had a thick mane of
hair, combed back in a long, sweeping blond wave which formed a
surprising contrast to his unattractive face and the small, darting
eyes under crinkled lids. His head was set on a scrawny neck which
emerged from a wing-collar, underlined by a bow tie. A small
toothbrush moustache bristled above an absolutely rectangular
mouth with full yet tight lips. These lips twitched incessantly as he
slowly turned the pages of my album and read the contents in
impassive silence without smiling once. If he didn't like the stuff,
why not say so and throw me out, but for heaven's sake let's get it
over! But he went on and on, as if obliged to perform an irksome
but sadly unavoidable task. I hunched ever deeper into my chair.
Time passed, slowly, interminably . . . When at last he had finished,
he raised those disquieting eyes of his and, with the first smile I
had seen on his face—it merely lengthened the rectangle of his
mouth without changing its shape—asked me if I would care to
join the staff of his bookshop.

He explained that once a month he welcomed among his book-
shelves personalities from the world of letters or the theatre who
gave talks. It had occurred to him as he looked at my drawings
that it might be rather an original idea to have me illustrate these

talks on the blackboard with thumbnail sketches. The album of course was just an amusing whim, his bookshop would probably sell quite a lot of it, but I ought to aim at something bigger. If I accepted his proposition we should meet regularly and he would be glad to encourage my career.

And so I became a regular visitor. Not for long, though. Lescure fell ill (I was told) and the talks were discontinued. They had lasted as long as autumn leaves. I received no sign of life from him while I spent the spring and summer working on my second album, *Conjectures on Modern Art Lovers*, and getting it printed. He came back, and wrote to me: how was I getting on? I went to show him my new work. He hinted that his long absence had not been due solely to illness but to more serious causes, coming from higher up. He had had to put up a fight, but everything was all right now. I tactfully refrained from asking for further enlightenment. There were no more *causeries*, but my book sold well. Lescure questioned me about my plans. We discussed them, I showed him my sketches, he gave me useful advice. One fine day he suggested that I should look into the possibility of creating a publishing business as part of the bookshop, to produce a few books for bibliophiles every year. I would be put in charge. I saw my future assured. At once we started to draw up lists of titles and illustrators. He would sometimes ask me to go to his flat near the Rue d'Assas, where I would find Monsieur Chasles, a burly man with a flowing beard, whom he called his right-hand man. At the shop he had taken on a young, slightly hunchbacked cousin, who was not unintelligent. Lescure suggested that I should make friends with him, but his presence made me feel inexplicably ill at ease. A contract was drawn up. Lescure reorganized the upper floor so as to make room for an office for me. Whereupon, he disappeared.

He had gone up north, the cousin told me, for a cure. Overwork. Depression. The tone of voice, the meaningful air, gave me to understand that these words were an understatement. Nobody knew when or even if he would come back. And indeed I received no sign from him for over a year, nor any reply to my letters. Whenever I asked for news of him, the significant grimace, the sorrowful shake of the head were the only response I got, and they kept me from pursuing my enquiries. Once, in the Rue d'Assas not far from his home, a taxi turned in front of me and I recognized

him through the window. He invariably wore the same Anthony
Eden hat with rolled-up brim, the same bow tie and wing collars;
the rectangular mouth was unmistakable. Had he come back,
then? Just before the taxi moved out of sight his eyes met mine.
For some time after that I waited for a message, but none came.

I had written him off, so to say, when my father died. Lescure
wrote me a few very moving lines, saying that rarely in his life had
he felt such spontaneous affection for anyone as he had for me.
Thereafter, for months again, there was complete silence.

And then suddenly one morning the telephone rang. He asked me
to come round to his flat. He had lost the bookshop after fifteen
months of exhausting struggle. Chasles, the faithful, zealous friend
and boon-companion, had in fact been nothing but a spy. And the
cousin had betrayed him. But the two of them were mere puppets
in far more powerful hands. Whose hands? Those of the Catholic
Church.

And he told me his story. Although his father had been an agnos-
tic and even rabidly anti-clerical, Lescure himself had felt drawn
towards religious questions. When still quite young, he had lived
in the shadow of a great Dominican, who had acquired fame as a
philosopher. Lescure had become his secretary. His trust and admiration for this man were limitless and he followed him in everything.
He was often invited to attend and even take part in his conversations with others. An extremely pious lady helped the reverend
father in his work. Gradually the boy became aware that he was
in fact serving as a chaperon, a screen for what was a licentious
life. Not only was the devout lady the mistress of the great theologian
but together they took a special interest in the very young ladies
whose father confessor he was . . . The horrified young man asked
for an interview with the higher authorities. He was listened to,
his testimony was taken down, and he was promised that something
would be done. Something was. He was at that time the editor of
the *Revue des Jeunes*; he was immediately fired and word was put
round that he was mad.

The same methods had been used against him once more, he
said. Since that disgraceful episode he had never ceased to be harried
by 'the Order'—always surreptitiously, of course. He would find
himself surrounded by spies, like that fellow Chasles, whom he
had welcomed like a brother in his seaside villa every summer;

or that deformed cousin who had been living miserably in the suburbs of Valenciennes. They would use every conceivable kind of
trick to trip him up. And this is what they had done once again.

I must confess that I felt a bit uneasy listening to his story. I
still did not know him very well. A man suffering from persecution
mania would have talked no differently. His small eyes gleamed, his
mouth twitched, his delicate hands fluttered; where was the impassive man who had received me at our first meeting? If our acquaintance had ended there, I should certainly have retained some doubts
both as to the truth of his story and his sanity. But when I got to
know him better and personally witnessed the further developments,
and when for a start his bookshop was taken over by a very Catholic
firm, I felt inclined to believe him.

He had asked me to come, he said, not just to put me wise to all
this but to acquaint me with his projects: his idea was to found a
literary periodical which, under the title of *La Quinzaine Critique*
(The Critical Fortnightly), would publish a large number of brief
but penetrating reviews of all the books that had come out in the
preceding fortnight, covering all subjects—science, literature,
philosophy, the theatre, the arts, religion. The various sections would
be taken charge of by the most highly qualified people. The list
he quoted—from Gaston Baty the producer to Gabriel Marcel the
philosopher—was indeed impressive. He suggested that I should
run the section dealing with de luxe editions and should also lighten
the somewhat severe pages of the magazine with amusing drawings
and cartoons.

Soon afterwards the magazine appeared and was very well
received. Not only was it a remarkably useful tool of their trade for
professional people; it was also a useful adjunct for the well-read.
Naturally, sales and subscriptions alone could not hope to make it
a paying proposition; but generous private subsidies and plenty of
advertising balanced the deficit without much difficulty. These
Lescure owed to his relations with the top figures in big business.
Doubtless this explained his sartorial fastidiousness—the Eden hat,
wing collar and bow tie, which always caused me such amused
surprise. They were so patently at odds with his opinions, which
were openly Leftist and fairly close to mine. He had, moreover,
under the shock of the great reverend's scandalous life, lost his
faith and had been a militant unbeliever for the past fifteen years.

In the interests of the magazine we now met several times a week, our acquaintance deepened and we became close friends. He would sometimes take me into the exclusive circle of his fund-providers, to some coal magnate or oil tycoon or to a high-society hostess who gave literary and musical evenings at her mansion in the Rue de Varenne.

For two years the magazine enjoyed a wide circulation among a large circle of cultivated readers, its standing grew, sales rose and then, in a matter of weeks, everything suddenly crashed; from one day to the next the subsidies stopped, the advertising vanished. And it all happened with such concerted unanimity that even I could not help suspecting some hidden influence at work. However a big conservative publishing house came forward with an offer to put the paper on its feet again and keep it afloat with all its contributors. Gradually the project underwent some changes; the magazine would become a big weekly of more popular appeal, something like *Candide* but more specifically book-minded. Lescure had laid it down as his primary condition that he should remain the sole editorial director, for the new owners' political and religious views were diametrically opposed to his. This condition was accepted. For some months we worked preparing the first dummy issue. I found a title for it: *Paru* (Just out). We were well paid. But neither he nor I had a contract. This surprised me a little but Lescure reassured me: with a firm of this standing a verbal promise was worth any amount of signatures.

When the issue was ready I was again to be surprised, for we continued to draw our salaries—for doing nothing. From week to week the company offered all kinds of explanations to justify the delay in publication: the season, sales promotion, advertising considerations . . . Lescure once again reassured me and regarded this caution as normal and wise.

Half way through the winter, with no move in sight, I went for a skiing holiday at Klosters. I had only been there two days when a telegram arrived: big meeting at the publishers', launching due any day. I wanted to have at least one shot at the 'Parsenn' and I chose the longest track, the ten mile one. I was out of training, and at the end of the run I sprained my ankle.

I arrived at the meeting limping on a stick. Lescure was radiant: everything was ready, we should be out in a week, big press

advertisements were already announcing the new magazine's birth.
The Chairman showered us with flowery compliments for our talent
and brilliant work; perhaps the pain in my ankle sharpened my
perceptions but the whole thing struck me as odd. Why these
excessive compliments? With some hesitation I remarked to Lescure
as we left that such a wealth of bouquets seemed to me to have a
funereal smell. Though he was startled at this observation, he had
no great job to persuade me that it was quite unjustified.

Two days later he sent me an urgent summons.

He had been to see the Chairman again the day before, to make
the final arrangements. Not the slightest hitch until the last moment
when he was already walking out of the door. As he did so, the
Chairman casually informed him that, as he was too busy himself,
Lescure would from now on be answerable to the literary director.

Lescure had blenched. The man under whose tutelage he was
being placed was noted for his extremism both in religious and
political matters and was moreover the recognized philosopher of
the *Camelots du Roi*, the monarchist right-wing movement! In any
case, any kind of control ran contrary to the undertaking that
had been given that Lescure should be the sole master of the ship.
Moreover, if he were to accept, four-fifths of his collaborators
would walk out on him. The Chairman said there was no need for
them to know. And as Lescure flared up, the other coldly uttered
his last word: 'Think it over.'

The first issue was set up in type, ready to roll off the press and
supposed to be 'put to bed' the following Thursday. It had been
announced in all the papers. The manoeuvre was plain: it was taken
for granted that Lescure would not dare call the whole thing off
at the last moment. And thus a weekly which from the look of its
editorial board was ostensibly left-wing would in fact be covertly
under the thumb of an ultra-clerical and monarchist *éminence
grise*.

To judge from my own reactions, anyone but Lescure would have
given way. There was no lack of good reasons for doing so: although
I had caught a whiff of the fishy smell underneath the bouquets of
flowers, the backhander now seemed to me a little naïve. A guardian
angel, so what? What could he do, single-handed against the lot
of us? It was he, not we, who would soon be 'gobbled up' and reduced
to impotence. I am afraid that underneath this fine show of optimism

there may have lurked another feeling: the somewhat cowardly desire to hold on to a soft job. Lescure placed his hand over mine and told me that, for his part, his mind was made up. To accept such surveillance was tantamount to going to Canossa. To refuse, he realized, meant losing everything: his work, his ideas, any future chance of starting a similar venture, not to mention his financial ruin. But all this counted for little compared to a much more important asset—his moral integrity.

He gave me, that day, an unforgettable lesson by his example. It has continued to guide my life. There was one comfort for Pierre Lescure: the entire editorial board walked out with him. The conservative publishers had to abandon the publication. It was put on the stocks again only much later, with a different policy, a different title, a different format, and moreover, no success. But Lescure's career was broken nevertheless.

This last misadventure produced a curious break in his mode of life. Up to then, in spite of his opinions, he had retained a great respect for the bourgeois virtues, as evidenced by the way he dressed. The fact that this great company, a concern of such high standing, this monument of traditional fair play, could have descended to such cynical double-crossing, could so shamelessly go back on its given word, brought everything crumbling down. A complete change came over him within a few days. No more Eden hat, no more wing collar and bow tie, no more smart double-breasted coat. Henceforward one saw him hatless, his hair streaming in the wind, in turtle-necked sweaters, baggy jackets, sometimes even wearing slippers. For a man of his age there was something childish in this sartorial revolt, a rather puerile ingenuousness, but the outward show was well in keeping with his unbending character, which was incapable of compromise. By his new way of dressing, he severed all links with a milieu which he had enjoyed frequenting but whose indignity, once perceived, forbade that he should even *seem* to condone it by his outward appearance. From then on he scraped a living by various means, turned his enforced liberty to account by devoting more of his time to actual writing. He wrote several novels, whose fame did not equal the influence they had on other writers. He was one of the pioneers of English literature in France: Keats, Katherine Mansfield, Virginia Woolf were his gods. He helped to form several novelists whose subsequent success owed much to his advice. Our friendship grew ever closer. As a result of our frequent discussions on the technique of the novel, I felt my own fingers begin to itch with the desire to swap my pencil for a pen some day.

As I eventually did, in fact, when in Besayes I began to set down the tale of my long-lost love.

IV

THIS, then, was the man who gave me the first inkling that one might act again, and carry on the fight by helping Britain. But his answer to my impatience was: we must wait, we'll talk about it when the moment comes. His rectangular mouth twitched with a fleeting malice that hinted at mysterious plans.

The Vichy lot, for their part, were losing no time. Industrialists, financiers, intellectuals got together to combine their efforts in favour of Germany, and founded the group 'Collaboration'. Hence the name of 'kollabos', which was soon applied not only to the members of that group, but to all those who fraternized with the Occupant. In addition to *Le Pilori*, *Gringoire* and *Je suis partout*, a new periodical, *La Gerbe*, had become the great eulogist of the Nazi leaders, and vilified the 'rotten intellectuals' who did not rally round the New Order. There was no possible answer to these insults since it would have required the Occupant's consent to publish it. And so every book or newspaper, even the apparently neutral, seemed to me suspect and blameworthy. It pained me to see in the bookshop windows an album by Masereel depicting the horrible scenes of the exodus, although all the plates, admirable in themselves, condemned war and soldiering. I feared, however, that their publication had been tolerated because German propaganda favoured these reminders so as to put the blame for them once more on the Jews and Communists. Since one could not speak freely and frankly, any attempt at public expression served the Nazis, who put their own interpretation on it which nobody could challenge. There was, therefore, but one duty, one law: to keep silent.

At Villiers, I spent the month of September reclaiming the jungle that had been my garden, and dug it up completely to plant potatoes. We would thus have at least something to eat in the spring, in spite of the predictable food shortage. I also built a rabbit-hutch and repaired the shed to house chickens and ducks. Thinking of the children, I wondered how to conserve the milk which was still readily available at the farm, though obviously this would not last. I had a brainwave: cheese! I bought, in Rue Jacob, the *Guide to Perfect Cheese-Making* and started to experiment. The variety of cheeses depends, in the main, on the temperature to which the milk-curd is brought: at 28° C you get a Camembert, at 33° C a Port-Salut, at 64° C a Gruyère. For keeping, the last seemed the best. But to make a 'wheel' of Gruyère requires 800 litres, and I was hard put to scrape together as many as ten. I had a shot at it, all the same. What I obtained was indubitably a Gruyère, but miniaturized to the dimensions of a straw-boater. The holes, not larger than pin-heads, were fortunately in proportion, but the rind, alas, was not! It was exactly as thick, no more no less, as the rind of a cheese of eighty kilogrammes . . . Which means that it left room, in between, for just a sliver of edible paste. I did not repeat the experiment, but chose instead to specialize in Port-Salut, which also keeps quite well. I even found a means of speeding up its maturation, which I managed to reduce from twenty-five days to twelve by hermetically sealing the cheese in tins. These I dated and numbered, to preclude any risk of error. Nevertheless, I somehow overlooked one of them which had slipped behind the others. It stayed hidden there for three months. I did not dare open it, in case the fermentation might cause it to explode. I told the children to keep at a safe distance, then cautiously unscrewed the lid . . . Nothing happened, so I opened the tin. The stuff inside was no longer a Port-Salut but, though a bit sticky, had retained its shape. The body looked firm. It had a strong but not unfamiliar smell. I plucked up courage, tasted a morsel. It was a perfect Roquefort.

I thought I had hit on a discovery: a Roquefort without ewe's milk, without temperature-controlled cellars, without *penicillum glaucum*, a Roquefort within the housewife's reach! I repeated the experiment and let a few of my Port-Salut ferment in their tins for three months. They decomposed most abominably. Fortune does not knock twice.

Having thus taken precautions to guard, at least to some extent, against the coming shortages, there remained the problem of finding work to retard the too-rapid melting of my slender savings. I did have an idea at the back of my mind, but dared not broach it to those on whom its materialization depended. A piece of luck came my way. The village boasted two carpenters, an old one and a young one. I was on friendly terms with the elder, but he was about to sell his business. With the younger one I merely used to exchange the time of day when we met in the street. One day he confided his troubles to me: he was up to his neck in work and couldn't find anyone to replace his companion, who was a prisoner of war. I promptly offered my services. I had always been fond of woodwork. I liked the touch and smell of timber. He had seen me build my *Paludes* and other boats, repair the *Chandernagor*, tinker about making the rabbit-hutch and pieces of furniture for my own use. Would he take me on trial, at the wage of an apprentice to start with? The deal was made. He suggested off his own bat that, in view of my age and lack of training, I should work only six hours a day. He also granted me one day off a week; I did not want to cut myself off from Paris.

As a first test, he made me plane the boards of a coffin. He spared me the task of measuring the corpse, but to plane oak-planks perfectly smooth, without bumps or hollows, is not a job for an amateur. He guided me, corrected my grip on the tool; I didn't do too badly. I had passed my *baccalauréat*.

I was to start at 8 a.m., go home for lunch, go back to work at two, and at five o'clock I would take pen and paper and resume the big novel about Stéphanie. I forced myself to write at least two pages a day, by way of practice, so as to keep my brain in condition; but in those days of dismal brooding, it was also pleasantly soothing, this self-imposed task of plunging into my memories and into the green paradise of my childhood love. I progressed fairly well, without bothering about a plan, a proper order or aesthetic considerations. I felt, however, a strong influence weighing on my pen: that of Joseph Conrad. For many years I had been a gluttonous reader of his novels. What I admired in them, apart from his powerful imagination, was their stringent, intricate technique, which seemed to me exactly right for depicting both living reality and the mystery of souls and individuals. Never was a character described from inside, as if the author were a godlike creature able to delve into the skull. Often indeed, a character was seen in action only through the account given by other characters, who in turn had sometimes gathered their information from what yet others had told them. This interplay of prisms, these uncertain echoes aroused

a curiosity, a mounting desire and impatience to meet the hero
'in the flesh', and when at last he did appear his vibrant presence
burst right out of the printed page.

While I was writing, I felt as if Conrad were looking over my
shoulder, preventing me from taking the easy way, that of a classical,
straightforward description. Stéphanie, under the name of Delphine,
myself under the name of Marc, appeared as filtered through the
memory of the narrator, the lieutenant to whom Marc had only
half opened his heart, who, for the benefit of the messmates of the
wounded man now slowly dying in Carcassonne, was trying to
reconstitute the hazy outlines of an evanescent riddle.

Every Thursday I went up to Paris for my regular meetings with
Lescure. For he had at last disclosed his mysterious secret: through
the intermediary of a cousin of his, a high official in a major
government branch and thus close to the horse's mouth for various
political and military information, Lescure himself had been
enrolled in one of the networks of the British Intelligence Service.
In his opinion, this was the only possible way in France of continuing to carry on the war: Britain's war. I could also join in, if I
cared to.

I should have preferred some network more directly linked to
the French in London; unfortunately there was none at that moment. Not yet. So, having no choice, I accepted. I thought he would
introduce me to his cousin, but he explained to me the first of the
rules of the Intelligence Service: never a name in a notebook, as
few names as possible in the memory. Consequently, never know
anyone beyond the immediate link above, in this case himself.
Therefore I should not be told the name of his cousin, whom he
nicknamed Robert. Later, in order to extend the network, I should
naturally have to make contact with other persons; none of them
would be allowed to know him, Lescure; and likewise, the people
contacted by those persons must never know me, Bruller; and so on.
This was an absolutely imperative rule, not to be infringed on any
pretext. Moreover, the first people who must be left in complete
ignorance were my mother and my wife. Not so much for fear of
any indiscretion on their part; but, for one thing, their ignorance
would be a guarantee of their silence if they happened to be
arrested and questioned, and, for another, if I had not confided in

them, I should feel all the more restrained from confiding in others less close to me.

This extreme caution which the Intelligence Service imposed on its members subsequently seemed to me, on many occasions, somewhat overdone by Lescure. There were times when quite a few of us smiled at his excessive precautions, his art of dragging red herrings across his track. But when I later saw how many needless losses, how many mass arrests sometimes resulted from the slackened discipline in French networks, I could only congratulate myself on having been subjected, right from the start, to the stringent rules of underground action. I remain convinced that it is to these rules that many of us owe our lives today.

The task assigned to us was twofold: the collecting of politico-military information, and the establishing of underground escape routes for hunted British agents who had been 'blown' and for airmen who had parachuted to safety from planes shot down on reconnaissance. I was to apply myself to the latter task, since the former required experience and skill beyond the scope of an amateur. This could always come later.

I therefore started to draw up a mental list of my friends, at least those close enough to deserve full confidence. They in turn would rope in those whom they could trust, and so on, in the two zones, North and South, right up to the Spanish frontier where the Intelligence Service had guides to smuggle them across.

But these trustworthy friends, as has been seen, were not so easy to find. Not counting those who weren't absolutely 'safe', many were too far away to be reached; others again presented risks due to their own situation and therefore had to be ruled out.

When nevertheless, after much effort, I managed to set up in the North the beginning of an underground route which my friend Pierre Dalloz, astride the two zones thanks o his job as an inspector-general of sites, was to extend into the southern zone, everything was stopped: 'Robert' was in flight and his network put in cold storage.

This was the end-result of the treachery of a young Englishman who, for love of money and also perhaps out of fear of his life, had begun to be a double agent. After three or four other agents had vanished without trace on their way to rendezvous with him, there was no more room for doubt, and it was decided to arrest the fellow and to have him tried and shot. He must have suspected, though, for he too disappeared without trace. Nevertheless, Robert wanted to carry on just the same. One morning, as he returned from La Rochelle and telephoned his home from the station as a safety measure, he understood from the way his wife answered that the *Abwehr* was in his flat. He therefore had to take to the *maquis*, as it was already called, and lead the life of a fugitive until he could at last reach London. I believe that our embryo route was in fact of some use on that occasion; but our group was now without a leader, and furthermore, the *Abwehr* had arrested Robert's private secretary. This man knew the whole set-up, and knew it, moreover, against his will: having no confidence in his own strength of character, he would have preferred to be left in ignorance; but Robert had not been able to do without his help. What would this weakling do in the hands of the Germans? Everyone expected him to come clean at the first grilling. For a time, Lescure and a few others no longer slept at home (I, being on a lower rung, was not yet endangered). But nothing happened, and eventually news leaked out: against all expectations, the weakling had held out. He had withstood all tortures without a word. At present he was in hospital with his nails torn off and a fractured jaw. That is how I discovered what was later to become a constant experience: that nobody knows in advance how he will react under torture. One whose strength seems unbreakable will cave in at the first twinge of physical pain, while another, who sweats and trembles in face of danger, will let himself be tortured to death without opening his mouth.

About this time the young English traitor was tracked down, caught and shot. But in Robert's absence all contact with British Intelligence was temporarily broken.

Fortunately, as these weeks and months went by, I had seen a good many people and discovered a good many things which would in any case have pulled me out of my state of abandon. The notorious handshake at Montoire, with which Marshal Pétain had promised Hitler not only the surrender of the French but their cooperation, had outraged the bulk of the people, as I could see even in my own village. But other people, other events were the source of less pleasant surprises. Both spurred me to carry on with the activity momentarily brought to a halt, but how, and what new form it might take, was something I still did not know.

I gradually found out which of my acquaintances were back in Paris and which were not. Among the PEN Club members was Aveline, whom I saw again. We made a date in a café near the Ecole Militaire, perhaps with some bravado, since the district was infested with German officers and troops. Although we did not hide from each other that we were both 'doing something'—'If I'm sent to a concentration camp,' he told me, 'at least it won't be just because I'm a Jew'—the rules of prudence forbade us to define what precisely we were 'doing'. Nor did it allow us to have too frequent contacts, since they had no object and were thus needlessly risky. Anyhow, he was obliged to escape to the free zone soon after, and it was only then that I learned, as will be seen, what he had been up to.

We exchanged news of mutual PEN Club friends, and of other writers. Jules Romains was in New York—which he was later to leave for Mexico. He had planned at first to stay in Paris in spite of the Germans, for when he had run into Benjamin Crémieux the day before the Germans marched in, he had said on leaving, with a wry smile: 'Let's at least try to get interned in the same camp.' Which shows, incidentally, how ignorant we still were at that time of what was going on in the camps: though we well imagined the hardships, the cold, hunger and odious lack of hygiene, we still naïvely presumed that friends might nevertheless chat and busy themselves with literature . . . Romains must later have changed his mind about staying, for one could now hear him on the American radio, broadcasting from New York. Maurois, Maritain, Julien Green were there too. Benjamin Crémieux was in the southern zone. The Secretary of the PEN's International House in Paris, Henri Membré, had found the premises looted and stripped of paintings, other works of art and of all the books. The Nazis had also ransacked the flats of Crémieux and Romains, destroying in both places some invaluable documents on the history of modern literature and their priceless correspondence with the best French and foreign writers.

Julien Cain, the director of the Bibliothèque Nationale, had helped to evacuate the PEN Club archives to a distant little port in

Brittany, where Membré had burned them just before the Germans arrived. He was a small, stubby Fleming, a good and likeable organizer, but little renowned as a writer. Without knowing it, he was to play quite a part in my own evolution, as was 'Flodobert', the rabid anti-Nazi, who had also returned to Paris, or had never left it, and whose recent signature under an article in the *Pariser Zeitung*, harmless though it was, had struck us with amazement.

In the village, during the rest of the week, I continued to lead the well-ordered life of a daytime carpenter and evening writer. My employer had promoted me to tasks more complex than planing coffin-planks, such as making door- and window-frames and cupboards. I was not yet skilled enough for such tricky work as drawing and cutting windows, but he now relied on me for the fitting and adjusting of shelves, panels and parquet in his customers' homes. I found this very amusing, for I could watch people living without constraint, quite unmindful of the workman, whose presence did not count. But I, who had never known any life but the easy-going one of a free-lance artist, now learnt the harsh discipline imposed by daily toil regardless of whether you feel well or lousy. On certain days it gave me a foretaste of hell: when you felt, not really ill but, as I say, lousy, and every stroke of the plane reverberated in the pit of your stomach like a boxer's punch. And you have to carry on none the less, not for ten minutes, but for ten hours (and I only worked six). My lack of training made those days more gruelling, and more than once I would gladly have given years of my life to be able to rest. But that would have meant losing face and so I doggedly carried on. I was well aware that, even had I weakened, the 'boss' would not have held it against me; whereas a worker, a proletarian, cannot afford to weaken, for he would lose his job. This impossibility of any appeal against unrelieved pain under unremitting toil is hell indeed.

On my way home at noon, I would often meet, near the Kommandantur, the officer who had occupied my house and had returned it so politely. At that hour he would be walking down the road to his mess. He would greet me in passing, but I never responded: this had become an immutable ceremony between us. The first time I had passed him, he had smiled at me broadly and put three fingers to his peaked cap. I had kept my head averted, so as not to be obliged to reply. The moment after, I was filled with remorse.

'I cannot hurt anyone's feelings even an enemy's, without suffering myself,' says the narrator of *The Silence of the Sea*. And that is how I felt for a long time. What harm had that man done me? Hadn't he behaved 'perfectly' so far as I was concerned? Hadn't he, with delicate tact, expressed a covert but no doubt genuine liking for France? He had put Pascal's death-mask on the mantelpiece; he had said, 'This house has a soul,' he had taken good care of it, even turned up the carpets. Was it just to pay him back with an insult? A courteous greeting, as from one man to another, would not involve any compromise. Next time I would respond to his greeting. With dignified reserve, unsmilingly. Just a nod.

But the next time I was not alone. I was walking up the road with the local builder. He was a short, stout man, with a bull neck and a face whose permanent flush was seemingly belied by the imperturbable air behind his steel-rimmed spectacles, and by his dispassionate, even voice, regardless of subject. Yet under that placid exterior simmered a violent sense of humiliation. He just could not stomach the defeat. He was wasting away. We never talked of anything else. We conjectured about Britain's chances of resistance. He severely blamed the Mayor who, though not exactly obsequious, was over-zealous to satisfy the Occupant's demands.

While we were thus discussing, we saw the officer appear at the top of the hill. He smiled as he passed us and raised his hand to his cap. But my neighbour walked by him stiff-necked, his eyes fixed straight ahead. He knew nothing of my thoughts about this particular officer: what inferences might he draw if he saw me greet him? To try and explain things afterwards meant giving my gesture undue importance. All this crossed my mind in a flash, but the result was that I too, and for the second time, passed stiff-necked, without a glance or a nod.

I realized at once that this repetition would leave me tied for good. My behaviour at our first meeting might pass, in the officer's eyes, at a pinch, for inattention, or an oversight due to surprise; so that my returning his greeting at our second meeting would merely have represented an exchange of courtesies. Whereas the renewed failure to respond indicated a deliberate attitude on my part, a well-thought-out determination. And if, at a third meeting, I should now change my attitude, this could only be taken as an expression of regret, of making amends, an admission that I now thought I had been wrong. To let the officer entertain this notion and possibly draw more far-reaching conclusions from it, was out of the question.

So the third meeting passed off exactly like the preceding ones, and so did the fourth and all the succeeding encounters, although with smiling obstinacy he would persist in saluting me, perhaps in the hope that his constancy might make me relent. He seemed unable to grasp that this very constancy hardened my own persistence, since any yielding on my part would have been tantamount to acknowledging that he had at last disarmed and convinced me. The slightest gesture would have implied a remorse all the more meaningful for having been so long delayed. It would have encouraged heaven knows what further approach from him, which I should have found that much harder to discountenance, except at the risk of insulting him more deeply. So the more he saluted, the stiffer I grew. It pained me, and it went on for weeks, until the troops at last were posted elsewhere, and he with them.

I felt all the more prompted to harden my attitude in that the village as such seemed little inclined to imitate me. Apart from the stout contractor, the cadaverously skinny road-mender, the diminutive station-master and the postman of nondescript appearance, I could not help realizing that the villagers, beginning with my own employer, were quite unruffled by the Occupant's presence. The farmer's wife went one better: she made the most of it quite shamelessly, letting her customers, her neighbours and even her own relatives go without the milk, butter and eggs which she could sell to the Germans at a higher price. Things were not much different in Paris, I felt. The Opéra, the Comédie-Française were playing to stalls packed with officers in full-dress uniforms. The cafés were crowded with shaven square skulls and Frenchmen unconcernedly drinking cheek by jowl. In the automobile-less streets, German soldiers, smartly dressed Frenchwomen and corpulent businessmen let themselves be towed in cycle-cabs, there being no taxis. I could not bear the sight of my fellow-creatures reduced to beasts of burden, even with their own consent to this degradation. However tired I sometimes was from traipsing interminably across a Paris where public transport had become scarce, I could never bring myself to be pulled along by another man. In this, as in so many other respects, I felt very much of an outsider, with only a few rare friends sharing this spirit of uncompromising non-acceptance.

Fortunately, this painful loneliness was soon to become much less pronounced. When the schools and the University re-opened after the summer vacations, it quickly became clear that a brazen attempt was being made to bring the French youth into step. The Minister of Education announced that 'Descartes must be flung out of the window.' Jean-Jacques Rousseau and other 'pernicious' writers were banned from the curriculum, while a new interpretation was put on the work of the great classics. Péguy and Anatole France were simply annexed, Mistral was roped in to support the ageing Maurras who had welcomed the downfall of France as a 'divine surprise', since with it had foundered the Republic. But the student body were in no mood to espouse these views and showed it on the first possible occasion.

I learnt of it in Lescure's home, from his son François, who was then the secretary-general of the Student's Union, though his unofficial membership of the Communist Party was a secret to no one. The authorities had just suspended the lectures of Professor Langevin at the Collège de France. François and a few fellow-students had duplicated leaflets in the highly governmental offices of a Mutual Aid Centre for undergraduates in the armed forces and in POW camps, a centre which Claude Bellanger was then running in the Place Saint-Michel. Other students had thrown these leaflets in handfuls all over the corridors of the Sorbonne, and on November 8th, several hundred undergraduates turned up outside the Collège de France. They were quickly dispersed by an enormous array of police, but it had been a useful way of making themselves felt. Three days later, on Armistice Day, they marched up the Champs-Elysées, ten times more numerous.

Some of them bore two poles on their shoulders—a pun incomprehensible to German ears[1]. They marched in silence up to the Arc de Triomphe. There they clashed with a gang of close-cropped young hoodlums, wearing shoulder-belts and giving the Hitler salute. They retorted with a full-throated rendering of *La Marseillaise*, and some blows were exchanged. Whereupon the Germans launched machine-gun carriers against the demonstrators, left the wounded lying on the ground, jailed a number of others, and tried and sentenced five of them, among them the seventeen-year-old Guy

[1]'Two poles' in French is: *deux gaules*, pronounced = de Gaulle.

Moquet who was later to die a hero's death. The rest of the demon-strators were 'put on cards' like vulgar streetwalkers. The University was closed, Langevin arrested, the whole Latin Quarter put under emergency law. 'France resists, you see!' said the young Lescure proudly.

That remains to be seen, I thought. The Sorbonne was not France. On the Champs-Elysées, the public had passively watched the students being mown down. 'Naturally,' François retorted, ' what do you expect in that posh part of Paris? . . . But just wait till something happens down in Belleville . . . ' I would gladly have believed him, but for the time being I was unconvinced.

Still, a few pointers here and there showed he might not be altogether wrong. On the stupid posters put up by the *Propaganda-Abteilung*, which only made Parisians laugh, or else on French propaganda ones with their fantastic swagger (one, urging de-mobbed soldiers to volunteer for the very Vichyist Servicemen's Legion, had the effrontery to depict Victory leading our streaming flags into battle!), the blank spaces became filled with comments and caustic exclamations. Sometimes it said: 'For de Gaulle make a stroke', and beneath it the poster looked like a page from a school-boy's notebook with its rows upon rows of downstrokes. At night the enemy had them erased, not with a rubber but with a razor, and the holes next day spoke even louder. Or else on the benches of Métro-stations one would find small handbills, duplicated, rubber-stamped or simply typed, giving 'Advice to the Occupied'. Such sheets would pass from hand to hand. Still, although Paris after months of cataleptic lethargy seemed to be recovering the power, if not of speech, at least of whispering, it was not yet even an embryonic revolt; and when, on December 13th, Pétain had Laval arrested and sacked from the premiership, the Marshal regained in public esteem all that he had lost after the Montoire handshake, and more. And I was sorely disappointed.

However, on Christmas Eve, under a clear winter sky, as I was approaching Boulevard Saint-Germain from the direction of Boulevard Raspail, I caught sight of a notice posted on a hoarding on the pavement opposite. This time the passers-by did not grin as they read it. All I could make out at a distance was a name and a word. The word in huge capitals was SHOT, and above it, in slightly smaller capitals, the name: JACQUES BONSERGENT. Dry-mouthed, I walked closer. It stated, in a few brief lines, that the young engineer, having struck a member of the German Army, had been sentenced to death two weeks ago. HE WAS SHOT THIS MORNING, proclaimed the last line of the sinister notice. I could not take my eyes off it. Around me people stopped, read, wordlessly exchanged glances, some of them bared their heads as if in the presence of the dead. I walked up the boulevard towards St-Germain-des-Prés. Every hundred yards or so the same poster was up, with the same motionless, silent crowd before it. At the same time as pain and anger, a feeling of excitement was coursing through me, as if I had thought, curiously: 'At last!' It was the first blood spilled. The first, anyhow, openly proclaimed by the Germans, who were at last lifting the mask of smiling flattery to growl a threatening 'Beware!' They were trying to scare us. But didn't that mean that they in turn were beginning to be scared of France, of the French? That they were not as victorious as they made out?

Scare us . . . ? Next morning, I found the posters surrounded by flowers, like so many tombs. Little flowers of every kind, mounted on pins, had been stuck on the posters during the night—real flowers and artificial ones, paper pansies, celluloid roses, small French and British flags . . . Right in the middle of the staid and stuffy Faubourg Saint-Germain! What must it be like in the popular districts of Belleville, Saint-Denis? I gulped down tears of pain and joy—joy at the first ripple perceived at last, under the flowers offered to her first martyr, throbbing through the invisible soul of my country . . .

V

A FEW days earlier, I had dined at the home of the poet René Arcos. It was a party to which Jean-Richard Bloch had suggested I be invited, and I met there Professor Wallon, Jean Cassou, Francis Jourdain, Frédéric Joliot-Curie, Jean Lurçat—all Communists or pro-Communists at that time. To raise our morale, each guest related some facts he knew from personal experience or had learnt from a reliable witness, or possibly gleaned from a local paper, inevitably Vichyite, which reported the news with due disapproval; and all of them heralded the slow awakening of a numbed population. Here someone had torn down official posters put up by the German authorities; there cables had been cut—in Saint-Malo, in Rennes, in Elbeuf. In Bordeaux, sailors had insulted German officers and spat at them. They were paying for their revulsion with a year in jail. In Soissons, the *Eclaireur de l'Est* felt outraged that young scamps had forced grizzled German colonels to make way for them on the pavement. In Rouen others had been caught in the act of putting up revolutionary stickers. While Jacques Bonsergent's blood was the first spilled in Paris, a mechanic in Brittany, Marcel Drossier, had already last September paid with his life for sabotaging telephone cables. All these actions, great and small, were an indication of many more of a similar nature, and this gladdened our hearts. But we had gathered there for a different reason, because of some very alarming facts which were a threat to the mind and spirit of France.

Not without regret, contempt and indignation, we had seen as far back as July the appearance of a new paper, *La Gerbe*, in which a man of the standing of Alphonse de Châteaubriand, unfortunately surrounded by a few writers of talent, was vying with publicists like Henri Béraud of *Gringoire* and Brasillach of *Je suis partout* as to who should denounce most virulently Great Britain, Jews, Freemasons, Communists and the corrupt Republic. But this had not perturbed us unduly; these fellows were vituperating in broad daylight, without disguising their opinions, and the people who let themselves be bamboozled were those who wanted to be.

We were far more worried by the existence of a press which, unlike those papers, *pretended* to be in opposition. In September the well-known daily *L'Oeuvre* had reappeared, in which Marcel Déat put up a show of carrying on the good fight and attacked the clerico-reactionary 'National Revolution' dear to Pétain and his clique with so much gusto that General de la Laurencie had come to Paris to arrest him (but released him soon after). Under the title *Aujourd'hui*, a new daily had been born and had rallied the misguided support of men like Galtier-Boissière and Henri Jeanson, who naïvely believed in the promise that they would be free to write as they pleased. And for a while it had indeed seemed that they were. In one of those papers there had even been an article in favour of the Jews! And so a number of readers threw themselves avidly on these ostensibly independent publications.

That was the trap. They would at first be given the kind of food they wanted and then, little by little, when they were sufficiently used to their paper to be relied on to stick to it, they would insidiously be offered other nourishment against which they would no longer be able to react. How could one counter this danger? A new publication touched us even more closely and risked doing even greater harm, since it aimed at the highest element in the nation— its mind.

The *Nouvelle Revue Française*, the most authoritative of French literary monthlies, had just taken on a new lease of life. Otto Abetz, Hitler's ambassador in Paris, where he had resided for several years, had entrusted Drieu la Rochelle with its management. Up to the war, with Jean Paulhan at the helm, no publication had exercised a comparable influence on intellectual circles. Abroad, the pulse of the French intelligentsia was taken by reading this monthly, which had been founded by Gide, Romains, Martin du Gard, Copeau. And although Gide and 'the spirit of the N.R.F.' had been denounced by Pétain as morally responsible for the defeat, Drieu now took support from those great names and declared that the sole purpose of the monthly was to keep alive throughout the present difficult years the great movement of thought which it had stimulated so powerfully during the last twenty. What seemed to give substance to his claim was the fact that Jean Paulhan, although he declined to figure in the review, yet kept his offices next to Drieu's own in the Rue Sébastien-Bottin. Former colleagues went to see him there and asked him what they ought to do. And Paulhan, with the quizzical ambiguity he liked to affect, would answer that he personally refrained from writing, but that everyone was free to use his own judgment, to obey his own conscience. Afterwards he would confide to his intimates, in that slightly precious, effeminate voice with its hint of a Southern drawl: 'So-and-so has greatly disappointed me. He's going to work on Drieu's muck-sheet.'

The 'So-and-so's' were not very numerous as yet. But there was a risk that they would grow in numbers. Writers who light-heartedly resign themselves to silence are rare birds. And the semblance of free speech, coupled with Paulhan's ostensible fence-sitting and the cordial professional relations most writers had till recently maintained with Drieu, formed all together a pretty formidable temptation. Had not even Eluard and Aragon yielded to it? The first issue of the N.R.F. under German supervision published poems by them both.

'A swindle!' Jean-Richard Bloch revealed to us. They were pre-war poems which had been in the files of the N.R.F. for months, and Drieu had shamelessly published them as if he had received them from the authors. The two poets were furious, but what could they do? They had sent two of their latest poems to Jean-Richard who read a few passages aloud to us. They were Aragon's '*Crève-Coeur*' and one of the first poems of Eluard's '*Poésie et Vérité*', of which we were thus the first audience. But where could their authors publish them? Where could they protest?

Francis Jourdain, with a mysterious air, produced from his pocket a printed double-sheet which he unfolded before us. It bore the title: *Pantagruel*. We passed it round, startled and moved. At a time when no stencils, paper or printer's ink were allowed to be sold and a close watch was kept on printing-presses, this sheet represented a feat of boldness and skill which commanded respect. Spread over its four pages were articles and information directed against Germany's war, news items received from England, subversive anecdotes, ironic observations, epigrams, lampoons. As for the leading article, I could have subscribed to every word of it; *Pantagruel*'s editor started by stigmatizing 'the spiteful, purblind obstinacy with which Republican Germany had been treated, the inanity of forcing an unworkable treaty down her throat, the too-one-sided attribution of war-guilt . . . ' and he went on to say that it was not a matter of wishing to annihilate the German people 'whose genius no one can deny', but it *was* a matter of saving France from slavery, and supporting for this purpose General de Gaulle, who alone upheld in the eyes of the world 'the French traditions of heroism and respect for the given word.'

So, with a little courage, such things could actually be *printed*! They could circulate, perhaps even be heard of abroad! The sudden buoyancy of this hope made us aware how heavily shame weighed upon us. Not the shame of having been beaten, that is merely due to the hazards of war; it may account for a feeling of humiliation, despair maybe, but not shame. The shame I speak of was no passionate sentiment of romantic grief, it was a daily, simple, familiar feeling, so familiar that its presence deep within (where it coloured all thought and actions) was hardly realized. This shame was for our image as presented to the world by the Pétain Government's press and propaganda: the image of a people submitting to its conqueror and thanking God for its punishment, submitting gratefully and almost gladly; for that is what the press throughout the country, what every radio station in all its broadcasts for the last six months had been trumpeting to the world, and first and foremost to yesterday's ally: that the citizens of France were submitting gratefully and almost gladly to the Germans, to Nazism. It was the shame of knowing that all the books, magazines, everything that could be published; all the diplomats who represented us abroad, all were repeating over and over again: 'We're glad to be beaten. We adore our conqueror, we applaud his crimes and want to take part in them.' And we, who read and heard all this, could do nothing, say nothing. Nothing. For six months now we had longed to shout at the top of our voices that it was not true; and there was not a paper, not a magazine, not a microphone through which we could try to tell the world that it wasn't true, that we did not submit, that we were still as proud as ever of being French, that we loved France even more in her misfortune than in her previous splendour. Compared with this gag, this nightmare, all other hardships seem footling. What do you care about shortages, about going without butter, sugar, coal, when you compare them to the agony of feeling you are an object of contempt for the rest of the world and cannot even protest?

And here, for the first time, a printed paper did protest! Oh, it was still a feeble cry, but in a cellar, an empty vault, a faint cry resounds very distinctly. For the first time we felt the crushing lid of silence lifting above us ever so slightly. Where could one get hold of copies of *Pantagruel*? We were impatient to distribute them.

But Francis Jourdain could give us no idea. He had received his copy through the post, naturally without the sender's name. He did not know the editor's name either, of course—and had he known it, he could not have divulged it. We only learnt that his name was Raymond Deiss a year later, after the Germans had caught him, sentenced him and beheaded him in Cologne.

As Jean Cassou and I walked home through the empty streets at curfew, we questioned ourselves about our duty. How long would the war, the Occupation last, supposing Britain held out? Ten years? Fifteen? If Britain yielded, French thought might have to keep alive amid the outer darkness for hundreds of years perhaps. The role of the intellectuals would be like that of the monks who, during the long night of the Middle Ages, had obstinately and secretly passed on the torch of classical thought, keeping it alight for close on a thousand years up to the Renaissance . . . But how could we manage to pass it on? Broadsheets like *Pantagruel*, however courageous, could not on their own carry the burden. Cassou too had sensed that his fellow-writers were weakening, wondering, wavering: was silence really a means of doing battle? Cassou tried to show them that if they held out so much as the tip of their little finger, they would soon find themselves dragged, body and soul, into the enemy camp, since their mere presence would attract others and they would have to connive at enemy propaganda without any chance of ever dissociating themselves. They did not always seem convinced by his reasoning.

Pierre de Lescure and I thus witnessed the slow dwindling of the batch of silent writers. Every week fresh signatures appeared in the press of treason. This shocked and mortified us all the more in that the Germans were now becoming tougher and more ruthless, and their accomplices therefore more despicable. While the grim, black-bordered red notices began to cover the walls, announcing more and more names of hostages who had been shot, denunciations poured in. Some of these were particularly revolting: an artist of Vlaminck's calibre calling down German vengeance on Picasso's head, poets denouncing poets. On January 1st, 1941, Henri Bergson, the great philosopher, died. He was Jewish. On the Minister's orders, his house was surrounded to prevent the forming of a cortège, and instead of receiving a state funeral he was buried with indecent haste. All those infamies made us even more sensitive to certain defections. One of Lescure's oldest literary friends, a man whom I myself respected greatly, one of the foremost critics of the 'thirties and an unrivalled authority on English literature, accepted the literary editorship of a newspaper that had sold itself to the enemy. We were at a loss to explain this weakness, which was not just a recantation as in the case of Durtain or Lenormand, for his articles always kept strictly within the bounds of pure criticism. He nevertheless consented to put his signature next to those of people whose virulent diatribes against Jews, Freemasons, democracy and Great Britain ought to have horrified him. And no doubt he was horrified, but if so, how could he . . .

One day, Lescure ran into Flodobert and, certain of finding him in accord with our own feelings (I had told him of our return trip through Germany, when Flodobert's wrathful appeals to the Czech air force had struck terror into the heart of poor Loewel), had talked to him about his fellow-critic. To his surprise, Flodobert had answered, with a musing look on his side-whiskered face: 'I wonder if he isn't right . . . ' And seeing Lescure bridle at this, he went on: 'He is a book-reviewer, after all. He's got to do his job. You don't hold it against a café-waiter when he serves a lager to a German. He thinks what he likes, for all that.' Lescure tried to hold him back from that slippery slope, but it was obvious that his colleague's example was undermining his last qualms. We did indeed see his signature appear soon after in the *Pariser Zeitung*, and later his name figured in large type among the new editorial board of *La Gerbe*, which huge posters publicized on all the walls of Paris . . .

'He's a goner,' said Lescure sadly. 'Perhaps he still genuinely believes that he'll be able to keep them at arm's length. But apart from the pressure he'll be subjected to, he'll find his friends condemn and shun him. He'll want to justify himself, and to do that, he'll have to adopt, little by little, the ideas he thinks he still rejects . . . *De profundis.*'

After Flodobert, others slithered down the same slope one by one. A fantastically luxurious album extolling Pétain was produced by one of the great masters of graphic art. Here and there were distressing signatures—Colette's, Paul Léautaud's, and those of Robert Desnos, the poet (but in his case we were horribly wrong) and of Léon-Paul Fargue, who could candidly declare, quite unaware of the appalling humour of his words: 'Speaking for myself, I take their money with a barge-pole . . . '

I for my part held back by his coat-tails that decent fellow, Henri Membré, the secretary of the PEN International House. I saw him repeatedly for professional reasons, the profession in this case being not literature, but carpentry. He had been both impressed and amused by the fact that I had turned carpenter in order to make a living without breaking my silence. And as he wanted to partition one of his rooms which he found too large, he suggested I should fashion the low set of shelves which would divide it. I had accepted, partly out of amusement too, but partly because it would mean a little jam on my bread: the wages I drew (and deserved) from my employer did not much exceed those of an apprentice. I sawed the shelves and uprights in my shed at Villiers, then went to his flat in the Rue des Renaudes to adjust and fit them.

While we worked, we naturally talked, and I found him very tolerant towards those fellow-writers who had sold out. 'I understand them, don't you see,' he would say. 'The Occupation may go on and on. Men like Duhamel, Mauriac, Malraux can afford to wait, they don't care if they keep silent, their reputation is established and will endure, they'll find it where they left it. But take me, for example. All I have to show is one novel, *Non-lieu*, which had an excellent press, and two others which attracted little attention. If I don't publish anything for five or ten years, I'll be forgotten, I'll have to start from scratch again . . . ' And he pleaded that writing a novel and getting it published was not really trading with the enemy, was it? I tried to convince him that it was already too much. He had seen, as we all had, a copy of the notorious 'Otto list', which the Publishers' Association had produced and which listed all the books due to be pulped. '*In their desire to help create a more wholesome atmosphere,*' so ran the foreword, '*the French publishers have decided to withdraw from sale those books which have systematically poisoned our public opinion; more particularly the publications by political refugees and Jewish authors who, betraying the hospitality France had given*

*them, unscrupulously incited us to wage a war from which they hoped to benefit
for selfish ends . . . .'* And the notice wound up with this fine compliment: *'The Occupation Authorities have expressed their satisfaction at the
initiative taken by the French publishers.'*

One hundred and forty of them had signed it, among them *all*
the major publishers, with the single exception of Emile-Paul
Frères. It was hard to say which was more distressing—their mass
rush into servitude, their breast-beating for their share in 'poisoning
public opinion', or the list of authors whom they had previously
scrambled after and lauded to the skies, and whom they were now
hastening to blacklist. Among them could be found higgledy-
piggledy Aragon, Julien Benda, Jean-Richard Bloch, Jacques
Kessel, Dorgelès, Istrati, Giraudoux, Maurois, Claudel, André
Malraux, with such odd bedfellows as Bainville, Henri Bordeaux and
even—the height of irony!—the ultra-Catholic monarchist Henri
Massis. Banned too were English authors, ancient and modern
(Shakespeare no less than Virginia Woolf), and banned of course
the German exiles, Ludwig Renn, Thomas and Heinrich Mann,
Zweig, Brecht, Wassermann, Emil Ludwig, Erich-Maria Remarque.
Forbidden to be sold or published were biographies, even those
written by Aryan authors, of Jewish musicians, artists, poets—
Offenbach, Heine, Meyerbeer, Chagall, Spire, Fleg, Darius Mil-
haud . . . Banned even—incoherence and ridicule could go no
further!—the Book of Isaiah! Everybody knew of this disgraceful
list, either through seeing it at home or at friends'. To publish
anything with these firms who were castigating their own authors
therefore meant publicly disowning those who had been sacrificed;
it meant approving the publishers' odious 'initiative' and generally
joining in the chorus of miserable cowards. Moreover, it implied
a belief in the 'freedom' of French thought, that it could be freely
expressed and circulated and preserve its influence abroad, when it
was well known that *all* French books—literary, historical, scientific or technical—were ruthlessly stopped at all frontiers to make
way for the export of German books only. Was Membré unaware
that a certain Kiesinger, attached to the Propaganda Department,
was taking foreign radio reporters round our country for the purpose of showing—as he wrote in his report—'to those who had
been used to believe in French cultural supremacy in Europe, how
false this notion was and why they had been misled into this error?'

In the heat of the moment, Membré naturally expressed agreement, but the following week he would say he had thought things over and would produce fresh arguments which I had to show up once more as being fallacious.

'You won't be able to restrain him much longer,' said Pierre de Lescure, with a sigh.

'Neither him nor many like him,' I agreed. 'We must find some outlet for their frustration before it's too late. But what outlet?'

Nevertheless, my thoughts would return to *Pantagruel* and other clandestine sheets which, we heard, were multiplying in the free zone. Mightn't those whose pens were itching with frustration find relief in writing for those sheets? But if those papers existed, they reached the northern zone only rarely. What was worse, friends returning from the unoccupied zone would paint a rather sombre picture. Their press, they told us, was in a deplorable state of confusion. There were two *Humanités*, one genuine, one phoney, and both letting fly at the British. A third 'Marxist-Leninist' sheet, *La Vérité*, made war on *L'Humanité*. *La Liberté*, though hostile to collaboration, nevertheless still put its faith in the 'victor of Verdun'. Many resisters, too, were still complex-ridden about Pétain and loath to believe that he was not an inveterate adversary of the Occupant. Moreover, many of those papers were ephemeral and disappeared after two or three issues. They could not provide a solution to our problems. Lescure thought so too and tried to make contacts elsewhere.

He never told me how he came across his eventual 'find'—perhaps through his son's relations with underground Communist groups. However that may be, on arriving at his flat one day, I found myself pulled into his room with a great air of secrecy. And there, behind closed doors, amid the pile of books and the prints tacked to the walls, he handed me a brochure of roughly the same format as the N.R.F., bearing the title, *La Pensée Libre*. 'Read it,' he told me. 'You can't take it away. I've only got this copy. But take your time, read it, and tell me what you think of it.'

I skimmed through the volume—some fifty pages—carefully read the first articles, glanced at the others, and soon my mind was made up. The contents, from cover to cover, expounded only Party viewpoints. That was better than nothing, it was even breathtaking, but wasn't there a risk that many readers might take it as confirmation of the enemy propaganda claim that only Jews and Communists were opposed to the New Order? I voiced this objection to Lescure, who agreed with me. What was more, he said, the editors themselves shared this view. And that was why they were trying to widen the range of their contributors and enrol writers from the whole gamut of Resistant thought, not even excluding the extreme right-wing, since the true patriots among them, appalled by the traitor Maurras and his 'divine surprise' as well as by Brasillach, Massis and other royalists of that ilk, had broken with them and were supporting de Gaulle. The editors had therefore requested Lescure, with his wide-ranging acquaintances in literary circles, to help them recruit contributors. Didn't this exactly coincide with our own plans?

However, the very first approach, which I myself made forthwith, disclosed the difficulties we were to encounter.

I sent a note to Georges Duhamel, who had always in the past expressed his liking for my drawings, and asked to see him. His ready answer, in his large handwriting, revealed a hint of curiosity. He received me in his comfortable study in the Rue de Liège, where he proudly showed me, on entering, a portrait of Arthur Rimbaud. I explained what we had in mind: how we wished to turn a clandestine periodical of Communist origin into an instrument for expressing all varieties of French thought. He listened to me very carefully, only once distracted by an importunate moth which engaged his attention until he at last managed to swat it. When I had finished, he replied very gently in that high-pitched voice which always sounded so surprising coming from a man of his corpulence, that he would never write for a journal run by Communists. He had had too many dealings with them in the past, he said, you couldn't do anything with those people, and he warned me to be on my guard. In any case, he told me, he personally intended to fight a different kind of battle. On the one hand, to maintain silence and refusal— he had already shown the door to several German writers who had come to him with requests for this or that—on the other, to take a firm stand inside the French Academy to prevent its take-over by pro-Nazi writers (already too numerous in it, as it was . . .) and therefore to block all further elections. He thus planned to fight in the open, however long that might last, and did not wish to jeopardize the success of his action by other, reckless activities.

Full of cordiality, he accompanied me to the door, stopping in the hall to make me listen to the first bars of the Kreutzer Sonata which someone behind a closed door had just begun to play on the piano. 'My son', he said, and nodded his head in time while we stood listening for a moment. On the doorstep, he said to me in parting: 'I haven't set eyes on you, of course!'—the very thing I had not quite dared to ask him.

I reported this fruitless outcome of our talk to Pierre de Lescure and together we drew a lesson from it. So long as all we had to show was a manifestly Communist *Pensée Libre*, we must expect similar reactions. Besides, Lescure considered my visit had been theoretically imprudent: complete confusion reigned in literary circles, and though the risk of being denounced, even by one's adversaries, was not very great, the risk that some undecided or talkative person might confide in others either to give himself airs or to ask for advice, was a very real one.

He therefore mapped out the following plan: first and foremost we must somehow turn out one magazine issue visibly emancipated from Party links; once this was published, it could be passed round the pen-pushing guild without the risk of scaring them off. And then, according to the way they responded, we could proceed to enrol new contributors.

This seemed to me a sound plan, except for the prerequisite: if we did not first recruit at least a few non-communist writers, how on earth were we to get out that first issue? Who would write the articles for it? 'Why . . . you and I, of course,' said Lescure.

A year earlier, such a suggestion would have seemed to me a sheer flight of fancy: I drew but I didn't write; how could I be suddenly expected to fill half a magazine? But for several months now, hadn't the memory of Stéphanie begun to turn me into a writer? I had submitted the first chapters to Lescure for his frank opinion as to whether there could be found the slightest trace of literary talent in this hotchpotch. When we met again the following week at the Café La Rotonde, he had dissected my work without indulgence or undue severity and had concluded: 'Keep on writing. We'll see,' which, if not strictly discouraging, at least left my question in suspense. His proposal now, out of the blue, that I should write a whole number of a magazine with him, thus had for me the value of an unhoped-for promotion.

We got down to work. We were not short of suitable topics, alas. Two novelists of great renown, whose silence during the last eight months had augured well for their future attitude, had delighted the pro-Nazi press by a sudden and spectacular volte-face. One of them, betraying the confidence placed in him by a mass of youthful followers whom his myth of earthy felicity had attracted, had attended a luncheon given in his honour by Dr Epting of the Propaganda-Staffel and had raised his glass, unconditional pacifist though he was, to the defeat of Britain. The other, whose books extolled the martial values of virility, had not withstood the victor's pressure and had recently attended the first night of one of his plays in the box of Otto Abetz—on the very day when a host of humble heroes were falling under German bullets on the nearby Mont Valérien. We felt that no physical nausea could equal the moral revulsion inspired by such craven self-abasement. Vengeful glee, however, filled me as I reported with gusto the entry of a new Minister into the Vichy Government: he happened to be a former schoolmate of mine at the Ecole Alsacienne, a boy of outstanding brilliance, but depraved and full of guile. One day, for fun, he had threatened to gouge out my eyes with a half-open pair of compasses, and the points were already pricking my lids when I started to defend myself, suddenly aware that this was not, perhaps, a joke. In his first interview with the press at Vichy he declared: 'I, who know England well, having lived there . . . ' What he did not say was that his stay there had been confined to a reformatory: the consequence of his burgling his father's safe, a misdeed of which he accused the servants. There had been a terrible scandal at school, for he had shared the substantial loot with some of his unscrupulous friends, and when they started coming to school by taxi every morning, the cat was out of the bag. Scandals piled up in his adult life too. Booksellers would put their rare editions and de luxe art books under lock and key the moment he entered their shops. After a couple of days spent at Jean Cocteau's home, he walked off with a Picasso drawing, which he subsequently sold, and when the theft was discovered, he once more ascribed it to the maid. From a doctor friend of his, he had filched the prescription-forms and used them as an order-book. That Pétain chose his ministers from people of such moral fibre delighted me. Actually, the cunning rascal was not lacking in talent, and in the course of several stays in Germany, had wormed his way into certain select quarters so that he now seemed well placed to negotiate France's entry into the war against Britain, a country with which, true enough, he had a long-standing account to settle. . . .

For Britain was putting up a valiant fight. The whole of France listened to the BBC programme, 'The French talk to the French', introduced by the four opening notes, several times repeated, of Beethoven's Fifth Symphony, and by a ditty, sung to the music of the *Cucaracha*, with a comical soft slur:

> *Radio-Paris m'ment . . .*
> *Radio-Paris m'ment . . .*
> *Radio-Paris est allemand . . .* [1]

The French people listened to de Gaulle and to his spokesman, Maurice Schumann, whose voice, which had at first struck me as pompous and over-emphatic, later seemed to me moving and persuasive, as I grew accustomed to it. Sometimes, as I walked up the stairs to the flat of some friends I was visiting, I could hear, from floor to floor, the same vibrant voice through the door of every landing so that I had the impression that my legs were moving at a standstill! Though the Germans tried to jam the broadcasts, they could still be picked by means of direction-finding frames, which were of course strictly forbidden. I had made one for myself, using with malicious glee the yards of black electric wire which the Germans had left behind in my garden. This I had wound round a low stool, and it appeared to be an ornamental feature. One autumn night, as I was listening to the British wavelength by the open window giving on to the dark garden, I suddenly thought I smelt tobacco smoke, and then saw a pale scroll dance in the light of the window. Was someone listening below? Taken aback, I cautiously tiptoed into the next room where the children were sleeping, sidled up to the window, cast a quick glance outside and saw the red end of a cigarette glow in the darkness. After a moment I could discern a motionless figure. It was obviously one of the officers billeted at the nearby château a little way up the hill, discreetly come to collect news . . . I feared I might be in for some trouble, but none ensued. I still do not know whether I owed my going scot-free to a 'gentleman's' dislike for playing the informer or

[1]'Paris Radio lies, Paris Radio lies, Paris Radio is German.'

to his unwillingness to deprive himself of a valuable source of information . . .

Another evening, I had heard the announcer say: 'You will now hear Lieutenant Brosset.' Brosset? My Brosset was a lieutenant-colonel . . . It was he, though. I recognized his ardent, ringing voice. He was addressing himself to his comrades in Africa, under Weygand's command. He had written to General Weygand immediately after the armistice—we only heard of it later—recalling their friendship and the memory of Mangin, his father-in-law. In his letter, he assured him of his esteem or his contempt according to which attitude Weygand would adopt during the rest of the war. By way of an answer, Weygand had him court-martialled *in absentia*, sentenced to death like de Gaulle, and to the confiscation of all his possessions. But at the time I knew nothing about Brosset since the letter he had sent me from Panama, and I wondered, though not over-anxiously, which side he was on . . . I was not really surprised to discover that he was in London with the Free French, but I was relieved and happy and proud that all my close personal friends so far had opted against the defeat. I had not chosen them too badly, after all . . .

VI

THE winter was severe, snow covered everything. In the carpenter's shop there was plenty of timber waste to provide us with sufficient heat, but I suffered from chilblains whenever I had to work in private houses. In my own home, where I now divided my late evenings between my novel and my articles, the only source of heat was an old coal-burning stove, without any coal. I fed it with logs of wood sawn into tiny chunks for slower combustion, and this produced an enormous amount of tar which trickled down the flues into a bowl I kept underneath. It also produced, I imagine, plenty of carbon monoxide, which may have been the cause of the intractable headaches which troubled me that winter and from which I still suffer to this day.

Lord, how interminable those days were, starting early in the morning in darkness and ending at night in darkness too! The winter dragged on and on, nothing happened, the war seemed to stagnate, to have frozen solid for decades. It was just one long icy night, I lived without a future, I wrote without joy. Writing those articles was better than doing nothing but I felt the effort was so disproportionate to the tragic sleep in which Frenchmen's minds lay wrapped. I felt, I knew deep inside me, that one ought to do something more, undertake some much vaster action. But what? My imagination too was frost-bound.

The people, suffering from the cold, were not spared hunger either. The food shops, which had been fairly well stocked up to the autumn, had emptied rapidly. Customers had to queue up for hours in the snow and slush and icy wind to buy a few wretched swedes. The meagre rations of sugar, meat and flour were obtainable only on ration cards; for these to be issued one had to produce identity papers on which the owner's religion was stated. As I have none, I asked my six-year-old twin sons, with somewhat grim humour, which religion they would like to see put against their names: Protestant like their mother, Catholic like their grandmother, or Jewish like their grandfather? 'Oh, no, not Jewish!' they said, unhesitatingly. That pricked my heart: so even in this outlying village they had already dimly grasped that to be Jewish in France was not a good thing these days . . .

Anyhow, with or without a ration card, there was little enough food, and in Paris even less than in the country. The Parisians took this semi-starvation in very bad part. The empty belly opened their minds. They no longer watched with a smile as the grey-clad, jackbooted soldiers went by. They called them *doryphores*—colorado beetles—because German requisitions made the potatoes disappear. They grasped at last that German purchases, paid for with the Occupation indemnity (four hundred million francs per day, at their 1940 value) were merely camouflaged looting. Relations were becoming taut, 'like a fiddle-string', according to Jean-Richard Bloch's prophetic expression. The Germans did not fail to notice it, their famous 'correctness' took a knock and gave way to more violent reactions. After the murder of a high-ranking officer in Nantes—a sordid business of underworld queers—fifty hostages, selected for the Germans by the French Minister Pucheu, with one of the foremost thinkers of the Communist party, Gabriel Péri, among them, were shot at the camp of Châteaubriant.

The text of the farewell letter written by one of the hostages, a youngster still at school, was passed from hand to hand, copied or typed out; its words, both touching and sublime, brought tears to the eyes. After saying throughout the letter how proud he was to fall for France, and comforting his parents with words of heroic dignity, he could not help, poor boy, letting his fear show for a moment in the last line: 'It is hard to die, though . . . ' This letter, and a poem by Aragon—received by Lescure through some channel unknown to me (his son again, perhaps?)—about the death of Péri, 'he who sang in the throes of death', moving in its deliberately naïve, popular ballad-style, were to be published along with the articles which we had meanwhile got ready. Lescure had added a short story and urged me to think about writing one as well, for the next issue. I promised to consider it. But I have no great powers of imagination and for a long while no inspiration came to my cold-benumbed brain.

It snowed and snowed . . . I can still see myself walking across the Place de la Concorde after nightfall, the vast square white and empty and still, without a light, without a car. How lovely it looked under its shroud! And the Champs-Elysées, the Rue Royale, the

bridge, statues, colonnades, so like the deserted, lunar town-scapes
which Chirico used to paint . . . Paris hushed and dormant like
the sleeping beauty was a sight of heartbreaking poignancy.
Walking by my side was Colonel Humbert who, passing through
the capital, had asked to see me. It was to him that I had turned
for my military transfer which had not come off. However, the
differences of age, career and situation, as well as the fact that he
had been my chief at the Officers' School of Saint-Cyr, combined
to put an intangible distance between us which kept our mutual
liking from developing into friendship. His sister Paulette was a
link between us. I wondered what he might have to say to me.
I knew he was in the Armistice Commission, which was charged
with protecting French interests (within the narrow margins left
to them) against the victor's demands. He had just returned from
Wiesbaden. We padded through the snow-muffled silence, he made
me tell him my 'campaign' until we reached the Weber, that
ancient café which today has disappeared to make room for the
Lufthansa's head-office . . . On its glass-fronted terrace, huddling
round the meagre warmth of a brazier, he told me of his own
sickening experiences: he would struggle for days and weeks to
wrest a few planes from the Germans, to save a couple of locomotives, to hold on to some reserves; he would report to Vichy the
concessions he had won and would receive orders, in reply, not to
bargain over anything. Sometimes Vichy even offered the Germans
things they had omitted to demand.

He was sick with stifled indignation. He did not utter the word
'treason', being too much of a soldier to dare make such a charge
against his superiors; but he felt a pathetic need to speak out and
confide his rancour and anxiety to someone. He had asked to be
relieved of his post, and on leaving Wiesbaden planned to head
south where he would take command of a unit of the Armistice
army. He hoped he would be able to instil his troops with a spirit
of resistance and the will to hold out. I feared—though I did not
tell him so—that here, too, he was indulging in wishful thinking.

Most of all, I wondered why he had chosen me of all people as
his confidant. Perhaps he distrusted his own milieu and had talked
to me like King Midas's barber confiding to a hole in the ground
the too-heavy secret of the asses' ears? Snow was falling again in
heavy flakes as we came out of the Café Weber. In the silent,

inky night it was sinister. I watched him walk away, until the slim, martial silhouette dissolved into the whiteness, the blackness. The idea struck me—but already too late—that he had perhaps not said all he had meant to. That he had wished to sound me out first; and that I might see him again before long. I did indeed see him again, but only after much time had passed.

From week to week my headaches grew worse, even after I had let the stove go out in the first warm days of sunshine, until a certain day in May, when the headache decided to settle in and leave me no more. One evening as Yvonne Paraf was correcting my English exercises in her flat (the German Occupation had made me decide to learn English) and saw me in agony, she had the curious idea— 'to get rid of everything', she said—of making me swallow a glass of water saturated with kitchen-salt. Instead of throwing up, I felt so ill that I had only one idea, to get home to bed. I had almost fainted in the métro on my way to her, so I borrowed her bicycle. Perhaps the fresh air and physical exercises did me good. The fact is that by the time I reached Rue Servandoni I felt fine. I rang Yvonne at once to suggest she send a report to the Medical Academy on the combined effects of common-salt-cum-bicycle, went to sleep perfectly happy, and woke up to find my migraine at its duty post, where it remained for years without taking a day off.

The events of that month of May were scarcely designed to dispel headaches. The charming and witty Francis Jourdain, who had come to lunch at Villiers one Sunday, had brought news of ghastly happenings. There had been a mass arrest (the first of its kind) of several thousand Jews who, he told me, had been parked not very far from us, at Pithiviers and at Beaune-la-Rolande. So Pétain was playing the running dog for his Nazi masters in this Jew-hunt from which he had pretended he would spare France! Shortly afterwards, he descended even lower in infamy: he handed over to Hitler the political and racial refugees; and by this act, the act of a despicable dotard who with a trembling hand offers his adopted child to the executioner in order to preserve his legitimate sons, he covered a traditional land of asylum with the gravest stigma of dishonour. The only piece of good news was that, as a result of Russian intervention, Jean-Richard Bloch had been able to pass through Germany in a sealed railway-carriage—like Lenin before him. He was now in Moscow, and his friends breathed more freely.

Hitler meanwhile was plastering Jugoslavia with German bombs, invading her territory, and then that of Greece. The swastika flying over the Acropolis—horrible, horrible, most horrible! I tried to comfort myself with the thought of the hero in Robert Ganzo's story, the one whose prisoner refuses to let him go. Perhaps Hitler's armies would get stuck in the lime of Europe which would not let them go? Unfortunately, for the time being their power seemed irresistible . . . And when, a month later, while I was shaving, stripped to the waist, my old friend Coronel, who was sheltering at Villiers in a house near ours, burst into the room with goggling eyes and announced excitedly:

'Have you heard the radio?'

'No.'

'Hitler has attacked the Russians!'

'It's not true!'

'Honest! Ask whoever you like!'

I just did not know what to think of this world-shaking event. Hitler's succession of victories for the last seven years had so warped my mind that I could not help fearing the worst every time. For never so far had he attacked any country without first making sure that it would crumble at the first shock: Austria, Czechoslovakia, Poland, Denmark, Norway, Holland, Belgium, France, Greece, Jugoslavia—not one had held out for more than a few days. Besides, he had foretold this in his talks with Rauschnig, when he explained that his strategy consisted of 'first destroying the enemy from within'. Had he not done so in every instance? And were not the Moscow trials, which at the time had been so inexplicable as to seem downright crazy, the ominous sign that this 'demolition from within' had not spared the Soviet Union either? If this were so, might Hitler not thrust his army, like a knife into butter, right into the heart of a country that had been politically undermined, decomposed by treachery, where a rebel Fascist government, after overthrowing Stalin, would be ready to capitulate without a fight —as Vichy had done—and go over to the enemy? If this catastrophe were to happen, what hope would be left for Europe, for France? With a whole continent behind him, assured of raw materials and industrial products, of oil, cereals, fats, perhaps of manpower

and fresh troops, in almost infinite quantities, who could still hope
to defeat Hitler? He would have been prophetic once again when
he proclaimed that the New Order would reign for a thousand
years.

Hitler's attack had taken place on a Sunday, of course—like his
actions in the Rhineland, the Anschluss, Prague, Poland. We were
expecting Léon Motchane and Yvonne for lunch. As I mentioned
before, he was of Russian origin, and though not a White Russian,
anything but a Communist. I was in the garden as he came in
through the gate. He walked up to me, joyfully rubbing his hands;
the smile on his long face pulled his full lips apart. 'So what do you
say?' he called out to me when still at a distance. For a moment I
wondered whether his good cheer was not caused by the prospect
of Stalin's imminent fall. He went on: 'The first good news for
twelve months!' 'But if Stalin should fall . . . ,' I said.

'What an idea!' he cried. 'You don't know the Russians. Never
mind if they like or dislike Stalin and his régime, that doesn't count
any more: Holy Russia is attacked, and they'll defend it. To the
last man! And they're invincible! When an army can manœuvre
over a territory covering two-thirds of Europe and half of Asia, it
can't be destroyed. Hitler has repeated Napoleon's mistake. Even
if he gets away with some early success, he has flung himself into
a bottomless pit. He's doomed. Let's drink to victory!'

The early days of the Russian campaign tended to confirm this
hope. The bloody reverses suffered by the Red Army, far from
weakening the central power, merely consolidated its cohesion and
also its popular support. Seeing the Soviet people put up such a
ferocious fight, the French felt a new surge of sympathy for them—
even the Frenchmen most hostile to Communism. 'Look at the lies
they've been telling us!' the little station-master of Villiers-Mont-
barbin would say to me indignantly every Thursday as I waited
for the local train to Paris. 'Are they still going to pretend those
people loathe their régime? They wouldn't be fighting with such
guts to defend it, would they now, Monsieur Bruller?' I nodded
agreement, deeming it unnecessary to repeat Léon's words about
Holy Russia. Besides, I shared the popular opinion: even a Russian
would scarcely fight so hard for something he hated . . . .

This new-found hope, the lovely sunshine over the flower-filled
garden, the presence of my mother, the children on leave from

school, all this coloured our quiet country life with a deceptive
holiday hue. There were times when, watching the twins rolling
in the grass, I would forget the Germans for an hour. At that period
my sons thought up so many pranks—the least of which was the
systematic demolition of the garden wall that overlooked the road
by stealthily removing tiny crumbs day after day, without ever
being caught in the act—that to spare myself the trouble of constantly having to punish them, I had thought up a tariff of indulgences for their 'good deeds' to be set against a tariff of penalties,
to allow them to redeem at least some of their deserved hidings. But
they never redeemed any of them, preferring to take their punishment. With growing alarm, I imagined that they were piling up
indulgences in anticipation of some colossal mischief. But not at all!
I had aroused an abstract passion in them—the passion for
hoarding! And like two misers, they never stopped piling up their
hoard of indulgences, unable to bring themselves to make the
slightest dent in it.

It was not without qualms, though, that I savoured those early
summer days with my family, and savoured, too, the hopes we
placed on the Soviet Union. I kept racking my brain: What could
we do? Lescure had passed all our articles to the editors of *La
Pensée Libre*. All we could do now was wait for publication before
tackling the next task of finding other contributors. This inactivity
weighed on me, I was sure there were better things to be done.
Lescure was still pressing me to write a short story, and I was
chafing more and more as I discarded one by one all the ideas that
came into my head, feeling that none of them was capable of making
the reader share the certainties that choked me.

VII

I T was then that I, too, happened to run into Flodobert. I was walking down the Rue du Vieux-Colombier when, outside the theatre of that name, I saw him coming towards me. His face, with its air of a Romantic intriguer, was already beaming at this happy coincidence. If he had not started writing for the German papers, how pleased I should have been to see him! We had enjoyed each other's company in Prague, and I retained some of my sympathy for him despite my disappointment. I could not bring myself to cold-shoulder him too ostentatiously. I therefore did not draw back when he took my arm and turned round to accompany me, talking all the while with voluble gaiety, perhaps because he really felt he had nothing to reproach himself with, perhaps because, on the contrary, he was trying to hide his uneasy conscience under a flood of words. I no longer remember all he said, but the gist of it was that one must bear up against bad fortune. Since Lescure and I were just then on the point of engaging in new clandestine work, it was not the moment to disclose my own feelings to a writer who, however likeable, had gone over to the enemy. So I answered rather coolly, with mere banalities. He did not seem to take this amiss. We had reached the esplanade at the intersection of the Rue de Sèvres and the Boulevard Raspail where the entrance to the underground station used to be, when he advised me to read the book he was carrying under his arm which, he told me, had just come out. It was *Gardens and Roads* by Ernst Jünger. With Germans like him one could really get along! Full of sensibility, of understanding, and such love of France! To make quite sure that I should read it, he thrust his own copy into my hands, said, 'See you soon!' and strode off briskly and full of cheer, his hair streaming in the wind, while I stepped down into the Métro.

The writer Ernst Jünger, who had fought in the French campaign as an officer, was the author of another book which had also been translated recently, a symbolical novel entitled *The Marble Cliffs*. I had not read it but had heard some people say that in its allegorical form one could detect a curiously independent thought concerning

the Nazi régime. I myself had found it rather odd to see in all the
bookshop-windows—notably in the one opposite the Senate where
Goering had his headquarters, Rue Vaugirard, and even in the
big German bookshop which had replaced the Brasserie Harcourt
on the Boulevard Saint-Michel—the jacket of this novel featuring
the translation of a verse by Goethe which read:

> *Things temporal and perishable*
> *Are symbols only, drifting sand.*

Could one imagine words more apt to convince us of the fragility
of military conquests? It certainly was surprising . . . I sat down to
read *Gardens and Roads*. It contained the daily jottings of Lieutenant Jünger, his—indeed very affectionate—thoughts about France,
discovered or rediscovered by him as he followed the army's movements, his contacts with French villages and their inhabitants,
a few love-affairs of short duration and many visits to churchyards,
which seemed to have an odd fascination for him.

I read this eulogy on defeated France by one of her conquerors
with a feeling of profound malaise, of mounting irritation. Not that
I thought it was a trap, written with ulterior motives. The author
seemed quite sincere, but his very sincerity instinctively released
my defence mechanism: he had been allowed to publish his book,
so . . . I imagined its effect on more impressionable readers: how
tempted they would be to see in this German the spokesman of
what cultured Germans felt about us! A most dangerous temptation.
If Jünger was not a party to this plot, he was at least its tool.

This book was still at the back of my mind when my friend
Jacques Vallette came to stay with us at Villiers in July as a paying
guest. He was a scholar of English literature, the present headmaster
of my old school, the Ecole Alsacienne, and the brother-in-law of
my publisher, Paul Hartmann, for whom he had translated Kip-
ling's *Puck of Pook's Hill*, which I had illustrated. I had decided to
take a holiday myself, and already foresaw that I would not resume
my work as a carpenter. Apart from the ordeal this job had become
for the last two months because of my headaches, I wanted to have
more free time. I was certain that the contacts gradually made by
Lescure would soon bear fruit, and that I should need to be ready.
From this point of view my illness, which had not escaped my
employer's notice, would serve as a good excuse for leaving him
without arousing curiosity or suspicion in the village. An idea had

meanwhile occurred to me how I might make a little money. I would illustrate by hand a very limited edition—twelve copies only—and sell it at a handsome price to as many collectors of rare books. I had chosen to start with three poetic tales by Edgar Allen Poe, of which the first, called 'Silence', had especially appealed to me on account of its title. Jacques Vallette corrected my translation.

As we were lunching under the lilacs one day, he told me a true story which had been reported to him by a friend, who had witnessed the event. He had been dining out one night in a black market restaurant when two Germans had sat down behind a pillar within earshot. One of them was in civilian dress, the other in uniform. As he spoke German fluently, he had no trouble in following their conversation. The army officer seemed perturbed. He had just returned from Poland which had been laid waste, divided up and destroyed, and found defeated France calm and almost flourishing! Everywhere people were talking of 'the hand-shake of Montoire' with the promise it contained of a French resurrection. Was Germany's arch-enemy really going to be allowed to rise again on the very doorstep of the Reich? Would that not be sheer folly? The civilian let him have his say before replying mockingly: 'Just leave the French to lull themselves with their illusions. We must draw their claws before we destroy them. Don't you realize we're fooling them?' And he had finished by quoting Racine in a guttural French: '*J' embrasse mon rival mais c'est pour l'étouffer!*'[1] The two of them had laughed heartily.

In a flash of light I saw that here was the subject of my story! For the benefit of those Frenchmen who were still wavering—still deluding themselves—and for the writers above all, this is what I wanted to express in the short story Lescure kept urging me to write. I would put that German officer into it, but instead of an enemy of France I would turn him into a man who loved France, who was under her spell as Ernst Jünger had been. A man who sincerely believed in a possible marriage between the two former adversaries within a happy Europe, a man who would be dumb-founded by the brutal revelation of the Nazis' true designs. Thus he would strive for months, in good faith, to persuade his French friends of Germany's noble intentions, only to discover in the end that he had fatally deceived them. His attempts to win them over

[1]'I embrace my rival, but only to choke him.'

must be so persuasive that they were almost successful. The German must therefore be likeable. The best possible German. The French, icily cold at first, would gradually be touched, almost convinced. This would be intimated through the feelings of a girl which would slowly evolve from frozen hatred to a sort of suppressed, unavowed attraction. And it suddenly came to me, as I was mowing the lawn one day and taking care to avoid the border of irises: 'She won't say a word!' For I realized that she would find herself in the same situation as that in which I had been with the officer who had obstinately persisted in saluting me and never received a reply . . . What would my German do in the end, when he had to admit that he had unintentionally been a deceiver all along? For a moment I thought he would revolt against the criminal designs and carry his hosts with him into rebellion. The young people's love could then break its restraint, burst forth into the open. But this happy ending soon struck me as a literary contrivance, historically incorrect. The last Germans to resist Hitler had disappeared in the course of the past six years, killed or swallowed up in the *Nacht und Nebel* of the concentration camps. Any German still at liberty could only show approval for Nazism or, failing that, knuckle under and obey. That vast German obedience was the tragedy of their country, and of Europe as well. Ernst Jünger loved France, but he obeyed. If my hero had been a man of character, he could not have been free, still less an officer. Incapable of disobedience, he could only go and get himself killed for his masters, however horrified he might be by their dastardly designs. When the girl became aware of all this, she would give him that wide-eyed look of a heart-breaking wrench, of hopeless pity which I had caught in Stéphanie's eyes when she had realized that I was too weak, too callow, too fickle to respond to the boundless trust she demanded. And the only word she would say, the farewell she would consent to utter at the last moment would be only the alms of charity from an impossible, wounded love.

Almost immediately I set to writing the story. As the German was taking shape, many memories returned to fill out the character. There was the man, of course, whom I had met in Montana years ago, our conversations by the fireside at night in the lounge of the old-fashioned hotel; his warm feelings for France, his hopes of an understanding between our two countries, and later, on his way to exile, his warning about the coming apocalypse when we had met on the café terrace on Boulevard Saint-Michel. I remembered the officer who had greeted me smilingly every day; and another German, much later during that bitter summer, who had walked into our garden dressed for tennis one day, having mistaken our house for the château. He had said to my wife, who did not answer, and to me when I joined them a moment later, how sorry he was not to have made the acquaintances he had hoped for in France, to discuss art and literature. And every two minutes he would glance at his watch and say: 'Ah well, it's lunchtime . . . ' in the hope of an invitation, and precipitately go on talking so as not to be sucked into that bottomless silence. There had been yet another German, tall, fair and smiling, who had also strayed into our garden on his way to the château and who, on realizing his mistake, had turned his eyes to the long, low house and said to us: 'How much I regret . . . This is a much more beautiful château . . . ' No doubt those two Germans, also, cherished no unfriendly feelings towards France, but 'good Germans' though they may have been, they yet served their Führer and accepted their role as tools of his damnable policy.

I also recalled a German nurse called Nana who had been with us for several months when our twins were babies. She was a big, buxom girl and an excellent, devoted nurse. But she began to worry us when, with the Christmas money we had given her to buy herself a present of her own choice, she had shown us on Christmas Eve what she had bought in Rue Saint-Sulpice: a frightful painted plaster head of Christ, its green face under the crown of thorns dripping with bright red blood that glistened as if freshly spilt, upturned eyes and a swollen violet tongue protruding between half-open lips. 'Isn't it beautiful?' We were even more perturbed when, some time later, she approached us with a mosquito between her fingers and said: 'Look, I'm going to punish him! I'm pulling his legs off, one . . . after . . . the other!' And we finally decided to part with her when she told us of a dream she had had in which, about to give our little Jean-Louis a bath, she had forgotten the tub on the kitchen-fire and found him later, would you believe it, madam, completely boiled. . . .

For the technique, I kept to the objective narration which, following Conrad's lead, I had adopted as a strict rule. I did not allow myself the licence under any circumstances of conveying a character's thoughts and feelings by an introspective description, but only—as in real life—by what an outsider can see or hear: people's gestures, their hands which betray them, their words always full of ambiguity, the silences which lay their hearts bare without their suspecting it.

I had to compose the whole story while in the grip of my racking headaches which even six aspirins at a time no longer managed to relieve. I had already seen a dozen doctors unavailingly before I thought of consulting a friend who made me undergo blood tests, found they showed excessive urea, examined me from head to foot and concluded that my complaint was serious and required urgent treatment: I was suffering from azotemia and ought to be put on a strict diet at once. Down in the village I sometimes met a fellow who spent his holidays there and whose business consisted of taking down the lectures given at the Medical Faculty, duplicating them and selling the copies to the students. 'Azotemia?' he said. 'I'll let you see the chapter on it.' And I was gratified to learn that my kidneys were affected by an incurable and irreversible process of disintegration which would necessarily lead to a fatal attack of uræmia in a few years.

After a month of severe dieting which, due to the general food shortage, practically meant living on vegetable soup and grated carrots (a diet which taught me that starvation by disgust can be no less cruel than starvation by hunger), my urea dropped so low that I had not enough left! I wrote to my doctor friend, who had meanwhile had to escape to the free zone. He coldly replied: 'A temporary remission, no doubt.' But as the reprieve, with a few ups and downs, has now lasted twenty-five years, I trust it will go on for a little longer. . . .

Unfortunately, the remission had no effect on my headaches which persisted with a vengeance. At times they became intolerable, and I had to stop writing. Yet events, with their daily crop of sadness and anguish, urged me to make haste. After the unsuccessful attempt on the lives of Laval and Marcel Déat by the young Colette, a fresh round up of Jews took place. The Germans were at the gates of Leningrad and threatening Moscow. I would go to bed early, taking refuge between the sheets like a dying matador on the merciful sand of the arena. Sometimes I would switch on the radio,

tuning in to a Swiss station, to fall asleep to the sound of music.
One evening I heard a feminine voice so fluid, limpid and crystalline that in my half-sleep I could hardly believe it was human,
so much did it seem to proceed from a celestial body. I thought I
must be listening to Bach (I later realized it was François Couperin).
I felt as if I too were disembodied, floating between heaven and
earth, as if the Cosmos were calling me to spread and dissolve in it.
It seemed to me that had I been able to die at that moment I would
have done so with serenity, even with joy.

Nevertheless, I managed to finish my story by the end of the
summer. I took a long time trying to find a title which would fit
the hidden violence of this tale without sound or fury. Every day
I lined up scores of them but found none to my liking. Then there
came to my mind a wild and poetic image which had often haunted
me: beneath the deceptively calm surface of the sea, the ceaseless,
cruel battles of the beasts of the deep. And I called my story *The
Silence of the Sea*.

I submitted it to Lescure, not without fear and hesitation: what
would he think of it? As it was fairly short, I stayed while he read it
in the austere, scholarly atmosphere of his tiny study. I knew from
experience, though, that it was hopeless trying to read either
approval or disappointment in his face. And indeed, for over an
hour, he remained perfectly inscrutable, while his rectangular
mouth under the bristly moustache twitched at times in an undecipherable grimace. At last he raised his head, gazed at me with
hazy, damp eyes and declared: 'It's a long time since anything
moved me so deeply.'

I expressed my gladness and relief. So the thing was fit for print.
We were expecting any day now the new issue of *La Pensée Libre*,
with our articles and Lescure's short story. My own would be
published in the next number. We were undecided whether to hand
it to the editors right away or hold on to it for the time being.
I eventually decided to hang on to it for possible cuts and alterations. Whereupon, a few days later, we heard the shattering news:
La Pensée Libre was smashed! The Gestapo had raided the printing
shop, seized all its material and jailed the printer. The editors had
got away after burning the manuscripts in a hurry: mine had had
a narrow escape! As Lescure, always sticking to his principles of
prudence, did not tell me their names, I found out only much later,

when they were caught and shot, that they were Jacques Decour and Georges Politzer. For, undismayed, they had immediately discussed with Lescure a new idea, which was to replace the defunct magazine by a literary and therefore unpolitical paper, to be entitled *Les Lettres Françaises*. But taking into account past experience and the fact that *La Pensée Libre*'s demise at its second number was due to its bulk, which required printing material and personnel beyond the norms of safety, they would cautiously revert, at the start, to a system of single stencilled sheets until they found another 'safe' printer. The trouble so far as I was concerned was that my short novel could obviously not appear in the new paper for lack of space.

Meanwhile, however, my own brain had not remained idle. The disappearance of the magazine had suddenly turned me into a writer without a publisher. Now this was no new situation for me, since I had always been my own publisher for my pre-war albums. Why shouldn't I publish my story in the same way? Too short to make a volume? André Gide's *Isabelle* and *Paludes*, Roger Martin du Gard's *African Confidences* were surely not much longer. I took the *Confidences* down from its shelf and counted the pages, lines and words: I found they added up to much the same length as mine. So the thing could be contemplated without being preposterous. My mind was made up.

I might as well admit that a drop of vanity, a whiff of slightly puerile romanticism were not entirely without influence on this decision. I remembered a story of certain rebels against Napoleon III who, at a dinner-party, were startled by their host putting in the place of honour, in the centre of the table, a bust of the abhorred sovereign. But when the dessert arrived, the host seized a hammer, struck the emperor in the face—and a hundred miniature copies of Victor Hugo's incendiary poem '*Les Châtiments*', printed in Belgium, scattered over the table-cloth . . . I could very well imagine my *Silence of the Sea* similarly tumbling out from a bust of Hitler at a party of Resistance fighters . . . and the story which would be told later of a fine trick played on the enemy.

But another, more serious thought had flashed through my mind; if in spite of all the difficulties I succeeded in setting up the organization needed for publishing my story—printing, bookbinding, distribution—the same organization might subsequently serve to

produce a series of other books! A clandestine publishing-house—
wasn't that precisely what was needed to still the hunger of print-
starved writers such as the worthy Membré and probably many
others? Besides, the birth, and later the existence, the practical
reality of such a publishing house, with the current of thought it
entailed—would not that be proof abroad that French intellectual
life survived under the Nazi heel? Would it not demonstrate that,
like the monks of old, France was keeping the torch alight in this
new darkness and passing on its flame from hand to hand, if necessary from generation to generation, until it could at last emerge
from the long tunnel into daylight? No broadsheets, no propaganda
tracts with their violence of tone designed to rouse the people and
fortify their resistance to the Occupying Power, could supply such
proof. They attested to Frenchmen's determination to go on
fighting; they could not attest to the fact that in this battle we
preserved cool heads and kept our reasoning faculty clear from the
errors and excesses engendered by passion. The point really was
to show world opinion that France, amid misfortune and violence,
was able to keep faith with her highest purpose: her claim to think
straight.

Now, books are indispensable for straight thinking, for this
requires a reflectiveness which cannot be practised by a journalist
hastily turning out fighting articles from day to day. It was a task,
moreover, well suited to a constant element in my character,
already evidenced when, long ago, I had dropped my collaboration
with *Vendredi* to return to the less topical themes of my own albums.
Yes, in the heart of the French Resistance which was coming pain-
fully into being, I had found my place and my calling: not in
active fighting, its violence and sometimes its mistakes; but in
safeguarding clear, accurate, persistent thinking in the face of
oppression, bondage, intolerance, the provocations of wickedness
and the pitfalls of anger. Wasn't that what I had already tried
to do in writing my *Silence of the Sea*? Hadn't I hoped that my book,
if it was still read ten years after the war, would not arouse the
contempt that after 1918 had engulfed the spoutings of jingoes like
René Benjamin or Marcel Hutin who had been gobbling up the
Boches as if they were so much marshmallow? If others, professional
writers this time, could be encouraged, by the existence of a press
capable of publishing their work, to write books in their turn which

though unmistakably works of opposition, would yet be lucid and thoughtful in their self-command, I should be more than repaid for my efforts.

For the first time I felt a lightening of the cloak of darkness that had been hanging over me for more than a year. And as can be seen, this had come about 'quite naturally'.

PART THREE

A GLEAM
IN THE NIGHT

In memory of Jean Lurçat

I

The first thing to do was to expound the gist of my project to Pierre de Lescure. He grasped its implications at once and, within a few minutes, he was as impatient to carry it into effect as I was. An obvious objection, though, came to his mind: how were we to succeed where *La Pensée Libre* had failed so rapidly and dramatically, when the complexities of publication in volume-form would also entail numerous risks? But I had thought of that and felt confident: we had to go about it differently, that was all, with security rules which the magazine editors had probably failed to apply—at least with sufficient stringency. Together we mapped out the main lines of the enterprise. I knew few authors, he knew few printers, so I would look after the technical side—manufacture and distribution —and he would go hunting for manuscripts. His job could only start after mine, of course; there was no point in canvassing authors until I had run to earth a craftsman to put them to press. Now this involved two big problems: one was to find printers who could be safely approached without the risk that fear or a hostile bias would send them straight to the nearest *Kommandantur* to denounce me. The other was, once the rare bird had been found, to persuade him to undertake such a perilous task. I mentally ran through the list of all the printers I knew and fixed my choice, for the first try, on Ernest Aulard.

Le petit père Aulard, as my publisher Paul Hartmann and I affectionately called him, was a Norman of working-class origin, with smooth fair hair and a corpulent chest, jolly without vulgarity, obliging without servility, and proud without insolence, in short the perfect good companion—and, above all, one of the best printers in Paris. Numerous albums of mine had come off his press, and in the years between the wars we had gradually seen his concern grow from a small backroom business in a courtyard off the Rue du Vieux-Colombier to the present spacious premises in Rue Tournefort. Though he was considerably older than I, we had thus in a way grown up together, and this had brought with it a mutual sympathy which made it very unlikely that he would give me away, even if he had turned pro-Vichy or pro-German like so many shopkeepers and small industrialists.

So I was not unduly apprehensive as I walked down the ancient street in the Mouffetard district one grey November day. I had not seen Aulard since the war. The pretext for my visit was that twelve-copy edition of Edgar Allen Poe's three tales which I had planned as a means of putting some jam on my bread without infringing my rule of public silence. After dealing with this we got round, as stealthily as Red Indians, to talking of 'one thing and another': food rationing, the black market, anything except politics. He held forth on his luck in having some relatives in Normandy, about his employees, most of whom also had friends or family in the country to send them food parcels . . . Not a word about the occupation, the Germans. What was I to make of this wariness? That he dared not give himself away, having no clue to my views? Or that, on the contrary, having guessed them, he feared I might disapprove of his? Hard to tell. I made a tentative move: 'Not too much trouble with the Occupants?' A glint in his eyes, a smile:

'Oh, the best thing, you know, is to keep away from them.'

'But what about paper?'

'I manage somehow without them.'

I returned his smile and the next moment we were chatting to our hearts' content, running down Pétain, the sacked Laval, Admiral Darlan, his successor, congratulating ourselves on the Red Army's resistance, on Britain's tenacity . . . There now remained the most ticklish point: old Aulard was all right, but he had just shown that he was the cautious type. How was I to frame my request? I mustn't scare him off by springing it on him too suddenly. We were already walking towards the door, making a date for my Poe edition, well then, so that's all right, see you soon . . .

On the doorstep, however, I made up my mind:

'Perhaps, one of these days . . . h'm . . . I might have something else to print, too . . . but something a bit . . . h'mm . . . see what I mean? Perhaps you could find me, among your colleagues, someone who . . . Well, er, think about it.'

I saw Aulard flush pink—with surprise—then he said calmly: 'Well . . . right here, of course.'

It was almost too easy! We looked at each other and grinned. He now knew why I had come. He made me sit down again:

what was it all about? I pulled my dummy book out of my brief-case and started to explain. What I had in mind was a small volume of a hundred pages or so, but not a hurriedly printed brochure: volumes on decent paper, with careful typography, tasteful lay-out, turned-in covers. Not just to gratify my taste as a booklover, but because I was sure that this elegance would catch the imagination. The appreciation of fine workmanship is also one of the great French qualities. It would be splendid if people noticed that the publisher, printer, compositors had not grudged the time, and had thus increased the risks, for the sole satisfaction of 'turning out a good piece of work'. Aulard agreed; he even seemed delighted. He sent for his foreman, his faithful right-hand man Pierre Doré, who enthusiastically approved. When did we start? Regretfully I had to pour cold water on their enthusiasm.

'How many people in your shop?'

'Fifty-odd.'

'That's what I thought. It's far too many. We cannot print here.'

I saw their faces fall. 'Everybody here thinks the same!' protested Doré, 'they can all be trusted!' I didn't disbelieve him. But a secret shared by fifty people is no longer a secret. How could they be sure that none of them would talk to his wife, his mates? That one of the wives would not take fright? Or, if some day the Gestapo were to search the place, that nobody would be scared enough to give the show away? If *La Pensée Libre* had foundered as soon as launched, it was undoubtedly for this very reason: too many people in the know.

Doré seemed discomfited, Aulard admitted that I was right. I explained that, to my mind, the job should be done in a very small printing shop, by someone working almost on his own. And that was why I had come.

'I'll think about it,' said Aulard. 'Come back in a week. I'll either have found one, or else made suitable arrangements here. Anyway, you can leave it to me. One more question. Have you thought of the stitching?'

'Not yet.'

'That's a tricky point. I've got twelve people on the job here. That's also too many, and they're all women . . . .'

'Oh dear!'

'Yeah. Couldn't Madame Bruller do it with one or two of her friends? I could teach them, it's not difficult.'

'My wife mustn't know anything: that's a harsh rule, but it is the rule. I have someone in mind, though . . . '

One evening in the previous winter, after leaving the Moulin-Rouge Cinema where we had seen some film I no longer remember, and dining in a neighbouring bistro on a soup of swedes and a hash *à la Parmentier*, in which the turnips were more abundant than the minced meat and potatoes, my old friend Yvonne Paraf had suddenly said as we were sipping a black 'coffee' made of roasted acorns: 'Jean, if one of these days you *do* something . . . you know what I mean . . . I wish you'd think of me.' So now I thought of her. I gave her a ring and went to see her in her two-room flat in Rue Vineuse on the hill of Chaillot. In a few words I explained our project.

'It sounds pretty audacious to me,' she said. 'Where will you find a printer?'

'He's already found.'

'And where will your publishing-house have its office?'

'Here, in your flat.'

'Ah . . . I see.'

A momentary surprise, and then a smile formed on her face, the familiar smile which always twisted her mouth a little to the left and produced an oddly-placed dimple, high over her cheekbone.

'What will I have to do?'

'First, stitch the volumes. The printed sheets will be brought to you. Together with a couple of girl-friends, you'll fold, collate and stitch them together.'

'But I haven't the faintest notion of how to do it!'

'Someone will come and show you.'

The smile broadened on her face. The prospect obviously delighted her.

'What about authors, manuscripts? Who will be the literary editor?'

'Pierre de Lescure.'

She pulled a face. I knew she had not much liking for him, not even genuine respect. She claimed that his Gorgon mouth inspired her with a sort of repugnance, which was nearly always proved right. None of the things I had told her about him had made her change her mind; for she was one of those very self-assured people whose convictions, once formed, were impervious to all argument. She once confessed to me that she was jealous of his influence: if I *had* to submit to someone's, why not to hers rather than to that pen-pusher's! I could never make her understand that in art, literature, politics and philosophy, I had more in common with him than with her. To have his name come up again spoiled her pleasure a little. Couldn't we do without him?

'Without him,' I told her roundly, 'this idea would never have occurred to me. You'll just have to get used to it.'

She heaved a half-serious, half-amused sigh, then cheered up again. It was only a passing cloud. However, I soon had to realize that if she did not appreciate Lescure, he warmly reciprocated her feelings, and, just as unreasonably, regarded her as a mere society woman of superficial intelligence. At the time this seemed to me of little importance, since Yvonne would have no dealings with him, her job being merely to assist me with the production and distribution. I could not foresee that Lescure would disappear for such long stretches that I should be obliged to saddle myself with the literary decisions as well and that, on his periodic returns, I should frequently find myself caught between hammer and anvil.

There remained the question of finance. Aulard had hopes of obtaining the paper for us cheaply—actually, he made us a gift of the paper for the first volume, out of his own pocket. For the printing he would of course charge only the time strictly spent on the machine. The total cost was estimated at about three thousand francs. That was still quite a sum in those days. It had to be found.

My banker at the time was an old friend, André Robillard. He was one of the gang with whom we spent those last happy days at Morgat on the eve of war. I knew his opinions well: every time I dropped in at the bank in the Avenue de l'Opéra, I looked him up in his office and we would try to boost each other's morale. There was only one point of difference between us: for me the people we were fighting were the Nazis, for him they were the Germans. For all practical purposes, it came to the same thing, and we shared the same hopes. When I told him of our requirements, the sum mentioned made him smile. Not that he could provide it all by himself, but he promised I could count on it within a week.

(And the following week I did indeed receive it from him, most of it subscribed by the chairman of his bank.)

Aulard, for his part, had lost no time. No sooner had I arrived on my second visit than, without letting me sit down, he took his hat and coat and steered me out again. 'I've found your rare bird.'

We walked down the *Mouff'*—the Rue Mouffetard—up the Avenue des Gobelins, followed the Boulevard de l'Hôpital. And there, almost opposite the Hôpital de la Pitié, which had become a German military hospital, and next to an undertaker's, he pointed out a tiny shop with its door wide open, above which could be read the word IMPRIMERIE—printing-works—in back-to-front capitals like typeset characters. The glass window bore a name in enamel letters: GEORGES OUDEVILLE. Inside was a small, stocky man of mature years, with a square head too big for his size. His sparse hair grizzled over a bulging forehead, more bumpy on the right than on the left; he had pale, dissimilar eyes, one of which tended to protrude. He worked on his own, printing exclusively wedding and funeral announcements (which in France are sent on folded cards to family and friends). His entire machinery consisted of one small Minerva press. Aulard had supplied him with the minimum fount of type of a fine Elzevir character, and some Garamond, just sufficient to compose an eight page forme: this was all that Oudeville could set on his press at a time. Whereupon he had to undo his formes, redistribute the type, compose the next eight pages, and so on. For a ninety-six-page volume plus the cover, at least twelve weeks would be needed. Three months during which, in between family announcements, Oudeville would machine the sheets, recto and verso, while German soldiers and medical orderlies kept passing his open door. This represented a risk, of course, but also a safeguard: who would imagine anybody crazy enough to print subversive material under the enemy's very nose? One would have to be just as crazy to suspect anything of the sort.

So it was agreed. Next Thursday I would bring him the first eight pages, he would set them up and destroy the manuscript. The Thursday after, I would come to correct those pages, which he would then put on the press, and bring him the eight following ones. Each Thursday he would thus get what he needed to set a new forme, and I should carry away the previous run and deposit it in some safe spot, to wit, Boulevard Raspail, in the very Vichyist Organizing Committee of the Building Trade, where a friend of Lescure's, Mme Zaclade, was working. Yvonne would collect them there or else someone would bring them to her. In this way, in accordance with security rules, the link would be broken between the binding and the printing side.

To Mme Zaclade as well as to Georges Oudeville, I introduced myself under an assumed name, of course. I maliciously chose Drieu, and gave as my address Rue Sébastien-Bottin—the N.R.F.'s headquarters. In this way, if by mischance they had to give a name to the Gestapo, the director of the pro-German N.R.F., Otto Abetz's friend, was the one who would encounter difficulties . . .

But that was my pseudonym as a publisher. I should need another as a writer. The fact was that I had not yet tried to find one, and the day was nearing when we should go to press. I thought up a whole row of them, but they were all swept aside when I called to mind the name of the majestic mountain-range which had played such an important part in my recent past, where I had almost taken to the *maquis* to preserve my freedom, a name full of rugged grandeur: the Vercors. What pseudonym, placed above my story, would ring as proudly?

So now I was Vercors, but Lescure reminded me of the duties imposed by prudence: this name must remain a myth. Nobody must be able to guess that it hid Jean Bruller. 'Drieu' himself must not know 'Vercors', and vice versa. My wife would recognize the locality, our house, certain words uttered by the officer? Then she must never read my story; nor my mother. Nor any of my close friends. Yvonne Paraf? I must somehow manage to make her believe that it was not me.

I was a bit dashed. It was hard to have to tell myself in advance that none of the persons for whom I had esteem or affection would ever know anything about my activity, would not even be able to read my story . . . But I knew that Lescure was right and did not find it too hard to extinguish this tiny flare of conceit.

Another problem: the publishing house had no name either. We tried out a few: the Underground Press, the Catacombs (and here I thought of reproducing as a trade mark the plate which, in the

Popular History of France long ago published by my father, illustrated
the episode of Sabinus, the Gallic Resistant, who, every day for nine
years, was supplied with food by his wife Eponine in the underground cave where he was hiding under the crumbling, ivy-grown
ruins, on the point of being discovered by the Roman legionaries
up above), the Freedom Press, the Press of No-Surrender . . . But
one day, in Rue Bonaparte, as I was toying with the words shadow,
darkness, midnight—the last word suddenly called to mind one of
Duhamel's titles, and another by Mac Orlan . . . *Midnight Confessions*
. . . *Midnight Tradition* . . . By God, that was what we wanted:
les Editions de Minuit—The Midnight Press! I was so delighted that
I promptly dashed round to Lescure, who was just as pleased with
it as I was.

So now all was settled. Yet there was one scruple on my conscience.
Did Oudeville realize the danger he was courting? Few people
knew as yet what tortures the underground fighters were subjected
to, when caught by the Gestapo. (Even we who thought we knew,
did not imagine one quarter of the truth at that time.) I considered
it only fair, therefore, to tell him what I knew before he started.
He listened with his back to me, busily assembling the type in his
setting-stick. I painted a particularly black picture so as not to
minimize the risk. My words bounced off his square back without
apparently producing an impression. I had not yet heard of the
ordeal of the 'bath' or of electricity, but I had been told of the spotlight torture, a blinding light less than a yard away directed at
the face night and day. Many victims went blind, their retinas
destroyed by the glare.

This time he interrupted his work and turned round. I found him
a little pale: no wonder, anybody would be! His left eye seemed to
goggle even more than usual.

'Night and day?' he asked.

'Yes. Several nights. Several days.'

'That must be dreadful for anyone with a tendency to conjunc-
tivitis?'

I could not help smiling. So what neither broken bones, nor
torn-off nails, thumb-screws or fractured jaws could do, a simple
spotlight had achieved because it was a pain he knew, he could
imagine it.

'If everyone acts with prudence,' I said, 'the risks are not awfully great. But they do exist. I wouldn't like to drag you into this without your having thought about it carefully.'

'Oh, I sort of guessed all this,' he said. 'Except the spotlight. Strong light hurts my eyes. I wear dark glasses in the summer. Never mind, I'm no more of a coward than the next fellow. May I ask you one more question?'

'Of course.'

'I've read the manuscript. It's a good story. But what does the author mean by the title? Why *The Silence of the Sea*? I'd rather say the silence of the niece. Wouldn't you?'

I told him that it was a symbolic image. But perhaps Vercors had not made his point sufficiently clear. I would mention it to him. (And I did indeed add three lines in the last few pages, where I evoked the silent battle of the beasts in the sea.) He questioned me again:

'Shan't we see him?'

'See whom?'

'Vercors.'

'No. He lives in the provinces. A very unsociable fellow. Vile-tempered, too. You know what writers are . . . '

'How old is he?'

'Fortyish. But he looks more.'

'Pity. I should have liked to shake his hand.'

I held out mine.

'I'll pass it on.'

II

I⟨T⟩ was an eventful week, the one during which Oudeville calmly rolled off my *Silence of the Sea* in his little shop wide open to the street. For some time François de Lescure, too prominent in his Student's Union, had felt the ground getting warm under his feet and no longer slept in his parents' home in Rue Duguay-Trouin. He had found a refuge in the premises of a laboratory behind the Panthéon, where a world-renowned electronic scientist was working —Fernand Holweck, director of the C.N.R.S. (National Committee for Scientific Research). We had been to see him there a number of times. And now we learned that Holweck had been arrested. François himself, if he knew that Holweck was 'busy' with something, did not know exactly what it was. We were to be without news for a long time—and then we learned that he had died at the Pitié Hospital (fifty yards away from Oudeville's shop . . .) with a smashed skull, broken ribs and jaw, charred feet.

By a lucky accident, François was absent on the morning of the arrest. But it had become too dangerous for him to stay any longer in the northern zone. He made for the south, almost officially, under the auspices of the Minister of Education—a relative of the writer Francis Carco—who, although a Vichyite, did not lower himself to act as the Occupant's hangman, as the fanatic pro-Nazi Abel Bonnard was later to do.

In the same week fell the thunderbolt of Pearl Harbor. The shattering of this military base by Japanese bombs without any declaration of war, was to be a turning-point of the war, for it brought the United States, under President Roosevelt's guidance, into the struggle against the Axis Powers. In the newsreels, great show was made of a terrifying picture: it featured the SS. generals signing a military pact with their Japanese counterparts. Above those fat, swelling chests wedged into the same black uniforms, never had human faces so arrogantly flaunted the cruelty of great barbarians. Such cold ferocity, such crushing callousness stared out of the rigid white faces and the adipose yellow ones, out of the frozen eyes of the ones and the unseeing slits of the others, that one sat fascinated by a kind of sacred terror. So much did this row of stony masks above the bulging ink-black tunics herald an irremediable slavery for the human race if those soulless bodies were ever to become the master of the world . . . .

Fortunately, between Germany and Japan lay all the breadth of the U.S.S.R. And the Soviet Army was fighting back fiercely, perhaps already victoriously . . . De Gaulle seemed impressed by it, for I heard him say on the radio that 'the mighty star of Russian power can be seen rising towards the zenith', that a people 'who has risen, armed, organized itself, and whose cohesion remains unshaken by the worst ordeals, is worthy of being called great because it knows how to fight'. It even looked as if this revelation was turning his thoughts towards a new conception at variance with his former ideas. For he had also had to realize that in France the public authorities, the high officials, the prelates, big business-men, and all those persons of standing and influence for whom he instinctively felt respect, had paid scant heed to his appeal and were complacently going along with Vichy's humiliating politics. Whereas the clandestine Resistance, by contrast, was to a large extent formed of 'other ranks'—workers, employees, railwaymen, humble curates and minor civil servants. Henceforward, judging by what he said, he seemed to be counting on the mass of French people to give birth to new élites.

Still in the same fortnight of December, I went to Oudeville to collect the first section of *The Silence of the Sea*, and to correct the second lot on the 'bed'. Bicycling along the Boulevard Saint-Germain on my way there, I met the poet Charles Vildrac under Diderot's statue. We talked about the two camps, the silent authors and the incorrigible babblers. He told me that he would resolutely remain with the silent men, if only out of respect for the memory of the aged poet Saint-Pol-Roux who had died at Camaret during the summer of 1940. Why in his memory, I asked; I thought that at the age of eighty-six he had died of old age? Not at all: the Germans had invaded his house, shot down his housekeeper before his eyes, seriously wounded his daughter Divine and set the whole house on fire; his own skull split by a rifle-butt, he had succumbed to the effects of this savagery in hospital at Brest. 'He is the Murdered Poet,' I thought, echoing the title of Apollinaire's most famous poem, as I rode on and greeted in passing Holweck's ghost at the

Pitié. In the chilly little shop, I asked Oudeville to insert on the fly-leaf a line of type dedicated to the aged bard of human love. He set it, showed me a pull, and then wrapped up his finished work. We placed the parcel on my carrier-rack—three hundred and fifty sheets just balanced on it provided I did not pedal fast—and off I rode to deposit it in Mme Zaclade's office. I gave my name (Drieu) to the commissionaire. She appeared but instead of showing me in, she pulled me into the corridor and said: 'Get away quickly! They've been to see my boss. They've left one of their men here and they'll be back.'

'Who?'

'The Germans. House search. They won't find anything. But I apologize for this imprudence.'

'Didn't you warn Lescure that you were "working" too?'

'I thought he'd guessed. Quick, be off, and again I'm sorry.'

'Good luck to you all.'

'Thanks.'

I had got off lightly. But here I was again on my bicycle, not knowing what to do with my parcel. Take it to Yvonne? That would be the simplest but it was no solution: we could not carry on every week with these too-direct contacts. All right, I would take it to my mother in Rue Servandoni. *One* parcel would not attract her notice. But if I added one more every week . . . We should have to find other means.

Oudeville himself found us one. He had a friend, he said, who ran a café a few yards from his shop, on the Boulevard de la Gare, under the sign of *La Halte aux Taxis*. Parcels were often left there for the carrying agents of the book and newspaper trade. The owner would have no suspicions, or rather he might have but he would ask no questions. So we went to see him and arranged matters. I suspected that Oudeville had not kept his mouth shut as tightly as he claimed, judging by the warmth with which the bistro-owner, damp-eyed, clasped my hand as we left.

I walked up the Boulevard to take the Métro at Place d'Italie. What a district! I had never seen walls covered with so many inscriptions in chalk and charcoal: the cross of Lorraine and the V for Victory, *Vive de Gaulle* and *Pétain to the gallows*, and *Vive Staline* and hammers and sickles. In a photographer's shop-window two large framed and coloured portraits showed respectively Pétain and Darlan. In the corner of each was a label. One said *For sale*. The other *Sold*. The Germans passed by constantly, but never saw the point.

All this I recounted to Lescure, though without mentioning Oudeville's name or the bistro-owner's, which he very properly preferred not to know. For his part, he reported the results of his as yet not very successful approaches. But the main thing was achieved: Paulhan had been roped in. Lescure, under the name of Larue, had been in contact for over a year with one of Gallimard's authors, who was well acquainted with Paulhan. His code name was Lebourg and he worked for the Ministry of the Navy, whence, for several months past, he had been able to supply 'Larue' with the movements of the French Fleet in the Mediterranean, for transmission to Larue's cousin and thence to England. Oddly enough, though Lescure himself was a Gallimard author, he did not know Paulhan, nor did he wish to, claiming that the latter was a dangerous man to know precisely because he was so useful. His office, by all accounts, was like a railway station—all the literary world passed through it, friend and foe alike, and views were expressed with incredible frankness. Paulhan was apparently untouchable, and this would be disquieting if there were not an obvious explanation for it. For —and Drieu la Rochelle must have made this clear to Otto Abetz —if a single hair on the head of 'the Pope of Literature' was touched, it would spell the end of the *Nouvelle Revue Française*: not a single writer would work for it any longer. Lescure added that this also explained why, though gravely compromised in an affair which will be mentioned later (the underground paper '*Résistance*') and imprisoned in Fresnes prison for three days, he was released without further unpleasantness. This apparent taboo, however, applied exclusively to his own person. It was therefore advisable that no one should ever see us in his office, a little too close to Drieu's own.

So it was Lebourg—whose true identity Lescure did not disclose to me—who went to see Paulhan. He explained our plan to him and reported that at first the other would not believe in its feasibility, since in view of the disastrous fate of *La Pensée Libre* and the difficulties Jacques Decour had still not overcome in producing even a stencilled version of *Les Lettres Françaises*, he feared that clandestinity and book-publishing were contradictory terms. He liked the title, *Editions de Minuit*, very much and he promised us his help (which later proved very effective) but preferred, like doubting Thomas, to touch a volume with his fingers before making any move himself.

Unfortunately, it was impossible to speed up the publication of the first volume owing to Oudeville's too-limited means. But at least there was no delay on the schedule, and by the end of January the entire lot had come off his press, been progressively stored at the café and finally delivered to Rue Vineuse. A friend of Yvonne's, Pierre Massé (the future post-war French Planning Chief), had taken care of the deliveries, thanks to the small car he was allowed to run by virtue of his high position at the Electricity Board. His wife Géka came to help Yvonne with the stitching. Aulard had gone to her flat to give them a demonstration. He had shown them how to fold, collate and sew the sheets with no margin of error and in a minimum of time. The most delicate point was the cover, which had to be turned in and stuck down without a smear so as to ensure an impeccable back. The glue itself had to be dissolved and heated to a temperature which left it neither too runny nor too thick. I decided to take charge of this myself, in view of my experience with glue as a carpenter. I would do the job in the kitchen to avoid making a mess.

During the whole week Yvonne and her friend folded, collated, stitched. With only two of them, the work did not progress very fast. On the following Thursday I found a respectable pile, which still, however, represented only a modest part of the edition. Yvonne clamoured for aid. A third woman-friend would soon join them, but could I not get hold of a fourth? I promised to do my best.

We were alone, Géka had not yet arrived. While I was warming the glue, Yvonne suddenly let drop: 'It's you, isn't it?'

'What's that?'

'The author of this story.'

I had expected the question and looked duly bewildered.

'What an extraordinary idea! I don't draw too badly, but whatever makes you think I can write? Is it because you've recognized my house at Villiers? That's how circumstantial evidence gets a fellow hanged! Hasn't it occurred to you that the author must necessarily be a friend, even a close friend, or how would I have discovered him? As a matter of fact, you've met him. If you had any flair . . . '

'That's just what I do have,' she interrupted, laughing.

'What do you mean?'

'Such a spelling mistake, right on the first page and almost in the first line, can only be *your* doing.'

'A spelling mistake?'

'Yes, *déguingandé*, with a "u", instead of *dégingandé*.'

I was floored, as one says. For it was true, I *had* written *déguingandé*. Everyone clings tenaciously to some such childhood errors. This was one of them, and it had given me away. What *was* I to answer? My brain works fast in moments like that. I pinched the tip of my nose and said, with an air of consternation:

'It's *dégingandé*? You're sure?'

'Now really! Do you want to look it up in Larousse?'

'Yvonne,' I said, sounding mortified, 'believe me or not, but it's I who added the "u". It wasn't there.'

' . . . ?'

'Yes, when I was checking the proofs on the "bed". I thought it was a misprint. So I added the "u".'

This was such a colossal cheek, and so much like what she thought of my spelling that she believed me and laughed even more: 'That doesn't in the least surprise me, coming from you!' And for a long time she kept racking her brains to find out which of my friends could possibly be the author of *Le Silence de la Mer*. It was much better this way, both for her and for me. It is easier to fend off inquisitive questioners when one really does not know the answer. And it was to be foreseen that the question 'Who is Vercors?' would be put to her more than once. Yet if my real name were bruited about once the book was in circulation and I got 'trailed' as a result, I should endanger Lescure, Aulard, Oudeville, the whole gang, and that would have been the end of the Editions de Minuit. As Lescure had rightly said, it was indispensable that no one should link my two identities.

It was Lescure who had meanwhile drafted the manifesto that was to be slipped into each volume. Short and simple, it summed up perfectly the underlying motives which had led me to conceive the idea, alongside the clandestine press dedicated to hatred and violence, of a publishing-house which strove to be faithful to clear, cogent thinking:

'*There was a time when people were exiled for preferring Euripides's Phaedra to Racine's. The glory of France was at stake, claimed the tyrant of the day. Today Einstein's physics, Freud's psychology, Isaiah's laments are all banned. It is forbidden to reprint Meredith, Thomas Hardy, Katherine Mansfield, Virginia Woolf, Henry James, Faulkner, all the others whom we love. "Do not display in your shop-windows Shakespeare, Milton, Keats, Shelley, the English poets and novelists of all time," commands the Booksellers' Association, acting on instructions from German Propaganda. As for French literature, it is now subjected to a quota when entering Belgium, Holland, Greece, wherever the New Europe is in the making. In September 1940, the Publishers' Guild signed a censorship convention with the Occupying Power. A notice to the public announced: "In signing this convention, the German authorities have wished to show their confidence in the publishing trade. The publishers, for their part, have desired to give French thought the possibility of continuing its mission while at the same time respecting the victor's rights", and "the German authorities have expressed their satisfaction at this initiative taken by the French publishers."*

'*There was a time in French history when government Prefects "annulled" those authors who refused to write in praise of their master. And the master said of the others: "I have thrown open my ante-rooms, and they jostle to get into them."*

'*In France today there are still writers who shun ante-rooms and refuse to write to order. They feel strongly that thought must be expressed, not simply to leave a mark on others' thinking, but above all, because the mind without self-expression is doomed to die.*

'*This, then, is the aim of the* Editions de Minuit. *Propaganda is not our domain. We mean to safeguard our inner life and freely serve our art. The names matter little. It is no longer a question of petty personal fame. Nor does it matter if the road is beset with difficulties. What is in question is man's spiritual purity.*'

Yvonne, her friends and I had finished our work by the day we had set on the '*achevé d'imprimer*', the date when a book comes off the press, obligatorily printed at the end of every French book-publication: the 20th February 1942. The date pleased Yvonne, whose birthday it was. Unintentionally, it also happened to be a historic date: on the day before, the State Tribunal at Riom met to try Léon Blum, Reynaud, Daladier, and with them the French Republic. On the eve of the 20th, too, Jacques Decour, founder of *La Pensée Libre* and of *Les Lettres Françaises*, had been arrested. He was to suffer martyrdom by torture, be tried, convicted and shot after having written to his parents a farewell letter of admirable modesty, which was a lesson for us all: '. . . *You know that for ten months I have been expecting what will come to pass this morning, and so I have had time to prepare myself for it. But as I have no religion, I did not sink into meditations about death. I think of myself a little like a leaf that falls from the tree to make leaf-mould. The quality of the mould will depend on that of the leaves. I am referring to the youth of France in whom I put all my hopes* . . .' Two days after the 20th, the ethnologist Boris Vildé, who had been arrested a year previously and likewise tortured, tried and condemned to death, fell under German bullets. Like so many leaves to form the mould, amid all these tragedies several hundred little volumes were now piled up on top of, inside and beneath a linen-cupboard. They now had to be distributed. The main object was to reach 'personalities' whom it would be useful to encourage or to persuade.

Paulhan had prepared a list of literary people, which Lebourg had handed to Lescure. Through André Robillard I had obtained a list of names in high finance, and through his brother-in-law, Maurice Darras, together with his colleague, the famous advocate Maurice Garçon, a list of lawyers and the judiciary. Claude Bellanger (in whose offices François de Lescure had at one time mimeographed his leaflets) had suggested approaching Holweck's successor at the C.N.R.S. for the names of scientists at the University and in research. Professor Robert Debré, France's outstanding pediatrician was to provide Paulhan with the names of leading doctors. I still lacked a list of major industrialists and top technicians.

I thought of an eminent civil servant, an ex-*Polytechnicien*, who had been a close friend of the former President Lebrun and had known my father well. He was Jewish and had been dismissed from his high office. I knew him only slightly, but I could expect to be received with open arms. In fact, I was practically shown the door: my venture was sheer folly, I should be arrested in less than three months. Pétain was doing his utmost to distinguish between people like him, Frenchmen since the 18th century, the nation's élite, and those Polacks and other riff-raff of recent importation. Under no circumstances would he have any part in such a puerile and unlawful undertaking. I emerged from this visit ashamed and infuriated. I remembered the words of another Jewish friend: 'Money corrupts everything.' Happily I obtained the required list from a third Jewish acquaintance, Jacques Goldschmidt's father, himself an industrialist, who gave a bitter laugh when apprised of this story.

Finally I thought of asking Pierre Dalloz and his wife, the painter Henriette Gröll, for a list of artists and architects. We lunched together in a small eating-house in Rue Mazarine near their flat, where regular customers were served with a thin sliver of real roast. While we sat chatting, I saw a tall, lanky man come in, whom I had met in pre-war days and whose career had always struck me as pathetic. In his young days he had written a play which the Comédie-Française had performed with marked success. And then, after that first splash, he had dried up and produced no more. He scratched a miserable living from occasional articles on any subject under the sun. His sorry fortune seemed inscribed on his long face, which two enormous pouches under his colourless eyes rendered appallingly ugly. One day in the 'thirties—at the time I was helping my publisher friends Ferenczi to raise the artistic level of their slightly naughty magazine, *Allô Paris*, by getting together, alongside some first-class illustrators, a few writers of quality— I had found the seedy playwright awaiting me in my office. We had never met and I had not thought of him. I had hardly walked in when he insolently took me to task: how had I dared overlook him? And with the same arrogance he went on to blow his own trumpet at length. This might have been excusable if the object in view had been, say, the French Academy, but in this lowly place, with the sole aim of making a few francs, it was degrading. So when I saw him come into the restaurant and scan the room with a sort of crafty watchfulness above those heavy pouches, I felt an instinctive mistrust and prudently turned to evade his prying gaze. I learned shortly after that the Germans had arrested him (perhaps on the evening of that very day), sent him for trial, sentenced and shot him.

I never forgave myself for this upsurge of injurious distrust. The period abounded in culpable misjudgments of this kind. Harry

Baur, the celebrated film actor, up to the moment of his execution for espionage, was thought to have wangled himself into the position of an 'honourable Aryan' for the sole purpose of making films in Berlin. And I myself remembered the evening when we were having drinks with friends at the Brasserie Lipp and the poet Robert Desnos had got up to greet us. He was writing in some German or pro-German publications at that time, so I did not shake his hand nor speak to him. How could I have known that his collaboration was a screen for underground work which caused him soon to be found out, sentenced and deported to Terezin, where he was to die? There are many of us whose memories are burdened with some such irreparable remorse. One day the BBC asked us to honour the memory of a hero who had been despised and heaped with obloquy by his fellow-citizens for many months. He was an important building contractor, secretly working for British Intelligence, and it was on their orders that he had sold himself to the Germans, collaborated with them, shown himself in their company, even procured girls for their entertainment. Nobody would greet him any more, people spat when he passed. Even his own wife had left him. He had to go about with a bodyguard. And now the BBC revealed his true activity, announced his death—beheaded by the axe. This type of heroism seemed to me entirely beyond my capacity: I don't think I could ever have summoned up the sublime courage to endure for months on end, without confiding the truth to a soul, such ostensible dishonour and my own side's loathing and contempt.

III

T HE volumes were ready, the lists drawn up, it only remained to distribute the former in accordance with the latter. This meant depositing the books in envelopes directly at the homes of the addressees or with the caretakers of their blocks of flats, and to drop the copies for out-of-town recipients into letter-boxes, one at a time. Now that the real danger was beginning with those distributions— and the first customers we meant to serve were Drieu La Rochelle and Otto Abetz—Yvonne had said: 'If I get caught, I guarantee you forty-eight hours to get to safety; after that I can't promise anything.' All I could do was to promise as much, for my part, and we agreed on a name we would give away in the event of our both being taken. We chose the name of one of General de Gaulle's companions (and later one of his postwar ambassadors), an old school-friend of mine, who, being in London, was out of danger and knew nothing of our intentions of which he is probably un-aware to this day ... We were a little naïve to imagine that a single name might satisfy the Gestapo, but we hoped at least, by means of this name, to misdirect their search long enough to give our friends time to get away.

There would be few helpers for the distribution at the beginning —Lescure had placed one of his women-agents at our disposal, a certain Renée, a mysterious blonde, and Lebourg promised us two or three voluntary assistants—but it would nevertheless be imprudent to arouse the curiosity of Yvonne's concierge by too much coming and going to and from her flat by strangers carrying parcels. It was more advisable to hand the parcels over somewhere nearby and to choose for this purpose some public place where it would seem perfectly normal for people to meet one another. I had a brainwave: the Palace of Chaillot was only a few steps away, we could make all our dates in the great hall of the Musée de l'Homme —the Anthropological Museum ...

For how was I to know, since we all lived in watertight compart-ments, each boxed up in his own secret, that the court case in which the young ethnologists Levitsky and Vildé, the lawyer L.N. Nord-

mann and four other 'accomplices' had been sentenced to death
was referred to by the Germans as 'the case of the Musée de
l'Homme'? It was there indeed—but I did not know it—that
Cassou, Aveline and Paulhan, with Professor Paul Rivet, the great
anthropologist, at their head, had founded the underground paper
Résistance, and set up their 'Committee of Public Safety'. I knew
that Cassou and Aveline had fled to the South, but I did not know
why. I knew that Vildé, Levitsky and their friends had been shot,
but I did not know why. No more than with Holweck, or with the
eminent physicist Solomon, or with the philosopher Politzer or with
the specialist on aesthetics, Valentin Feldman, who in the face of
the firing squad had uttered the magnificent cry: 'Idiots, it's for
you I am dying!' And it was almost at the very hour when the
conspirators of the Musée de l'Homme fell on the Mont Valérien
on February 23rd that I was innocently preparing my series of
rendezvous there . . .

If we had been given the opportunity, as had been decided, to
meet with our parcels ten or twelve times successively in this closely
watched place, our adventure would have come to an end there
and then. But just at that time Lescure sent me an urgent call, and
I went to see him at the Café Flore, a frequent meeting-place of
ours. The Flore at that time was a very different place from what it
is now. It was a hotbed of the fighting intelligentsia, and there was
a smell of rebellion in the air. Sartre—still little known to the great
public—used to write there every day and surprised me by his
extraordinary ability, after staying his pen to greet a friend, exchange a few words or engage in an entire conversation, to go on
with his writing as if nothing had happened, as if the interruption
had taken place on a different planet. I would have dearly liked to
introduce myself to him and to Simone de Beauvoir, her head un-
failingly swathed in a white turban, had it not meant trespassing
on Pierre de Lescure's ground and running counter to the rules of
security.

Lescure gave me no time to sit down and hauled me off to the
Rhumerie Martiniquaise, a little farther down the Boulevard
Saint-Germain. An alarm had been given, and he no longer slept
at home. A radio operator of the Intelligence Service with whom
he had been in constant touch had been arrested. Lescure had
given him a message to pass on to London, announcing the publi-

cation of the first volume of the Editions de Minuit. If the man now talked and if the Gestapo laid their hands on a volume and on Lescure himself, what could he say in his defence? We must therefore halt distribution and store the volumes in a cellar until the alarm was over.

I imagined this meant a delay of a few days, a few weeks at most. It was at that period that Lescure's caution seemed to us all rather excessive. He prolonged the ban on distribution from week to week. It did not look as if the wireless operator had talked, but he might cave in any moment. Lescure had gone back to his home after sleeping out for a month, so as to pick up the threads and resume his contacts. He deemed that his principal activity had priority over the Editions de Minuit, and I was in no position to contradict him.

But it was no longer weeks, it was months. March, April . . . Lescure's caution, meanwhile, extended to another domain. We had learnt of the existence in the northern zone of a text by Jacques Maritain, the great philosophical writer, which had come from America via the southern zone. We knew its title: *A travers le désastre* (*Through the Tunnel of Disaster*). We even knew in whose hands it was: Pierre-Aimé Touchard's, the writer. But how were we to approach Touchard without rousing his misgivings? Lescure did not know him any more than I did. For certain reasons which I have forgotten he was not keen to use Paulhan as a middleman, so we looked around for some safe friend whom Touchard might know well. We still had not found anybody when Lescure disappeared in May.

A sudden disappearance, of which he had given nobody a warning. All I was able to find out from his wife was that 'he was in the mountains taking care of his health', without leaving any address, or rather, without giving her permission to divulge it. He would surely write to me, she said. But I received no word. The worst of it was that he had left me without any contact, I did not even know Lebourg's real name, and I could not go to see Paulhan directly without violating all the rules.

There remained Claude Bellanger. I did not know him. I had no idea that under the cover of his functions at the Mutual Aid Centre on Place Saint-Michel he was engaged in one of the first Resistance movements, the group called Maintenir (which later merged with

the *O.C.M.*—the Civil and Military Organization). All I knew was
that he was 'working' with Lebourg and Lescure. The latter's
daughter agreed to announce my visit to Bellanger under the name
of Desvignes, for I did not wish my various jobs to get mixed up—
the technical side where I was Drieu, and the literary management
which, in Lescure's absence, I was now obliged to assume *pro
tem.*

At Place Saint-Michel I found a round-faced, smiling fellow in
his thirties, with a pipe on which he drew incessantly and a voice
not exactly lisping but accompanied by a sort of buzzing noise like
a flight of insects. I explained my situation which he understood
very well, and he gave me Lebourg's real name: Jacques Debu-
Bridel. I had read the latter's book, *Frère esclave*, the strange tale
of a youngster who enjoys being tormented by his younger brother.
Bellanger 'phoned him in my presence and told him I would come
to see him.

We then began talking, and he said a great many very nice
things. Our venture, which I believed to be still virtually unknown
since no book had as yet come out, already enjoyed great renown in
his entourage. I was even more surprised to learn that *Le Silence
de la Mer* was already circulating in unexpected forms—mimeographed or typed or even copied by hand from the single proof
which had been passed by Lescure to Lebourg, by Lebourg to
Paulhan and by Paulhan to Professor Debré who had had it duplicated. Bellanger had read it. 'The author,' he told me, 'can only
be a writer of the first rank.' And as I tried to moderate this bold
judgment with a gesture and a smile, he asserted: 'Why, it sticks
out a mile!' and returned my smile in such a way that for a moment
I feared that he knew whom he was talking to. Had Lescure for
once not held his tongue? But the questions that followed (What
sort of a man was Vercors? How old?) made it clear that he saw
in me only Desvignes, the publisher. I savoured that wonderful
experience: to receive to your face a tremendous compliment that
is not addressed to you and leaves you in no doubt of its sincerity!
I discovered the joys of anonymity (and have retained a lingering
nostalgia for it for the last twenty-five years). He also informed me
of the general desire that the Editions de Minuit should consider
drawing up the main lines of a great publishing house after the war,
with the support of the whole Resistance, so as to spike the guns of

the existing publishers who had practically all disqualified themselves by signing the Otto list.

I left him, as can be imagined, in a very cheerful frame of mind
—a little flabbergasted to find myself already acclaimed as a writer
and a publisher without having had an inkling of it, and went to
my date with Debu-Bridel in his office at the Ministry of the Navy,
in Rue de Grenelle.

He gave me the same warm welcome as Bellanger. The first thing
he did was to hand me, on behalf of Professor Debré, five banknotes
of one thousand francs—a tidy sum in those days—which already
more than paid for the cost of producing a second volume. He too
had read *Le Silence de la Mer* and told me that around him the
game of guessing the author's identity was already in full swing.
The names most often mentioned were Gide and Martin du Gard.
He himself wavered between Schlumberger and Marcel Arland.
Saying so, he closely watched my face so as to detect a smile or a
twitch which might corroborate one or other of the names he had
dropped. As for Paulhan, for reasons best known to himself, he
would murmur to his intimates in confidence: 'Vercors *is* Maurice
Bedel'—which was ideal for me but not quite so for that writer's
safety . . . Happily, his intimates must have been discreet, for Bedel
—who was sleeping soundly, of course—was left unmolested. But
all this gossip proved how salutary Lescure's precautions had
been.

Together we examined the situation. Lescure had left Lebourg
no more instructions than he had left me. So he, I and Jean Paulhan
through his intermediary, would henceforward have to keep in
constant touch. It was already early May: couldn't we now get out
Le Silence de la Mer, since Lescure was anyhow out of danger in his
hide-out? He had a notion that Lescure would be back soon, so we
might wait a little longer; on the other hand, there was nothing to
prevent us from getting on with the next volume without him. I
mentioned Maritain's text. He did not know Touchard. Paulhan
himself had not yet ferreted out a new manuscript. It would be
easier to make a collection of shorter essays. It was known, too, that
Paul Eluard was compiling poems from different authors. All this
remained pretty vague.

Every week I returned to see Lebourg, who had nothing new to
tell me. But there was no lack of news in the outside world. In his

vast dusty office at the Ministry we never stopped discussing it. In Prague two students had assassinated Heydrich, the Butcher of Bohemia. In reprisal, the small town of Lidice had been wiped out with its inhabitants, the aged, women and children included. Laval had returned to power on Otto Abetz's armoured bandwagon. He had appealed to French workers over the radio to go to work in Germany for '*La Relève*'—the relief of the French P.O.W.'s there —one prisoner being sent home for every five voluntary workers. It was our first duty, he said, to participate in Europe's defence against Bolshevism, and he had had the odious courage to declare: 'I hope for Germany's victory!' But the French workers stayed put. Perhaps it was to compensate for this failure in Hitler's eyes that a fortnight later a decree came out making it compulsory for Jews to wear the yellow star. We felt personally disgraced by this spittle in the face. Debu had seen his first star as he was leaving his home in the Boulevard Saint-Michel, on the chest of an old man who looked so humbled and furtive that Debu did not at once recognize in him a professor of the Collège de France, the great institution for advanced studies. I had seen mine, I told him, on the very day the decree came out, worn by a young woman-friend who flaunted it like a provocation. She was paying a bedside visit to a sick man whom we were very fond of, but whose Vichyite opinions greatly grieved us. I saw her walk in, head held high and sticking out her chest which was adorned with a star framing the word JUIVE (Jewess) as if it were a topaz brooch. Out of the corner of my eye, I saw our bedridden friend give a start, his face on the white pillow flushed crimson. That was what she had intended, I suppose. He muttered through compressed lips:

'Why do you wear that thing?'

'Out of pride, dear.'

'Damn nonsense! It's foolhardy.'

'With a name like mine?'

Lebourg and I both agreed that no Jew should have complied with the order; far from saving them, it would simply seal their fate. There had been some fine examples of public protest: people sporting stars which, instead of JEW, featured the words CHRIST-IAN or BRETON, or else BRAHMIN, or even ZAZOU (Teddy-Boy). Some people put stars on their dogs. A few people had been jailed. This might have been effective, perhaps, if the whole population had started wearing stars, as only the Danish people, led by their King Frederik, were to prove. But how could one get the word around?

Other news was more inspiring. For the last fortnight, a unit of French combatants, under General Kœnig's command, was holding out in the desert sands of Bir Hakeim against the onslaught of Field-Marshal Rommel's mechanized army. Their heroic resistance earned the world's admiration; it was called the 'Desert Verdun' and, by this exploit, France made a glorious comeback into the war. Did it mean the end of the gloomy purgatory 'through the tunnel of disaster'? I learnt that Maritain's text bearing this title was already circulating in the southern zone. We had been beaten to the post! Pierre Dalloz, back from a trip to Grenoble, told me the name of its publisher: it was my own, Paul Hartmann! He had taken refuge in Savoy, at Chambéry, in the house of his father-in-law, the rector of the University of Paris. Since Touchard seemed definitely out of reach, I decided to cross the demarcation line and fetch the famous booklet myself. I had another reason for doing so. It was being gleefully bruited about that the *Nouvelle Revue Française*, spurned by numerous readers, was in a sorry plight. To stem the adverse tide, Drieu la Rochelle announced a complete reorganization of the editorial board and appealed for the collaboration of outstanding writers in the other zone, with the promise of complete neutrality in all matters relating to politics. Some were reported to be wavering. And among them was mentioned Roger Martin du Gard.

It was urgent, therefore, that someone should go and warn him, and give him a true picture of intellectual life in the North. For between Frenchmen in the two zones there reigned a total ignorance, a mutual incomprehension which bordered at times on antagonism: Hitler had known what he was about when he had cut the country in two—half occupied, half so-called free. Those in the 'free' zone would say scornfully that they failed to understand how the people in the occupied zone could put up with the presence of the Germans. In Marseilles, they called that zone, with their inimitable accent, 'the defeated zone'. Conversely, the French in the North accused, with like contempt, those of the 'nono' (short for: non-occupied) zone of getting accustomed to their easier life, and even of accepting their lot with positive gusto. They were said to have developed an appalling flabbiness: many of those 'Southerners' saw in Pétain's 'National Revolution' a retaliation for February 6th, a punishment for the Popular Front, and congratulated themselves on it as if peace had been signed and France no longer had anything to fear from Germany.

There were only two ways of getting from one zone to the other: either you crossed the line with an Underground guide, a *passeur*, or you got yourself an official mission so as to obtain an *Ausweis*. The former was the quicker method, and the risk involved was minor, that of doing a short spell in prison if you got caught. Yet in my case it would mean attracting attention to myself, which might subsequently hamper me in my activity. But how was I to get a permit?

Géka Massé had told Yvonne of a shady office in Rue Mouton-Duvernet, where a semi-rogue named Hubertus facilitated, against cash, the delivery of an *Ausweis*. It was an unpleasant *démarche*, but I should not be making it for myself alone. The wife of Louis Martin-Chauffier, the journalist and writer, also wished to cross the line in order to join her husband in Lyons, where he was already giving shelter to Aveline. I was received by a smiling German whom one might have credited with acting out of sheer sympathy for the poor French if his very first demand, before going into details, had not been for a substantial advance on his 'fees'. I had brought with me, against all eventualities, a letter from a wholesale firm of furnishing fabrics which declared me to be its artistic manager and stated that it was necessary for me to go to Lyons to contact various suppliers there. This was not entirely without foundation: the firm in question belonged to an old friend who, being Jewish, had fled to Marseilles after my brother-in-law and I had agreed to become his fictitious successors to save his company from being sequestrated and robbed. The German scrutinized the certificate, pulled a face, and said he would see his friends at the *Kommandostab* about it, to find out if it was good enough. We made a date for the next Thursday but one. When I showed up on the appointed day, I found the door locked and affixed to it the ominous seals with the eagles of the *Abwehr*. The fellow had been pinched. I did not wait for explanations and decamped in haste.

Another plan was suggested to me by a timely letter from Jean Chazal, my charming mess-officer of the 15/9 Battalion, who announced his transfer to Nevers as an examining magistrate. Nevers was in the northern zone, but Thiers, his previous appointment, was in the South. Could he not request his successor there to send me a Court summons and thus get me across the line in both directions on official business? Chazal complied, and in early July I received a summons ordering me to appear in court at Thiers three days after, as a witness to a serious motor accident.

I went to the *Kommandantur* in Meaux, where the official stamps on the document had the desired effect. I was urgently sent on to the competent service in *Gross-Paris*, with a pass which spared me the trouble of queuing up for hours. In front of the interrogating official I feigned a great reluctance to comply: 'If I can't get my *Ausweis* at once, no need to trouble yourself: I'll be spared an awful lot of bother, that's all.' I have rarely seen a man so baffled. Ought he to refuse the *Ausweis* or grant it without prior investigation? This usually meant a long wait. But my own attitude seemed deeply reprehensible to this punctilious functionary. A Frenchman summoned by a French court was in duty bound to obey! 'You must go,' he kept saying. 'But if I can't catch the train tonight, there's no point, is there?' I persisted. Eventually he told me to return after lunch when the *Ausweis* would be ready. It was indeed, and that very night I sat in the train.

IV

I FIRST stopped at Nevers to thank Chazal and take his advice.
I found, come to meet me at the station, a woman in advanced
pregnancy, but very pretty. She walked up to me, spoke my name.
She told me that the only indication her husband had given her
was: 'Watch out for a profile like a medallion', but actually she had
spotted me, as she explained with a laugh, because of my rucksack
and my air of looking for someone. Chazal was beginning to meet
with serious difficulties as a magistrate and told me that, a few
weeks later, he might no longer have been able to help. He had
just released thirty men from jail—to save them being handed to
the Germans—by dismissing the charge against them, which had
infuriated the *Préfet*: they were thirty Communists accused of acts
of sabotage. He had requested them to go and blow up trains in
some other *département* for a while, but he feared he was now under
close watch and likely to be transferred elsewhere.

I asked him if, before going on to Lyons, I ought to play the
game right through and report to his colleague in Thiers, but he
assured me I could make straight for Lyons. Next day I crossed the
line at Moulins, without any incident. Imagination has much sway
over us: the mere fact of *knowing* that I should meet no more German uniforms or yellow stars made me feel there was a different
light in the air. Something brighter, more transparent—but also
less sharp and tonic, as if I already felt tempted to forget, to relax,
to be lulled by the gentleness of a fallacious freedom . . .

I reached Lyons in the evening, spent the night at a hotel near
the station, and went to my first date the next morning, in a café
on Place Bellecour. That is where I was to meet Suzanne Paraf,
one of Yvonne's sisters. I was not quite sure if she would turn up,
for the inter-zone correspondence was strictly limited to family
news on ready-printed cards: all one was entitled to do was to
strike out the words that did not apply and complete a couple of
dotted lines. It was quite a *tour de force* to impart, by means of news
about Baby and Granny's health, the date, place and exact time
of a discreet rendezvous. But Frenchmen had become experts at

this little game, and I did not have to wait long on my café terrace. It was a lovely day on Place Bellecour and I was tingling with happy excitement: how wonderful to be waiting for a friend who is late, without fearing she might have been arrested! I had no longer realized in Paris how much this fear was latent in us, even when one gave it no thought. It seemed to me that on that terrace I recaptured, with this tranquillity of mind, almost the pre-war atmosphere.

Suzanne soon joined me, we ordered two vermouths (which could no longer be obtained in Paris) and described life in our respective zones. She took me to lunch in a small restaurant, where we had *boeuf bourguignon*—braised beef—which seemed to me a feast. And we got down to business. It had been decided, until Lescure's return, to suspend distribution of *Le Silence de la Mer* in the North and send part of the edition to the South: people would presume it had been printed there, and this would keep Lescure out of danger. A suitcase would therefore be forwarded to Suzanne by rail and she would receive the corresponding consignment slip, which she was to hand to a porter. If everything went without a hitch, she would get possession of the case, take it home and wait for the books to be fetched by the people charged with the distribution. It was one of the objects of my journey to find such people, and I hoped to do so mainly with the help of Martin-Chauffier. She would then have nothing further to do till the next parcel came along.

As we walked out of the restaurant, she pressed my arm and said: 'A moment ago you asked me how you can recognize a member of the Milice. Look, there are four of them.' And indeed, at the street-corner, four fellows in black berets with a white 'gamma' on them were getting out of a Citroën. They affected the strutting swagger of the German SS. but could not quite keep up the resemblance: their faces did not bear the mark of icy cruelty but were rather those of brutish ruffians. They were none the more reassuring for all that.

I left her and took the tram to Collonges on the Mont d'Or, where the Martin-Chauffiers lived. I did not know them well at the time—I had seen Simone only once to help her cross the line—but Aveline was staying with them. I knew now why he had fled and had no doubt that they were all still active in the Resistance. And

so they were, even overdoing it a little: the absence of the Gestapo
had dispelled their caution and I heard more names and facts
mentioned than I would have wished. I did not repay them in
kind but merely told them what was indispensable. When I mentioned Maritain's text, Aveline smiled, opened a drawer, and showed
me a brochure in a pink cover. He himself had had it reprinted after
Hartmann's edition, but he had no other copy and could not spare
this one. This was of no consequence, since I should be going to
Grenoble to see Battail. Hartmann in Chambéry was only an
hour's distance by train; it would be easy to make a date. Besides,
I had not come to see my hosts about this, but about distribution in
the southern zone. Could they arrange it or refer me to someone
who could? Aveline promised to make contact with more qualified
people; we planned to meet again at Lyons-Perrache, on the
station platform of my Paris-bound train on my way back from
Marseilles. He would then give me details of the person who would
take my business in hand. I was also given Roger Martin du Gard's
address and wrote to him in Nice that evening, asking him to see
me.

In Grenoble, Battail and his young wife met me at the station.
We first went to have a drink at the *Trois-Dauphins*, the famous café
on Place Grenette, where we told one another our life-stories since
the armistice. For their household few things had changed; they
were both still teaching at La Tronche. A bed was prepared for me
there in their little flat on the upper story of the school-house.

Just as we were about to board a bus at the terminus to take me
there, I felt myself held back by the arm. It was the young Lescure.
I was not too much surprised, knowing that he was in Grenoble,
but he could not get over his astonishment at seeing me and kept
saying: '*Ah! mon petit vieux . . . mon petit vieux . . .*' with a huge grin
on his face, and since I was his senior by twenty years, I found this
greeting rather rejuvenating. He was with a girl of his own age, as
pretty as a picture. We made a date for the next day and I only
just caught the bus as it was moving off. Battail and his wife were
already worrying lest I missed it.

While Marie-Louise was cooking the dinner, Battail suddenly
blurted out, with a hint of anxiety clouding his eyes: 'I say, those
Germans . . . you aren't too well in with them, are you?' And I
was able to measure the distance that separated Frenchmen in the

two zones by the fact that he had been able to entertain the slightest doubt about my feelings. But all around him, in teaching circles, he saw so many Socialists hoping against hope that Hitler's Europe might, after all, help somehow to make Briand's dream come true. He hinted that even his own wife at times felt tempted by this hope. It pained him. Thus the harm done by Pétain insinuated itself right into people's homes and families. I explained to Battail the reason for my coming, and asked him to help a little in Grenoble by drawing up a list of useful people to reach among school-teachers and masters of the *lycées*. He agreed enthusiastically, and in return confessed his own hesitations. It had been suggested that he should enter a secret military organization—what did I think of it? I asked him for details of the set-up and personnel. In his area, the group culminated in an active army colonel whose name he mentioned. That settled it. I made a grimace and strongly advised him to keep away: anything to do with Vichy could only be of a dubious nature and, moreover, might lead right up to the Germans some day. Besides, the fact that everybody knew everybody else revealed a lack of seriousness. I expounded the rules of underground action and advised him to keep aloof from any movement that did not strictly abide by them. I would try to help him.

Next day I met Hartmann at the station when the train from Chambéry drew in. He looked a little aged, had lost weight, his eyelids were puffy. We sat down on the parapet along the Isère, behind Stendhal's house, and he pulled out of his brief-case, besides the Maritain, a sheaf of printed and stencilled papers which showed the extent of his activities. I told him about mine. It had meanwhile occurred to me that it would be better for Battail to be in touch with men like Hartmann than with regular officers. Hartmann was all for it. I had asked Battail to wait for us in front of the Museum, and I left them there together while I went off to meet François de Lescure. I had hoped he would give me news of his father, but he knew no more than I did—or so he said. He told me of his nostalgia for the occupied zone, and how difficult it was to do any serious work in the 'nono' zone on account of people's inveterate imprudence.

Before leaving Grenoble, I telephoned my doctor friend at Besayes, whom I remembered, together with his wife, with so much gratitude. They were still allowed the use of a car, which ran on compressed coal-gas contained in three long cast-iron cylinders on the car-roof. They came to fetch me and drove me once more through the Vercors before taking me to Valence. I found it rather piquant to be the only one to know that the writer whose mystery was beginning to intrigue Paris was riding again, as of old, through that mountain fortress whose name he had adopted, in the company of such cordial and attentive friends who had—must have—no inkling of the truth. Seldom have I so regretted having to keep my mouth shut! I myself did not guess that, a short distance away, in a hamlet perched on those mountain-slopes, my friend Pierre Dalloz and Yves Farge were secretly preparing in the heart of this bastion the organization of the armed maquis which was to become, two years later, the most tragic and the most glorious maquis of France.

At Valence I boarded the train for Marseilles where I was expected by Coronel and his wife, who had been living there for the past five or six months.

If Lyons and Grenoble had given the impression of taking me back to the pre-war atmosphere, what am I to say of Marseilles? As I walked out of the station, my lungs filled with an air of freedom which I knew to be spurious, but which I tried to believe in all the same. Just as a schoolboy, at the start of the summer holidays, tries hard to believe that they will last for ever. Like him, I spent a few days nursing sweet illusions that would help me to be happy. On the Canebière an animated crowd was loitering, apparently as carefree as they used to be. The cinemas featured films by Frank Capra which had been banned up North, such as *Mr Deeds Goes to Town* and *You Can't Take It With You* which had delighted us in the last years of peace. On the Vieux-Port, the old harbour, jolly, vociferous fish-wives offered for sale at their open-air stalls all kinds of molluscs and shellfish—sea-urchins, big bitter mussels that are eaten raw, clams, cockles, *violets*. The restaurant menus announced *bourride* and *bouillabaisse* (but at what price! . . .). Gay music rang out from the eating places. To someone freshly arrived from hungry, empty Paris, it seemed almost unbelievable.

Behind this outward lavishness, little of the people's actual and extreme want of food showed: no milk for the children, no meat, flour or butter. My painter friends, Henri Goetz and his wife, told me years later that they lived in those days on rabbit-fodder which could still be found for sale. You closed your eyes and swilled it down with a lot of water, and it proved a filling meal. Another thing that should have brought me back to reality was the number of Parisian friends, among them a great many Jewish ones of course, who had come to the South for safety. Once more I was able to assess the widening rift of misunderstanding that separated the two zones. An old acquaintance of my parents, a lady who was a co-religionary of my father's and one of their dearest and most intelligent friends, had somehow got it into her head that my mother, who was of Catholic origin and hailed from the province of Berry, had been persuaded to drift into the wrong camp. She wept as she talked of it and I had to go to great pains to undeceive her. 'Your father!' she kept saying, as if my mother had betrayed his memory—a very unfair suspicion since on the contrary, my mother's flat in Rue Servandoni had become the almost daily shelter of her few Jewish women-friends who had been unwilling or unable to leave Paris. One of them filled me with pity for culinary reasons. She was a very kind soul, but inordinately stupid. She had always been extremely fat, for 'delectable dishes' were her only aim in life, her be-all and end-all. The want of food literally killed her: I have never seen any human being waste away so quickly, her emaciated face positively dripped with sagging folds. And one day she died—even more of despair, I believe, than of inanition.

'Your father!' the old lady kept repeating and, conjuring up his memory, she told me all kinds of details about his life which I did not know; how he had trekked on foot from his native Hungary at the age of sixteen to follow his star to the land of Victor Hugo and the French Revolution. How it had been the German poet, Hauff, with his 'Orphan-Girl of the Pont des Arts', who had irresistibly drawn him towards that show-place of the world, like a moth to lamp-light. How, by the most extraordinary chance, the first person he had met on that bridge was the only Hungarian friend he knew in Paris. In fact, I knew much less than this old friend about the youth of my father, who was a very reserved man, and being too reserved myself I had refrained from questioning him. The little I knew from what my mother had told us on various occasions remained full of gaps. I promised myself I would question her on my return and learn from her at last all that she remembered.

I knew that close relatives of Stéphanie's were living in Marseilles. I naturally looked them up. Perhaps I had nursed the unadmitted hope that I might approach her at last? They gave me good news of her, mentioned that she too was in the South but not in Marseilles. On the Côte d'Azur, perhaps? The reply was evasive. I felt some sort of reticence, so that I dared not ask for her address, sensing I should meet with a refusal. Was it merely out of habitual prudence, or was it considered undesirable that we should meet again, even after all those years? The intensity of my disappointment made me realize how powerful had been the hope I had harboured. Without that hope, would I even have gone down to Marseilles, where I had no affairs to settle? I was not so certain of it.

What *was* certain, though, was the pleasure I felt at seeing once again so many friends whom events had scattered. Coronel and his young wife were going through rather hard times, I discovered. They lived in a tiny lodging near the Vieux-Port and eked out a meagre living by his taking a succession of mean jobs—at the moment at a paint-manufacturer's—while she, a Londoner by birth, was giving English lessons. I had given Martin du Gard their address to reply to. His letter disappointed me. He had moved from Nice to La Napoule, in order to keep his door locked against even his best friends, because, against all hope, his recent creative sterility, which he had feared might be permanent, had given way to a new urge to write, and he had launched into a long labour which he might not have time to finish in the years left to him. So it was he, after all, who had chosen the hermit's life that I had dreamed of for so long . . . There followed four pages full of friendship and questions about my own life. Nevertheless, he did slam the door in my face, assuming no doubt that the purpose of my visit would be to urge him to speak up—one way or other. And indeed, had I seen him, I should have pressed him to let us have a text for our Editions de Minuit. All I could do in the circumstances was to send him another letter warning him against Drieu La Rochelle's invitation to join the editorial board of the *N.R.F.* I won't flatter myself that my letter was the cause of his subsequent refusal, but he did in fact decline to authorize the use of his name.

Together with the Coronels, I spent the Sunday at the headland of La Madrague, amid scenery evoking the loveliness of ancient Greece. We swam all three in the warm, crystalline sea at the foot of an imposing steep and rocky island which rose, white as marble, from the blue water like a vision of the Sporades. One could have imagined Sappho hurling herself, with her lyre, from its jagged peak into the sea. They were moments out of this world, and in my memory that day glows like a shimmering oasis in the long deep night of the occupation. That bathe was my only contact with the sea throughout four years, and this privation was perhaps the one I felt most cruelly—more, certainly, than the privation of food.

That evening, as if to bring me back, by contrast, to the labyrinthine darkness of clandestine life, Coronel took me along to a strange building where a friend of his was living, a man who was more or less a Communist. It was situated in a narrow street behind the embankment of Rive Neuve in the Old Port (opposite the squalid, picturesque quarters which the Germans were to dynamite the following year—not out of concern for social hygiene but because quite a few of their men disappeared there, getting murdered or choosing to desert). We stepped under a grimy, sweaty porch, which was prolonged by a dark, narrow corridor leading on to yet more corridors, passed under vaults where the unexpected light of a window would sometimes pierce the murk, and the whirr of a sewing-machine could be heard in the silence; then climbed a decrepit, dank, lugubrious staircase which led on to more corridors from which other flights of steps ascended. We had to walk down one of these, and a little farther on, climb another three. At what floor level were we? At last we found ourselves before a row of doors painted a uniform sullen grey. Coronel knocked at one of them, and I saw it opening on to an exquisite and cosy interior, a pearl encased in this hideous oyster shell. The walls were lined with books, among them the complete works of Marx as well as numerous revolutionary writings. When we left our host late at night, he piloted us down other steps and along yet more corridors until at last we found ourselves, not in the narrow street, but on the quayside. The building had two exits.

I was so deeply pervaded by this atmosphere, with its reminiscence of underworld novels, that afterwards, whenever I heard of a place being raided anywhere, the picture, the constant phantasm that would spring to my mind like a remembered film sequence, was that sumptuous library in the heart of the sinister building, with its array of tell-tale books (which the police discover and smash up while the suspect escapes through the black maze of stairs and corridors before slipping out of the porch on to the harbour and disappearing in the darkness of the deserted city . . .).

Dark and deserted, too, was the night when I walked back to my hotel. As I climbed the narrow stairs to my room, a couple walked up in front of me, arm in arm. The tall, very fair-haired man had a close-shaven neck and spoke with a harsh, guttural accent. The night was hot; I read a few pages in bed, leaving the window open. No sooner had I turned out the light than the yard resounded with a woman's long-drawn-out moan of voluptuousness, as if calling the hotel, the neighbours and the world to witness her lust. A lust experienced, I had no doubt, in the arms of the tall, blond German. I fell asleep in anger and disgust: I detest shamelessness, and this exhibition of it struck me like a provocation.

I had only one more day in Marseilles, for I must cross the line—after my date on the station platform at Lyons—before midnight on the day after. It was then, in Coronel's flat, that I had one of those idiotic, exasperating misadventures which, in the Resistance movement, so often foiled the best-laid plans. A former schoolmate, who had also fled from the North, came to see me. We had been out of touch for ages. I remembered him without displeasure, although his ragging and self-conceit had often annoyed me in our school days. Later they had made me smile. And here he was, not in the least subdued by the country's defeat but contemplating the world with the roving irony of a superior fellow who stood high above those trifling concerns. Coronel and I imprudently discussed the Maritain book in his presence; he asked to have a look at it, briefly skimmed through the pages, and then declared he would take it away to read at leisure. I told him this was out of the question, reminded him that I had to leave before noon the next day, and tried to retrieve the book. He refused to let it go and swore to high heaven that he would return it to me that very evening. His calmly insolent smile exasperated me. Surely we weren't going to have a fight? I had the inexplicable weakness to give in, and let him leave with the precious book.

Evening came, but of course no sign of him. I chided myself

furiously for my craven acquiescence. For once I hadn't held my tongue: it served me right! Next morning, Coronel and I went to look for him. He was not in, and nobody could tell us where to find him. It was impossible to delay my departure by even an hour— there was that date in Lyons where I was expected on that particular train. In the end I had to leave empty-handed, without the only spoils I had garnered. I never knew whether I had been the victim of a 'good joke' or of something worse.

It was a dramatic loss, but fortunately I knew that Yvonne had hopes in her turn of going South soon, thanks to a friend in high places. In any case, however, the delay was disastrous. I was still chewing the cud of my rage when the train pulled into the station at Lyons-Perrache. Everything had gone wrong: Stéphanie, Maritain, Martin du Gard—if Aveline too let me down now, I should have made the whole journey for nothing . . .

He *was* there. We only had a few minutes. I told him of my mishap, asked him to contact Hartmann and get him to send another copy of the book to Yvonne's sister. He then slipped me a card, with quick explanations. On it I read a name unknown to me and an address: YVES FARGE. I wrongly gathered that he was a professor of literature; in fact he was an artist and journalist, a resistance fighter from the first hour who, after Liberation, was to become first a commissar of the Republic and later Minister of Food. It was he, Aveline told me, who would handle the distribution of our books in the Lyons area and find correspondents in the other regions. The train whistled, started up, and I caught it on the move.

V

I FOUND Paris on my return all agog with excitement. A British
commando, part Canadian, part Scots, had made a landing at
Dieppe. In spite of the scant forces involved, the optimists already
imagined the great moment to have come. I was not one of them
and did not grasp the point of that raid—in fact, I still haven't—
which was doomed to failure from the outset. It was in fact thrown
back into the sea, with heavy losses, after only a few hours ashore.
It was said afterwards that one of the Scots had nevertheless found
time to post a bottle of whisky to his sweetheart in France, who
had safely received it. This was probably a myth, but everybody
cherished the illusion of having received that fabulous bottle himself. The day after the raid, the Field-Marshal at the head of the
State thanked the German army for having saved France from the
invaders' clutches.

A week later, on August 26th, the biggest round-up ever of Jews
was unleashed, this time regardless of age, sex or origin. Throughout
the whole territory, Pétain was setting the ultimate seal on his
infamy by delivering into the Nazis' hands even the survivors of
Verdun whom he himself had decorated. For a fortnight, a train
packed with children waited around for lack of orders, until Laval
suggested off his own bat that they be deported like the rest. It is
to the honour of Frenchmen that quite a few Jews at least received
timely warning, enabling them to escape. Others preferred to die.
Solemn old men stepped over balconies to hurl themselves into the
street. Screaming women battered their heads against the stone
pavements as their offspring were wrenched from them. French
policemen took part in this dirty business. An old friend of my
father's, over eighty, blind, and an eminent physicist, was thrown
into a truck with sobbing, half-naked girls who had been raped one
after another. Tristan Bernard, arrested together with his wife, upheld her with words of poignant wisdom: 'We have lived in fear, we
shall now live in hope . . . ' By tens of thousands, Jews were packed

into the Vélodrome d'Hiver, the covered sports stadium of Paris, before being dumped, some at Drancy, some at Compiègne, like so much cattle destined for the gas ovens of Treblinka and other places of horror.

Some time after, I had a strange dream. I found myself in a kind of seaside resort and was due to take the tram to some ill-defined destination. To reach the tram, I had first to pass through a waiting-room of vast dimensions, something like the monumental station hall of the Gare d'Orsay in Paris. In it reigned an atmosphere of mass emigration; the place was crammed with people sitting on their luggage, amid stacks of cases and bundles. I was searching for Stéphanie among the groups of people. At last I discovered her mother seated on a folding-chair, next to a woman-friend. She smiled at me, her head shaking, as it always used to, with a tiny, ceaseless tremor, which seemed to be the effect of a constant, gentle uncertainty. She motioned me to turn round. I saw Stéphanie by the wall, her head supported on a sort of low pillar or sculptor's turntable. As I walked up to her, she gazed at me with knitted brows as if trying to remember who I was. I greeted her, she smiled at last and, in her motionless face, her eyes directed my glance towards a painter who was doing her portrait. I then noticed that she had no body. Her head alone was placed on the console, like a wax model, with a filmy gauze wrapped round it. Her skin, despite her mute, lifeless immobility, had a lovely fresh tint. I turned to look at her mother, who did not seem in the least surprised and gave me an encouraging nod. But I had realized, with a stricken heart, that I ought never to have been there. I apologized, Stéphanie smiled at me in a blaze of loveliness, I stammered that I would be back later. But as I went out to where a tram was waiting for me, her hesitation to recognize me wrung my heart, and I knew with sorrowful certainty that I should not go back.

On waking, the remembrance of this dream seemed to me both sweet and sinister. The vision in that vast dusty hall, amid the crowds waiting for God knows what departure, of the face I loved, had found and lost again, gripped me with anxious fear and a vague foreboding which kept haunting me till the day when Stéphanie's tragic fate became a certainty: arrested in Dordogne,

she and her mother had been taken to Auschwitz, where they both
died.

September was drawing to an end, Lescure had still not returned
nor sent any news. It was now six months since the distribution of
Le Silence de la Mer had been paralysed by his prohibition. Should
we now disregard it? Yvonne came back from the southern zone
and suggested we should send there not just part of the edition,
but the whole of it. 'Lots of people down there,' she told us, 'still
believe in Father Christmas. The Vercors story might open their
eyes. Whereas over here it's already old history: people have
realized, don't you think?' I was not sure that her view was correct;
but I was the author, after all . . . So I gave in to her arguments.
Nevertheless, it was agreed that we should keep at least a hundred
books or so for Paris: Paulhan and Bellanger had promised copies
to some eminent personalities whom they did not wish to dis-
appoint.

Yvonne had brought back from the South the Maritain concealed
in the lining of her toilet-case. One incident had made her tremble
for a moment, at the crossing of the line. Why had she roused the
suspicion of the fat uniformed German woman in charge of searching
the passengers' luggage? Anyhow, she made Yvonne open all her
bags and started to rummage in them when she came upon an
hotel bill with the expense item: one bath—8 francs. Indignation
made her forget her suspicions. Treating Yvonne as a 'capitalist', she
gave her a talking-to on the need for austerity in wartime—and
forgot to search the toilet-bag.

When I brought the booklet to Oudeville, he told me a piece
of good news: he had unearthed a linotypist by the name of Maurice
Roulois, who was a home-worker and able to typeset our 96-page
Maritain at one stretch, which would save us a considerable amount
of time. I could not blind myself to the fact, however, that it also
made for greatly increased risks: for nothing is easier than to trace
the type of a lino machine, if you just take a close look at the
printed page. It is impossible to avoid its containing a crooked or
broken letter here and there, which will keep on showing up all
through the print. And as Paris did not boast of an unlimited
number of linotype presses, it would only require a thorough inspection of those presses to detect the faulty type-mould. I there-

fore had fears for Roulois's safety and never stopped trembling for him a little until the very last day. I can only presume that nobody gave the Gestapo this infallible tip, for he never had any trouble.

Thanks to him, the Maritain would take only two weeks to print. After this there would be a long time lag until we could round up the material for our third volume. This was natural enough and ought not to have worried me: a writer always has something more urgent to do than write for his bottom drawer and, failing any chance of getting into print, who would waste time and trouble in producing an unpublishable piece of work? Authors had first to learn of the existence of the Editions de Minuit, be invited to give us a manuscript, then sit down to ponder, hit on a worthy subject (had I myself not taken weeks to think of one for *The Silence of the Sea*?) give it time to mature, then write, revise, correct it before it was ready to be handed to Paulhan; the time for him to study it before passing it to Debu-Bridel, who would then at last pass it on to me. . . .

Yes, I knew quite well that all this took time; but as I went to see Lebourg at the Ministry of the Navy week after week, I nevertheless grew more and more impatient and worried. I would explain to him, helpless though he was to do anything about it, that it was a blessing after all that the distribution of *Le Silence* had suffered such a long delay for, in the eyes of people abroad, it was better that no book should come from our press at all than that we should publish one volume and then have none to follow it up; since this would have proved the very opposite of what we had set out to prove; to wit, the absence, rather than the existence, in captive France of a vast national movement of thought opposed to the Nazi stranglehold. Was I going to be in the same desperate position as Malte Laurids Brigge? In my impatience, I could not help paraphrasing Rainer Maria Rilke's hero . . .

. . . Is it possible to put up with such a situation? Their flags now hang out everywhere. People no longer seem to notice them. Perhaps out of habit, from having seen them too much. Is it possible that they don't jump, don't weep, don't shout at the sight?

Yes, it *is* possible.

Is it possible that, on the contrary, there are so many people who think: 'I can rob that Jew since it is permitted. It is even recommended,' and can afterwards strut before their mirrors without blushing?

And that so many others can say to themselves: 'Let idiots die for such stupidities. I'm doing all right and am lining my pockets?'

Yes, it *is* possible.

Is it possible that it is *this* face of Paris, of France—and not the true one—which is all the world can see? Only this gangrened piece of profile, while the other, the proud and unblemished one, remains shrouded in shadow and silence under a veil of shame which ought rather to conceal the disgusting tumour from sight?

Is it possible that all those publishers, at the first beckoning, and even before, should have rushed into the ante-rooms to take their orders? And have found so many writers already waiting there?

And again: that the others found nothing better to do than keep their mouths shut, or else whisper so softly that one can hardly hear them?

Yes, it *is* possible.

But then, if all this is possible, Rilke himself had already written, *if all this has even a semblance of possibility, why then, for the love of everything dear to us, something must be done! The first nobody who has these disturbing thoughts must begin to do something to repair these neglects. However unimportant, however unqualified he may be*—since no one else will. *This Brigge, this stranger, this insignificant young man must sit down up there, on his fifth floor, and write, and write day and night. Yes, he must write, that's what it will come to.*

And, as it had for Brigge, this is what it had come to for me, over a year ago. But after more than a year, no writer had taken up the torch. And although this was explicable, I nevertheless feared it might begin to look odd and disastrous to the outside world. Especially since the 'Kollabos' on the other hand had no scruple about exploiting to the enemy's advantage any line that could be so construed, and had annexed for this purpose the French writers from Péguy right up to—the limit of effrontery!—Victor Hugo, whose giant portrait loomed on posters in the Métro above a well-chosen quotation against England. One chapter from the *Scènes de la Vie Future*, in which Duhamel had somewhat rough-handled America, had just been reproduced in the German-language *Signal* (without permission of course) and with his name in large type. Which writer had not on occasion penned a paragraph that the

Germans could now misuse? It was a threat that hung over all of them.

Fortunately, I had other preoccupations to distract me from my worries and keep me calm: the despatching of *Le Silence de la Mer* to the free zone, and the printing of the Maritain. The latter was run off eight pages at a time, like the previous volume (but at a quicker rate, thanks to Roulois), and I corrected the proofs progressively on the 'bed'. The forwarding, on the other hand, raised the problem of the means of transport that would best conform to the norms of security.

We had to discard carriage by rail: it left too many traces, and we knew that the rather stringent check at the crossing of the line would make such traces risky. Bellanger, for his underground network, had centralized a line-crossing organization. He sent me to a well-intentioned forwarding agent who, at perfectly normal rates and with the help of accomplices in key positions, arranged to transfer the luggage of Jewish and other clandestine fugitives by lorry under the nose of the Germans. I went to see him to enquire exactly how to proceed. All one had to do, without giving one's name, was to send the consignee the number of the consignment on an interzone card, and the same number would appear on the parcel itself. The whole thing was perfectly anonymous. I had put my questions simply, and the answers had been given just as simply, so that I began to fear I might not have made quite clear the delicate nature of the consignment. Quite needlessly I felt compelled to add some words of explanation which my interlocutor tactfully pretended not to have heard. I left in embarrassment at my own insistence.

We needed very big trunks. I had one such trunk, but it had some peculiar features. I should explain that it had been left to me by Kalidou. Kalidou was Kébé's brother, and Kébé was a noble Senegalese whom Diego Brosset had chosen as his batman because of his intelligence and athletic prowess. Kébé had followed Diego to France and for a while had been in the service of Madame Mangin, the general's widow. I had 'inherited' him when my boys were born, and he had practically brought them up. He had then left us to return to his country and had sent me his brother. But if Kébé was a Moslem of strict obedience, a total abstainer and virtuous to a degree, Kalidou was not carved out of the same wood. Why had he left that trunk behind when he went home? I no longer remember, but when I opened it, one can imagine my amusement on finding that its inside was entirely papered with suggestive pictures, probably printed in Casablanca—representing houris, odalisques and nautch-girls with lavishly pink bellies, breasts and bottoms under gaudily-coloured transparent veils. Partly for convenience and partly for fun, I carried the trunk to Yvonne's flat and while we were packing it with books, we laughed in anticipation of Suzanne's surprise when she came to open it. And if, peradventure, the Germans opened it first, would they ever suspect what contraband it contained. . . ?

Suzanne's reaction surpassed our hopes. She lived in Lyons in the flat of a very kindly but very strait-laced lady and, during the few days that the trunk was in her room, she trembled at the idea that her landlady might open the lid in her absence. So, without further waiting, she removed it herself to Yves Farge, our correspondent, whom she had never met before. No sooner had she dumped it down than, to Farge's and Fargette's suspicious surprise, she took to her heels. Apprehensively they opened the trunk, found in it *Le Silence de la Mer* amid the houris and nautch-girls, and asked themselves all sorts of questions, as can be readily imagined.

What they found in a subsequent case was a baby's layette. The consignment numbers had been mixed up. Farge boldly went to claim his own: the numbers were checked, and he was sent to the home of a police inspector recently promoted to fatherhood, who was much relieved to swap cases without manifesting any curiosity.

Kalidou's trunk, once it was packed with books, was horribly heavy. As Pierre Massé was ill, we no longer had the use of his car, but we found someone to give us a hand. It was Oudeville once again who unearthed this new helper to whom he introduced me in his shop. The fellow was a book-keeper in a medical bookshop on Place de l'Odéon. He was small and square-shouldered, with very bright eyes behind thick glasses. He wanted to 'work', he said. He seemed to me a bit highly strung: to hear him talk, the things he would have liked to transport were bombs and hand-grenades, and also to use them, if need be. I did not much care for his bragging, and apologized for having nothing more exciting to offer him for the moment than a peaceable trunk to be taken to a road carrier's. We fixed an appointment at the Carrefour de Passy, just above the

Métro station. It was quite close to Yvonne's place but the weight of the trunk almost tore my arm off. A cold October rain was falling, in a gloomy, relentless drizzle. When the man felt the weight of the trunk, I saw him go pale. What did he think he was being asked to transport? 'If you have the jitters . . . ' I said, but he shook his head. And I saw him walk away to the Underground through the pelting rain, an open umbrella in one hand and, in the other, that tombstone which he seemed to be dragging almost along the ground like a reluctant mastiff. Till the evening I kept thinking, with uneasy concern, of the pathetic, pitiful figure shambling past suspicious-eyed policemen.

We had fixed the next date for the coming Thursday, to transport some packages of the current Maritain this time. He did not show up. That sort of thing was always unnerving. Alarmed, I went to his bookshop and asked for him. He was there! His face sagged when he recognized me. What had become of my grenade-carting *guerrillero*? He told me curtly not to count on him in future and left me standing.

Still, who has not panicked at least once in his life? I have not forgotten the fear that for ten whole minutes paralysed me one day, along the pavement of Avenue Duquesne. Pierre Massé still being off sick, it fell to me to transport with minimum delay and within the day twelve enormous parcels of one of our editions temporarily stored (for some reason I don't remember) in a bookshop on Boulevard Montparnasse belonging to the poet Georges Hugnet. Each parcel weighed 20 kilograms; this meant 40 to be carried in the two saddle-bags of my bicycle, and to make six outward journeys and six returns, with the hill of Chaillot to climb each time, I had to choose the quickest route for every jouney if I wanted to finish the job before nightfall. The quickest route, however, passed in front of the Ecole Militaire, a district teeming with Germans. Outside each little hotel reserved for the Wehrmacht and outside the two big cafés where Resisters had thrown bombs not so long ago, SS. guards were standing watch. Twice, three times I passed both ways without rousing their attention; but on my third return trip it seemed to me that their eyes were following me suspiciously. On the next transport, at the moment when I had to pass before them for the seventh time with that overladen bicycle, I was taken with a trembling fit. I tried to continue regardless, but found it impossible: my legs were shaking, my bike began to wobble, and I had to get off, lean it against a tree, and sit down on the kerbstone. It took me long minutes to control myself, calm my heartbeats, recover my strength and be able at last to remount and ride on. I passed unhindered before the sentinels, whom I did not have the honour to interest. My panic promptly subsided and, although a bit knocked up, I made the last journeys without further apprehension.

I remember this case of jitters because, during more than three years, it was the only one of its kind I experienced. Normally, in the humdrum routine of work, though one knows of course that it involves some danger, it is an abstract, purely intellectual knowledge which does not affect the centres of emotion. Now what you don't feel does not exist, so that the feeling I had in general— even though I knew it to be false—was that nothing could happen to *me*. Many people imagine that to face the perils of clandestine action, sanctioned by torture and death, a certain dose of courage is a prime necessity. That is a fallacy: in fact, you act most of the time with a kind of calm unconsciousness, and what courage there may be is of little merit, since it does not require the effort to over-come fear. From this point of view, compared to the smallest armed action by the maquis, ours was a positive rest-cure.

That is why my personal life could follow a well-organized, stable rhythm: two days in Paris to attend to publishing, five days in the country to work as an illustrator. For during these last weeks I had been able to get back to etching and was busy with a project particularly close to my heart: the illustrations for *Hamlet*. The book would not be published so long as the Germans were there, but during the two or three years it would take me to complete the work, my livelihood would be assured. My publisher Goldschmidt, evacuated to Algiers, had given me the green light. I thought I could detect in this decision the benevolent hand of his mother, who had just joined him there. She was of Russian origin and must have been a remarkable beauty in her youth. I felt an almost filial affection for her and was moved by her confidence in my talents: 'After the war, you'll become famous, you'll see!' she had told me with a sweet smile a few days before leaving Paris. Her departure worried me, for her heart was frightfully delicate. She was subject to frequent fainting fits, and I was afraid she might not stand up to the excitement and strain of a clandestine voyage. In answer to my last 'au revoir' she had said with the same sweet, sadly affectionate smile: 'My husband will see you again, not I . . . ' Happily I learnt that they had both safely reached port after great hardships. Her will-power had upheld her to the end. And then, having seen her children and grandchildren again, and lived with them through a week of happiness, one morning . . . 'She forgot to wake up,' the friend told me who had been instructed to settle the financial questions with me. That faraway death affected me greatly.

On my way home to Rue Servandoni, I was stopped in my tracks at the corner of Rue Jacob and Rue Bonaparte by the photograph of a Crucifixion which, though I could not identify it, I ascribed to some German primitive (it was actually a Grünewald painting). The terrible, wasted body seemed almost reduced to a mineral state. Blows and falls had marked it with such innumerable bruises and a thousand minute scratches that it looked like the crackled glaze of old porcelain, or the worm-eaten wood of old furniture. It was so symbolical of the long martyrdom, the slow flaying alive of the Jews before their final immolation, that I remained obsessed for a long time by this dreadful evocation of bestial fury bent on the degradation of man.

Another time, passing across Place du Carrousel to bring André Robillard the volumes he had asked me for, I noticed that the pedestal of Gambetta's statue had been tarred with a huge star of David and the word 'JEW' daubed in its centre. I was baffled for a moment: whoever had wanted the great French statesman of the last century to wear the star? If it was an anti-Semite, wasn't he thus proclaiming that a great patriot could be Jewish? Perhaps it was the act of a Resister, and meant to ridicule the anti-Jewish laws? Only when, a little farther on, I spotted a poster for the pro-German Légion des Volontaires Français picturing a fluttering sheaf of French flags—royal, imperial and republican—and saw that the republican one had been daubed with the same inscription, 'Jew', did I realize that in the eyes of a monarchist converted to Hitlerism, the Jew Gambetta must necessarily seem a traitor twice over: by his determined resistance against the Germans and his restoration of the Republic.

VI

ONE day, on my way to Rue Vineuse, I saw a couple of grey-clad soldiers—a rare sight in that district—planted in the middle of the roadway, trying with a loonish air to decipher the name of the street. Had it not been for their uniform, they might have been a pair of bored French *poilus* in a music-hall sketch wearily dragging their feet on the pavements of any garrison town. And suddenly the thought struck me, really without any reason: 'They're making the most of the little time left to them.'

I had almost thought it aloud and it amazed me. For two years now, the presence of German uniforms had seemed to me, as to everybody else, a curse hanging over Paris in mourning for an endless period—a hundred years' war. When I reported my curious impression to Yvonne a few minutes later, she teased me: 'Are you hearing voices now?', for there was really nothing that could conceivably justify such a hallucination. Germany and Japan were continuing to score points everywhere. Besieged Leningrad was starving to death. Moscow held fast, but had been outflanked in the south, the irresistible stream of the German Army was nearing the Volga, the Caucasus, the Black Sea, was coming within reach of the Caspian and would soon lay hands on its oilfields. After Indo-China and Singapore, the Japs were occupying, one after the other, all the islands of the Malayan archipelago. Rommel, in spite of Bir Hakeim, was at the gates of Alexandria. The British, in a little ballet figure, had led him a dance back to beyond Benghazi, but the bells of London had pealed too soon and Rommel in his turn had conducted them back all the way to the Egyptian frontier.

In France itself, Nazi and pro-Nazi propaganda had never flowered in such profusion. It was almost impossible to go to a cinema: with rare exceptions, they all showed ponderous Germanic flops headed by the infamous *Jew Süss*, which was programmed in all picture-theatres in succession, while anti-Semitic displays of rarely attained crudeness filled the show-cases of public buildings, offering to the eyes of the passer-by anatomical details of the kind usually reserved for a museum of freaks and horrors: a heavy eye, a thick-lobed ear, a bulbous nose, protruding lips, to 'teach Frenchmen to spot the Hebrew enemy'.

Commandant Paul Chack, for his part, an author of successful seafaring tales, had taken it upon himself to organize great anti-Bolshevik exhibitions, which were on a par with the anti-Jewish ones in abject mendacity. The New Order reigned everywhere and nothing, really nothing, justified my strange vision.

I had forgotten all about it, anyhow, when, a few weeks later, on the morning of November 8th, we were roused by a thunderclap: the Allies had landed in North Africa! It was a Sunday once again. For years Hitler had accustomed us to view this day with misgiving. Was it possible that for the first time a Sunday could be auspicious? And what would Pétain do now? We were not long in finding out: he gave orders to fire on the 'invaders' (though he had surrendered Indo-China to the Japanese without a shot). When the Germans in turn invaded the free zone to strengthen the Mediterranean coast, he did not lift his little finger. For a brief moment, some people still tried to believe that he was playing for time to hoodwink the Germans and make good his own escape to Africa: Giraud had just landed there by plane; Darlan, who had chanced to be there for family reasons and scented the changing tide of victory, decided, on the throw of a dice, to cast in his lot with the Americans who set him up in power. This was simply revolting, but perhaps Pétain too was on the point of rallying to them? What would become of de Gaulle if he did? And of the Republican régime?

Needless worry: Pétain stayed put. So as to remain among the French people, he said. Because he was scared of flying, sighed those of his close associates who had believed in him. At least this put an end to all doubts. As a clandestine journal wrote, those people who, before joining the Resistance, had waited 'for the day when the pilot would change course', now realized at last that he never would. And henceforward the ranks of the Resistance swelled, in a ceaseless flow of one-way traffic, with crowds of Vichyites who had woken up from their illusions.

But even more than those events, the drama of Toulon was to rouse the waverers from their fool's paradise. The man charged with the defence of this naval base against Allied action was

Admiral Marquis, whose orders were not to oppose any German intervention. Thus Vichy decreed. All the stronghold's firing-power was directed seawards, withdrawn from the direction of the land, and the citadel dismantled. At 3 a.m. one November morning, six armoured columns moved towards Toulon. At 5 a.m. they entered the port without a cannon-shot and immediately occupied the Arsenal. But on board the ships, the reflex of naval honour had proved stronger than all signals. At the first shot, the *Strasbourg* blew herself up. One after the other, the *Dupleix*, the *Marseillaise*, the *Foch*, the *Vienne*, the smaller destroyers and torpedo-boats keeled over on their flanks. The submarines made for the bottom (six of them managed to escape). The sailors had pulled up the gangways and were destroying the vital parts of their craft. Laval telephoned from Vichy: 'Above all, no incidents, do you hear? But what is that noise? Those explosions?'—'The ships have scuttled themselves.' The line went dead, Laval had hung up in a fury. The blaze of burning ships lit up the darkness. As the sun rose amid the smoke that enveloped the wrecks, the French Fleet had ceased to exist.

As I listened in to the Free French on the BBC exultantly reporting in detail this heroic scuttling, I was less stirred by admiration and pride in this ultimate upsurge of national honour than by suppressed, dumb, trembling rage. All my thoughts fomented and fed this rage. What a cruel confirmation of the criminal stupidity of Pétain and his clique! What had those Machiavellis obtained with their *Realpolitik*? What had they saved? What had they made of us? The Germans had demobilized the Armistice army down to the last man. What had become of all that Vichy trumpet-blowing, those stuck-out chests, those flapping standards, like the entry of circus clowns?

Now, with no more Algeria, no more fleet, no more army, Laval had nothing left, not the meanest bargaining counter for his horse-deals. We were in the same plight as Poland, Greece, Norway—nothing stood any more between the Germans and us.

In Algiers, a murder put paid to the Darlan scandal. A shady business . . . An unknown young man walked into his victim's office without let or hindrance, waited there without anyone taking notice of him; and then was tried and executed within forty-eight hours; his name could not be revealed for 'security reasons' . . . *Cui prodest?* Who profited by it? Giraud? De Gaulle? Pétain? One thing was certain: this was pure Shakespearean drama, where power was no longer delegated, but *seized*, as profit, intrigue, violence commanded.

In the East the German communiqués, after proudly announcing in September the capture of the 'Red October' factories on the outskirts of Stalingrad, now had a less victorious ring; and though they extolled the heroic fight of the German combatants, they implicitly paid the same tribute to the Soviet soldier who defended his city house by house. It was a Dantesque struggle, commented on, with its ups and downs, by Jean-Richard Bloch on Moscow radio, to which I sometimes managed to tune in. October, November, December . . . The battle was still raging at Stalingrad . . . But were the Germans still the attackers? Wasn't it the Red Army now? Their offensive south of Voronezh might have weighty consequences if the Soviet counter-attacks—to adopt the metaphor of Geneva Radio's commentator René Payot—not only started like avalanches, but invariably ended like them, too . . .

And what was meanwhile happening to us, to our publishing-house? I learned from Bellanger that our too-restricted distribution of *Le Silence* was causing a row in Paris. People were annoyed: why did So-and-so get it, and not I? We should have to reprint it to soothe hurt feelings. The motive which had prompted us to send the bulk of the edition to the southern zone was considered specious. The general opinion was that, on the contrary, *Le Silence de la Mer* would have been a much more suitable choice for Paris, less dated (as Yvonne had persuaded me into believing) than the Maritain . . . I gently laughed in my sleeve.

And now Bellanger too mentioned Maurice Bedel's name! Or rather, he showed himself as surprised as I at the rumour of this authorship. It appeared that a link had been spotted between some detail in my story and a similar one in one of his books . . . By what a thin thread a literary reputation hangs at times!

So far so good, but we were getting on to the third winter of the Occupation and—the Maritain apart—we were still unable to put to press a second manuscript composed on French soil! This could not go on, we must do something to save face. Following Lescure's example, I decided—as he had done for *La Pensée Libre*—

to make up a collection of essays and articles with what little material we could lay hands on. Jacques Decour, after three months in
prison, had just been shot, and Jean Paulhan, his co-founder of
Les Lettres Françaises, would give us, under the pseudonym of Lom-
agne, a study on the young martyr's writings. Yvonne, under the
name of Queyras, would contribute an essay on the need for
Indignation, which the welter of infamies ought to arouse but which
was so often smothered by what might be called the Great Torpor
of the Conservative-minded. Debu-Bridel, calling himself Argonne,
would give us some of his *Pages of a Diary*, written under the shock
of the defeat. He would choose in particular the pages in which
he pilloried *Paris-Soir* and *L'Intransigeant*, the two most-read evening
papers, whose first concern, in their issues of May 10th, 1940, was
to reproduce in huge print Hitler's proclamation to the German
soldiers in which he accused France of having declared war on
Germany thirty-one times in the course of the last two hundred
years . . . Once every seven years! Why, with what ulterior motive,
had they seen fit to publish this grotesque calumny, without even
a rectification? Debu also passed on to us an anonymous poem,
transmitted to him by the poet Francis Ponge, on the subject of the
ill-famed *Relève* which despatched French workmen to work in
German factories.

> *Les wagons s'attelant*
> *trinquent avec l'enfer.*[1]

I would add one of my own poems, also anonymously, and contribute a short novella too, which I would sign *Santerre* instead of
Vercors, in order to make us look more numerous . . .

All this might add up to quite an honourable though somewhat
slender volume. Yvonne had to journey to the former free zone
once again in January—the total occupation of France had at least
the advantage of facilitating travel throughout the country, though
in exchange the trains were under close surveillance. At a meeting
of the recently formed National Committee of Writers, Paulhan
had entrusted her with a letter addressed to the aged philosopher,
Julien Benda, who had retired to Carcassonne. She dropped him
a line from Toulouse, requesting him to be on the station platform
at the passing of her train. She did indeed find there a little man
with a perfectly round face and white hair combed in a funny

[1]'The coupled wagons/clink glasses with hell.'

fringe down to his eyebrows. Would she have time first to explain things to him, then to persuade him, and all this in less than five minutes? The wizened philosopher perused the letter, skimmed through our manifesto, approved it and promised his collaboration without further waste of time. With the result that, at the end of three minutes, they had nothing more to say to each other and actually found the time dragging until the train's departure . . .

Suzanne Paraf was the one who brought us Julien Benda's text when she came up to Paris a few weeks later. It turned out to be an essay of chilly, dry humour on the German nation, under the title *Uriel's Report*, and was to appear under the pen-name of Comminge. (It was Yvonne's suggestion that all authors' names, following my own example, should be those of French provinces, an idea which we were to adopt throughout.) We had also hopes of receiving from that brilliant young writer, Jean Prévost, who had gone to live in Grenoble and was to meet with a hero's death in the Vercors, a scathing indictment against a celebrated author who was befouling himself by his submission to the conqueror, and who is still alive today, adulated and honoured. However, the expected text did not reach us and we had to go to press without it. The third volume of the Editions de Minuit, such as it was, was typeset by Maurice Roulois, near the church of Montrouge.

Pierre Massé's absence and the defection of my *guerrillero* obliged me once again to resort to my bicycle for transport. Which weighs more, 40 kilograms of paper or 40 kilograms of metal type? To judge by my tyres, the metal wins by a long shot: with a mighty explosion, the inner rear tube gave up the ghost just opposite the statue of the Lion of Belfort. Rather shaken, I clattered past the traffic cop in a din of clanking metal with the most dignified and casual air I could muster. I managed to keep my balance until I had reached the Avenue Denfert-Rochereau and finished the journey pushing the bike, a bit exhausted but without any further incident.

I was not bound for Oudeville's shop. Apart from his too danger-ous link with Roulois, the printing delays were too long. Good old Aulard had meanwhile organized himself for the job: he would print our stuff himself on Sundays behind closed shutters, with the sole aid of Pierre Doré, his foreman, and an absolutely reliable old compositor. In the evening all the used paper would be burnt and on Monday morning the rest of the staff would have no inkling. He had admirably calculated his timetable, and one Sunday in March, at 8 a.m. I attended the 'make-ready' of the *Chroniques Interdites*, 'The Forbidden Chronicles', on his largest press, able to run off thirty-two pages at one go. No hitch. I left and returned in the evening at the same hour. Everything was ready. The rate of printing, moreover, was such that it would permit fifteen hundred copies of every book to be printed, which meant three or four times more than had been possible for *Le Silence* and the Maritain.

But how on earth were we going to transport them to Yvonne's place for stitching, and return the type to Roulois, all in one evening and with a single bicycle? And how were we to distribute fifteen hundred copies, when the job of distributing three hundred and fifty had already been none too easy? We should have been obliged to forgo the chance of printing this quantity if, in the meantime, I had not had an encounter of the utmost usefulness.

At sunset one evening in the previous autumn, as I was coming out of the underground station at Sèvres-Babylone, I noticed outside the Kodak shop at the corner of the Boulevard a man examining the window-display. His back had a familiar look, I waited till he turned round. It was Jacques Lecompte-Boinet, General Mangin's son-in-law. It will be remembered that, shortly after the defeat of France, he and his wife Francette had come up to see me at a friend's flat for the sole purpose of hearing me confirm their own feelings about Laval and Pétain. He flung himself on me, we shook hands, and in a mysterious but voluble tone of voice he informed me, without delay and without bothering to sound me out further, that he was now 'in it up to the ears'.

And he went on to explain that the object over there, in the shop-window, was the code sign indicating that the way was clear and that the rendezvous in Rue du Four was on . . . And to apologize for being unable to take me along, the meeting being top secret . . . . It was my first experience of the excessive talkativeness that was so current in the French networks, in flagrant contrast with the rules of the Intelligence Service which Lescure had imposed on me. With the result that this prompt confidence struck me as so fool-hardy that I had some doubts about his business being serious. 'We must see each other,' he said. I dared not refuse, we fixed a date, and did indeed meet in a small café near Saint-Augustin, on the corner of Rue de Rigny, which was to become our habitual rendezvous. For a long time I let him do all the talking, being little inclined to confide my own occupations to this too-likeable chatterbox. About his own work he gave me countless details of which I should have preferred to remain ignorant, but which obliged me to admit that they knocked a breach in my previous incredulity. Besides, I noticed that his indiscretions were not as uncontrolled as they had seemed at first sight, for in the end I had learned no name or address, merely pseudonyms, and in fact most of his high-spirited talk concerned his own tragi-comical adventures.

Under the assumed name of Mathieu he had found himself one day, without really meaning to, at the head of a network called *Ceux de la Résistance* ('Those of the Resistance movement'), which had succeeded a group in the North created for the purpose of extending the southern movement '*Combat*'. After a series of arrests, all that remained of the original team was himself and one other; and eventually he remained all alone. With the help of three friends, whom he christened Lebreton, Charpentier and Vaillant, he went about reconstituting the movement, extending it especially in Normandy and in the East, which were now again almost entirely under his control, and where he disposed of military groups as well as of an intelligence network. Apart from these, he controlled some combat groups in the Paris suburbs of Poissy, Aubervilliers and in the 7th arrondissement. But he had no newspaper of his own and was looking for a printer.

I felt a little guilty at my over-long prudence and took the plunge. 'One good turn deserves another,' I said. 'I can help you find a printer. Will you give me a hand with my publishing?' He jerked away from me on the bench on which we were sitting, with that way he had of staring you up and down when he was surprised.

'What publishing? The *Editions de Minuit*?'

'Ah, you know about them?'

'Why! So that's you?' he cried. 'You're a sly one! But I should have guessed, of course! Come on,' he said, getting up. 'Come along, you must tell me about it.'

We walked out of the café. At the Métro he pulled me back. 'No, no! let's walk. Down there it's teeming with inquisitive fellows

who search you when you come out . . . ' Heavens, how he made me
trot! It was not to be the last time, either. And every time it wore
me out, and increased my headache which I could have done without. But I knew he was right, that the Métro was an unhealthy
place for people like him. On Boulevard Haussmann he said all of
a sudden:

'I say, in that case you must know who that fellow Vercors is?'

'You don't know him. Besides, in any case . . . '

'That's true, you'd have no right to. What do you think of his
Silence?'

'Why? Don't you like it?'

'Personally I do, but lots of people object that his German is
too decent.'

'Never mind. They'll understand later. Have you read the
Maritain?'

'Not yet. But tell me, why does the printer's end-note say:
"published under Nazi occupation"? Why "Nazi", and not German? This distinction makes people uneasy.'

'Ah! That's because I'm still trying to believe that the German
soul, the old Germany of Kant and the Humanists has not yet been
entirely engulfed in the Nazi maelstrom. That deep down it is still
holding out and that we'll find it alive some day. So what I'm
trying to show is that we are still making a difference between
the two, and shall go on making it as long as it proves possible.
That we don't wage this war as one power against another, still
less as one people against another, but that for us it is a war of the
spirit against the crimes of oppression.'

'I wonder if you're right. The "good Germany" no longer exists.
Anyhow, good or bad, it's Germany we must smash for a start.'

'Of course. But suppose I receive a manuscript from, say, Thomas
Mann or Bertolt Brecht, in short from a German exile? I want to
be able to use the same formula. Now, wouldn't "German occupation" be rather embarrassing, even cruel for them?'

'That's not our fault! But forget it. Have you something in the
press at the moment?'

'A volume of essays. And that's the point: we are short of people
to help with transport, distribution. Couldn't you now and then
lend me two or three men from your group?'

'What will they have to do?'

I explained my problems. Transport the metal first, then the parcels; afterwards distribute the stuff. We walked and walked, I was dragging my bad leg. By the time we had reached his destination, we had been able to settle the ways and means by which the indispensable break of connections was ensured between the various agents. As for the day-to-day details that might crop up, we would meet at regular intervals in the same pub.

I left him knock-kneed but with the feeling that henceforward, short of some serious hitch, I should have unlimited means at the disposal of my business. We were about to emerge from the handicraft stage.

VII

The beginning turned out to be less auspicious than expected. First, the chap who ought to have collected the type from Roulois, stood us up, and so I had to transport it myself. As against this, the parcels of the *Forbidden Chronicles*, removed from Aulard's press on Sunday night on a hand-barrow which, as arranged, was left under an archway on the near-by Place Lucien Herr, were taken away at dawn next morning after curfew and duly found on their cart at the appointed hour at the corner of Rue Vineuse, whence Yvonne and I took them up to her flat. Nobody had seen anybody, the whole thing was perfectly anonymous. The new stitchers in Yvonne's 'bindery' worked at the double (and so did I in the kitchen, where I pasted the covers with Suzanne Paraf, while she roundly criticized *Le Silence de la Mer* with its 'silly little prude of a niece', whom I was ill-placed to defend . . .). In a fortnight the volumes were ready; one part would be distributed by our own means, as before; the other entrusted to Lecompte-Boinet's network, where it would be further subdivided, part in his own ranks, part in other resistance groups with which he was in touch.

I passed him the suitcase in a *café-tabac* facing the Palace of Chaillot, where his contact man would pick it up. Thereafter I had no news. The man had vanished. And Mathieu was obliged to inform me that the fellow had got himself nabbed while on an assignment. The suitcase? Parked in his room no doubt, but the hotel was watched day and night. It was impossible to lay hands on the case for a long while, till one day another of the lads boldly walked up to the hotel-room, found the case there, and brought it back. This was a lesson for us: no more suitcases from now on; we must divide the risk into several packages. Unfortunately, this did not always prove practicable.

The fact was that all clandestine action was getting more complicated, more hazardous, from day to day. The sinister Darnand had been appointed Secretary in charge of Public Order, the whole of the French police was placed under the domination of the Milice which out-gestapoed the Gestapo, both in efficiency and savagery. Apart from chasing Resistance fighters, it also tracked down French art treasures on Germany's account. Private art collections were looted, those belonging to Jewish owners first, of course. Abel Bonnard, the new Minister of Education, even planned to deliver up to Goering, to Goebbels, certain masterpieces of our museums as he had already done with the nineteen panels of the *Mystical Lamb*, which the city of Ghent had entrusted to France. One day at the Deux-Magots I ran into a former comrade from my regiment, Germain Bazin, since become a curator. He told me about the salvage action from the Louvre and the provincial museums: how Huyghe, Jaujard, himself and some others, in face of the Minister's felony, had secretly removed the masterpieces coveted by the Occupant to the cellars of châteaux situated in Lot and in Dordogne. The *Mona Lisa* alone had changed her *maquis* three times already, passing from Chambord to Louvigny, from Louvigny to Montauban, from there to a place in Aveyron. . . .

I listened to his account one February day in the company of Pierre de Lescure, who had returned for a brief stay before disappearing for a second time. I am afraid that it was during this period that the first seeds were sown of the misunderstandings that were to grow later into a serious rift, which, by parting us, caused me one of the great sorrows of my life. Deep inside me, I reproached him a little sadly with lacking confidence in me, as evinced by the care he had taken to abandon me without prior notice, without a contact and without leaving me an address. But it is one of my weaknesses that I am loath to remonstrate with people I am fond of, to 'have things out with them', and I prefer to let bygones be bygones. It is a weakness, I say, for it does happen that a friend will repeat the same offence more than once with an easy conscience, and thus unwittingly undermine my equanimity, force me to put my foot down at last and become angry, with the result that we may fall out for good, when a friendly warning in time might have prevented this. So I left Lescure in ignorance of the little grudge I bore him for his cavalier silence of almost a year, on my own account and for *Le Silence de la Mer*, as well as for our publishing business. He, on the contrary, let me feel that he was piqued at my failure to wait for his return and consent before circulating my story against his orders, and before compiling the volume of the

Chronicles. He did not say so openly; but one evening, as we were dining together at Bellanger's place with Debu-Bridel, he half hinted at it. The talk had turned on an important subsidy (50,000 francs) which had been offered to me some weeks before, through an intermediary, by one of the leaders of the *Organisation Civile et Militaire.* The condition attached to the offer was that, instead of the mention 'printed at the expense of a patriotic book-lover', the printer's note should state in future: 'at the expense of the *O.C.M.*' I had told Bellanger to transmit the reply that I would gladly accept the subsidy but rejected the condition, since it would put us under the allegiance of a single sector of the Resistance, and I had heard no more about it . . . . So when Bellanger had referred to the matter at dinner, Lescure retorted, putting some emphasis on the adverb: 'On this particular point, I *fortunately* happen to be in agreement with Desvignes,' which let me more than guess what he felt about the other points that I had had to decide without him.

This little incident apart, the dinner passed off in high spirits. Stalingrad had just fallen entirely into the hands of the Russians, Field-Marshal Paulus had surrendered with fifteen generals, one hundred thousand men, enormous war material. Four days of mourning had been decreed by Hitler (how well we understood him!) and Bellanger was celebrating the capture of Rostov and Kharkov with a magnificent dish of cabbage and cold meat when, crash! the dish came to pieces in his hands, spilling its contents all over the tablecloth. We all had a good laugh, but Debu afterwards confessed to me, when Bellanger was arrested in March, that he had seen it as an evil omen.

At about the same time, Yvonne Paraf also encountered a pretty sticky moment. Before the war, she had worked for a Franco-British company, now dormant of course, but Yvonne still dropped in occasionally to see a former colleague there. On her last visit she had been warned that the *Abwehr* had raided the offices the day before, taken down the addresses of the entire former staff, with Yvonne's name at the head of the list. If the *Abwehr* were to poke their noses into her flat, they would find some thousand copies of the *Forbidden Chronicles* in process of being bound, stacked all over the floor, the furniture and on the cupboard-tops. . . .

Down in my country-retreat I was unaware of all this, working away at my *Hamlet* in blissful ignorance. When I went up to Paris on the following Thursday as usual, I rang Yvonne at the arranged time. No answer. Perturbed, I telephoned Léon Motchane. Yes, he told me, Yvonne was at his place; they were expecting me. His voice had been odd, a little chilly and peeved. And it was a chilly and peeved Léon who opened the door to me. It must be said that, from the outset, I had made Yvonne promise that she would not take Léon into her confidence any more than I had taken my mother or my wife into mine. He therefore had no idea of our business when she had urgently called him to the rescue. Together with her, he transported the *Chronicles* to various safe places, but felt outraged that we should have kept things from him for so long. Was he not particularly well placed to render us all kinds of services? This was true, for he had widespread connections, was in contact with the American services through Switzerland and Sweden and was moreover in touch with a German officer at the Hôtel Majestic who was secretly opposed to Hitler: Léon had thus been able, during the whole of the war, to supply the Allies with valuable information, and for us too he had been a source of news, often giving us advance notice of events. Moreover, he now effectively helped us to improve our distribution and, under the name of Thimerais, he gave us a piece of writing entitled *The Patient Thought*, in which he dealt with the future of France and the world after victory. This contained many forecasts and intuitive guesses which events subsequently confirmed.

The *Forbidden Chronicles* came out on April 10th and—at last, at last!—Paulhan was able to hand Yvonne two manuscripts during a meeting of the Comité National des Ecrivains. She read them that same night, and gave them to me to read the next day. The first was *Les Amants d'Avignon* ('The Lovers of Avignon') by Elsa Triolet, which I liked—and so did Yvonne—for its vitality, finesse and warmth of feeling. The second manuscript, somewhat spoiled by platitudes, left us hesitant. However, since Lescure was back, the decision lay with him. I had no doubt what it would be. His choice dumbfounded me. The fact that he warmly approved the text which had disappointed us was rather in the nature of a pleasant surprise, but when he flatly turned down Elsa Triolet's fine tale, I was struck with amazement. I tried to plead in its favour, but he cut me short with a smile and said I had been too much subject to Yvonne's influence. On various occasions already I had sensed his hostility towards her, but this time I had the painful impression that, in making this surprising choice, he was actually violating his true opinion and fairness itself in order to make me feel the weight of his authority. Being on the point of rejoining the maquis once more, he appointed his deputy: the great poet Paul Eluard. This meant openly putting a guardian over my head. I nevertheless welcomed this particular one with joy, and so did Yvonne. We had never met Eluard but had the greatest admiration for his poetry. When Lescure had gone, Eluard wished to form his own opinion of *Les Amants d'Avignon* discarded by Lescure. His reaction was the one I had expected: 'To be published forthwith.' But I was saddened that for the first time I had seen Lescure, for a momentary whim, abandon the virtues he had taught me to prize.

It might appear from the foregoing that relations between us had become somewhat strained. Actually, everything so far had been said or done under the cloak of friendship—one might even say of affection, some sort of lover's spite. I remember one day, when we were walking across the Place du Châtelet, telling him of a remark that had come to my ears: Marcel Arland, the noted critic, did not believe that the author of *The Silence of the Sea* was a professional writer. 'You see, it shows through,' I said, and Lescure had been fervently eager to reassure me. More than that: when I related to him, in the Luxembourg Gardens, what my mother, whom I had meanwhile questioned, had revealed to me about my father's youth, his arrival in France at the age of sixteen to find— just like Alexandre Dumas's Gilbert and in his footsteps—equality liberty and fraternity, he urged me to write the story of his life. 'You owe it to his memory,' he said. So it was thanks to him again to his encouragement, one might even say his imperious demand that some time later I got down to drafting *La Marche à l'Etoile* ('The Guiding Star'). And even my *Hamlet* illustrations, the first of which were just then making me sweat and slave, may possibly be indebted to him for what quality they have. I was struggling along, full of self-doubts, and eventually showed my drawings to Lescure to get his verdict. It was blistering: I had completely 'missed the mark', they were fit only for the waste-paper basket!

All except one. But that one, he said, was great; it would show me the way. My bewilderment may be imagined: four months of work for the garbage-heap! His severity at least guaranteed the quality of the one that had been spared. I started afresh from that basis. Three weeks later he 'couldn't believe his eyes', he said: it was altogether a different artist! For the last time he manifested an excitement and joy equal to mine.

However, he went back to his hideout in the Jura mountains, leaving me once more without any news; and when, after sharing the life of the *maquisards* for eighteen months without putting aside the novel he was engaged on, he returned after Liberation, I found a man I hardly recognized: vengeful, merciless, implacable, ready to declare anyone who had committed the slightest error fit to be shot; and when I showed myself less relentless and did not measure all the 'sinners' by the same yardstick, he would needle me with barbs and darts that were only slightly blunted by the quizzical smile that played on his rectangular mouth when he remarked to Debu-Bridel: 'At lunch today, I once again gave Vercors much pain . . . ' I took it lying down and I was wrong: far from preventing the split, I only provoked him to tear it open more violently.

Today I wonder if the first crack did not appear on a certain evening when I was seeing him home at curfew-time, after we had been to see Musset's *Lorenzaccio* performed by Marguerite Jamois. To be frank, I had been distracted all through the play by the presence of some uniformed officers in the stalls. This was because I was still shaken by a scene I had witnessed, though I had played no part in it, on my way in the Métro.

I was standing near the carriage-door. Opposite me stood a man in the uniform of the Waffen-SS. When the train stopped, a very young lad, almost a boy, had got on. What did he do? I don't know, I didn't see it. But the next second the SS. man's fist cracked down on his jaw, splitting his lip. And while the boy was wiping the blood off with his handkerchief, silently and fearfully, the brute heaped on him a shower of threats and abuse. And I? I just stood there. I did nothing, said nothing. Nobody in the carriage said anything, did anything. For there were other Germans right there watching us, one hand already on their revolver-holsters. If there had been a fight, we all knew that the upshot would be the firing-squad, and for the boy even more surely than for the rest of us.

So this smack in the jaw which I had not received but had not returned either still racked me with pain and humiliation as I sat in my seat at the Montparnasse Theatre; and it went on throbbing as we walked through the deserted streets towards Lescure's flat, while he was telling me of his hopeful expectations: Marguerite Jamois had read a play of his which I greatly liked myself. Its title was *Julma*. It was a poetic piece set in the mist of Flanders, about two lonely creatures' unavailing search for each other; for while the man is dying of his loneliness, Julma knows she would be unable to survive the loss of her own solitude. Lescure seemed much elated as he told me that Jamois seemed willing to produce the play in which she herself would play Julma.

'After the war, of course?' I asked.

'Why no, this season.'

I registered the blow.

'But, Pierre, that's impossible!' I objected. 'What about your silence? You wouldn't publish a book, would you?'

'That's not the same thing . . . '

'To me it seems worse: there will be Germans in the theatre, SS. officers, Pierre—torturers! Are you going to play for them?'

He smiled, but I thought I detected a note of irritation in his voice.

'That's not the right way to look at it. But we'll discuss it some other time.'

And the next moment he had disappeared behind the heavy door of his house. I was disconcerted, ill at ease. Perhaps, without that crack of the fist in the Métro, I should not have reacted the same way. But I also reflected that there was no longer a single Jewish actor in Jamois's company, perhaps she had not been able to act otherwise if she wanted to keep her theatre, but all the same . . . Yes, this certainly needed discussing, the decision was far too important.

But he did not give me a chance, never mentioned the matter again. In any case the play was not produced, and he had to return to his hideout. Nevertheless, I am afraid that my reaction, the reprimand I seemed to give him, may have left him secretly wounded and resentful. For it was after that night that he began to harry me with his more or less barbed darts. But it may also be that I am barking up the wrong tree, and that the fact he never mentioned

Julma again was due to his lack of genuine interest in this plan and, consequently, in my remarks about it.

In March, a year after the publication of *Le Silence de la Mer*, I was still voicing my anxiety about the lack of manuscripts to Lebourg; but a complete change came about in April. It was as if *Les Amants d'Avignon* had thrown open a door which was never to close again. Lebourg informed me in May that Eluard was expecting my visit in order to hand me an anthology of clandestine poems which he had compiled. I was received in his flat in Rue de la Chapelle, which has since been re-named Rue Marx-Dormoy (after the Socialist M.P., murdered by a gang of former Cagoulards—right-wing terrorists—in the very place assigned to him by Pétain as a forced residence). In the tiny apartment, books, paintings, strange curios jostled each other in a veritable bric-à-brac museum of art in the inter-war years. No less unusual seemed to me his wife, Nusch. Her face, under her frizzy mop of hair, had the fine, sharp features of Colette's in her young days. And with Colette, too, she shared a fruity accent—although hers stemmed from the eastern regions, and not from Burgundy. But her body was thin as a wire, and her limbs elongated. She wore beach-pyjamas with bell-bottom trousers, and gripped a cigarette-holder of astonishing length between her teeth.

This apparition, straight out of the 'Twenties, invited me to sit down while Eluard was finishing a telephone conversation. This was the first time I saw the poet. Goodness knows why the name 'Eluard' had always conjured up in me the vision of a very 'proper' young man, a trifle sickly, with a wan face and rather indistinct features. The man sitting by the telephone, on the contrary, had a well-knit frame, a seraph's face which age had filled out a little but which still retained a striking beauty. His free hand shook a little when it moved—a sequel of the First World War—it fluttered and came to rest again with wing-like tremors. I introduced myself under the name of Desvignes. We sat down at a table piled high with papers. We had to cast off the poems so that they would not exceed ninety-six pages, which was the maximum that could be run off the press in one day. When the cast-off was done, we found there was plenty of space; so, emboldened I slipped in two extras, one by Pierre Massé, the other by myself, though of course I did not tell him so. He read them and approved. Phew! There still remained the task of finding pseudonyms—some thirty of them—for all those unsigned poems. He invented them all within the hour. I found myself the richer by one more name: Roland Dolée. I took the manuscripts with me when I left him to pass them to Roulois, and was to bring him back the proofs the following week.

I don't remember what prevented me from keeping the appointment and made me send Yvonne instead. The prospect thrilled her. She found Eluard surrounded by other poets—Hugnet, Frénaud, Jean Lescure (no connection with his namesake), Lucien Scheler, Jean Tardieu . . . She must have stammered something about being sent by me as she stood on the doorstep. Anyhow, Eluard announced as he showed her in: 'This is Madame Desvignes.' Still flustered and caught unawares, she failed to protest; the name got around and so, in the eyes of many Resisters, we were officially bound in wedlock, in spite of our protests and denials, for the rest of the war.

Eluard, in compiling his anthology, had wished to stress how far the French poets, under the shock of disaster, had travelled from their previous dedication to 'Art for Art's sake' (or, as one would say in today's jargon, poetry talking to itself), and to demonstrate that spiritual purity no longer implied, as once it had, non-involvement in things temporal and perishable, but demanded on the contrary that poets must once again revolt against and expose evil, since it was threatening man in his very essence. This is why he had entitled the volume *L'Honneur des Poètes*—'The Poets' Honour'.

> *Puisque les morts ne peuvent plus se taire,*
> *Est-ce aux vivants à garder leur silence?*[1]

—thus cried Jean Tardieu in the opening pages. And each poet after him loudly proclaimed that his honour lay in expressing rage, pain, passion and hope. Ten thousand kilometres away, another poet, a friend of Eluard's, who had fled to Panama, considered that this return to worldly affairs outraged his Surrealist creed, and he published a pamphlet which he called 'The Poets' Dishonour'. His name was Benjamin Péret. In his eyes, for poetry to descend to topical events instead of *transcending* them was a fall from grace.

[1] 'Since the dead can no longer be silenced,
Are the living entitled to keep their mouths shut?'

Had I not harboured somewhat similar feelings a few years earlier? And even in creating the Editions de Minuit, had I not been prompted by the same concern to transcend the cataclysm in order to attain clear, dispassionate thought—'to think straight'? And yet, in the present dispute, I sided unreservedly with Eluard; I thought as he did that a poet's honour no longer resided in his being true to his former solitude and detachment, but in going back to his people who were exposed to suffering and martyrdom. And indeed it was in reply to myself just as much as to Benjamin Péret that I set out to write, a little later, a short novella entitled *Les Mots* ('The Words'). It showed a poet living just outside a little village chosen for its isolation, and maintaining there, despite the Occupation—just as Péret would have liked him to—that precious detachment necessary for penning his solitary poems. And he does maintain it until the day when he becomes the horrified witness of the savage destruction of the village with all its inhabitants whom he loves: the men mown down, the women and children burnt in the village church before his eyes. At this sight, he too 'dishonours' himself: he can no longer do otherwise than scream his horror, his hatred, his despair. Words of vengeance surge up and overwhelm him, and all the time he keeps thinking that perhaps just one kilometre would have made all the difference: one single kilometre away, he would have seen nothing, heard nothing, but would have gone on serenely composing his poems dedicated to Words; he would have continued to despise the 'betrayal' of those who, just as he had now done, sacrificed transcendency and lofty indifference to some derisory spurt of indignation . . . . How could Péret be expected to understand under Panama's blue sky, ten thousand miles away, that if his friends had *not* 'betrayed' their former poems when they were scorched by the flaming hell of yellow stars, torture, shootings, gas chambers, they would have felt traitors to more than their art: to the whole of mankind, without whom there is no poetry?

This participation, this communion with the horrors of our times was also the subject of a manuscript which Yvonne triumphantly brought us in the early days of July: *Le Cahier noir* ('The Black Notebook') by François Mauriac. For some time Paulhan and Debu-Bridel had been 'pummelling' him, as one might say, for a piece of writing; and during a fashionable tea-party, behind the back of an Admiral who had opened fire on the troops of the Free French Forces and was boasting about it, Mauriac had promised Lebourg that he would give us a text. Jean Blanzat had informed him one evening: 'Mauriac wants to see you', and the next day Lebourg had dashed to Rue Théophile-Gautier.

It was the hour of the BBC news and, however impatient, he first had to listen, through the jamming devices, to 'The French talking to the French'; then followed the news from various battle-fronts; and then the horrible, heart-rending account of the heroic end of the Warsaw Ghetto and its thirty-five thousand Jewish survivors. After they had watched four hundred thousand of their own people disappear, in one transport after another, they had sworn that they would resist to the last drop of blood. And in order to smash their resistance, the Germans had been compelled to resort to artillery and aviation which had annihilated the ghetto with iron and fire. And when all had died under the rubble, the infuriated Germans had gone on to crush the ruins with sledge-hammers and bulldozers until nothing was left standing over an area as large as a district of Paris, and there remained only a mountain of pulverized dust.

When the speaker had finished, and after a pause in which grief and horror battled with helpless rage in the listeners' breasts, Mauriac began to read aloud, in that hoarse, passionate croak which moves an audience far more than a melodious voice, the stirring text of his *Cahier Noir*, which was to be one of the highlights of our publications. For safety's sake, Lebourg advised him to cover up certain too-revealing details by which fellow-writers in the pay of the Germans might identify him. A superfluous precaution, for nobody failed to spot the author of those pages by the nobility of his style and thought, and his name soon flew from mouth to mouth. Mauriac had to live in retirement for a while and wait for things to blow over.

However, the manuscript had first to be retyped at his flat, and it was agreed that Lebourg would come to collect the type-script. But no sooner had it been typed out than Mauriac received the visit of an unknown lady, who brought him a copy of *The Poets' Honour*. They talked of Debu-Bridel whom she claimed to know, and so, for the sake of convenience, Mauriac handed her his typescript. But the moment she had left, he sent an urgent message to Lebourg.

'I have been frightfully imprudent. Suppose it was a Gestapo snare? I mentioned your name . . . .'

The lady, as will have been guessed, was Yvonne, but right up to the moment when she handed us the typescript of *Le Cahier Noir* the two men were weighed down by misgivings. This trifling incident illustrates the state of perpetual worry we lived in for four years. Each night we chided ourselves for some imprudent step or word that might have compromised a friend; in the daytime, we avoided as much as possible the Métro, cafés, theatres; carefully weighed each word we uttered in public places or on the telephone. This was not really a hardship: it had become second nature. But looking back on it now after twenty years, it seems to me almost unreal.

My life, in any case, had become that of a split personality: when I was at home in Villiers, I would forget everything else and live immersed in rural tranquillity. My former employer, the village carpenter, came to see me to complain of my successor, a young fellow slow in the uptake. Ah, if only I'd agree to come back, he would pay me twelve francs fifty per hour! (That was four times more than I had been earning when I left him.) I had to plead my bad health, show him the *Hamlet* etchings I was engaged on. But what a testimonial! I would have looked down my nose at a king . . . This was not his only worry. For that clumsy companion of his was at least better than nothing, yet there was a risk that he too might be taken away. Laval's *Relève*—the exchange of voluntary workmen for POW's—had misfired, so now workers were being deported by force for work in Germany under the label of the *S.T.O.*—*Service du travail obligatoire* (Compulsory Labour Service). The cobbler was removed from his bench, the salesman from his counter, the undergraduate from his desk, a passer-by was high-jacked at a street-corner, another at the exit of a cinema. Men with specialized skills were rounded up and despatched pell-mell to Germany. However, after the first shock of surprise, it proved increasingly difficult to catch the bird in his nest. All the young who felt they were in danger made for the *maquis*. With this new intake, the Resistance movement grew from month to month. The Germans revenged themselves by tightening our belts a little more every day. On the radio, their spokesman Dr Schmidt addressed himself to the French people, laying the blame for their near-starvation at their own door and declaring that if they wanted more fats, all they had to do was grow poppy-seed for oil!

During that month of July we published in quick succession our fourth volume, *The Poets' Honour*, and the reprint of *The Silence of the Sea*, to satisfy the demand of the deprived Parisians. The former bore the date of the National Holiday (July 14th), the latter that of July 25th, 'the day of the overthrow of Rome's tyrant' (after Sicily had fallen to the Allies, the King had summoned Mussolini and had him thrown in gaol. Badoglio was said to be bargaining for capitulation—which seemed to be a speciality of field-marshals . . .).

In Paris practically nobody had as yet read *Le Silence de la Mer* but everybody was talking about it, mixing up fiction and fact. That is what usually happens to myths. One Sunday, Robert Ganzo came to see us in Villiers. A perfectly harmless visit since, a fervent trout-angler, he had come to borrow *Paludes*, the canoe I had built myself. But the talk under the shade of the big apple-tree naturally centred mostly on Resistance and collaboration and all the latest news and rumours. Under the seal of secrecy he informed me of the existence of a clandestine publishing-house and of its publication of a masterpiece by Roger Martin du Gard. 'It's called *Vercors*—an extraordinarily moving story. Someone's going to lend it to me, I'll pass it on to you.' My wife, who was pouring tea for us, told us in strict confidence: 'The Editions de Minuit are in fact Gallimard.' Ganzo made a sceptical grimace. 'Do you really think so?'—'That's what everyone says!' I thought to myself that Paulhan must have been shooting his mouth off. I congratulated myself on never having met him and on obeying Lescure's injunctions on this point. But I also thought that we should have to scotch that particular rumour.

Nevertheless, I never dreamed that this budding fame which Paris was beginning to talk of, might already have spread beyond the city gates, much less beyond the bars of captive France. One evening just like any other, in my bed in Villiers, trying as usual to catch above the jamming noise the deep, slightly declamatory voice of 'General de Gaulle's spokesman'—nobody knew at the time that it was Maurice Schumann—I was listening a little absent-

mindedly as he spoke of the clandestine press, the ever more
numerous newspapers circulated by the Resistance, when I suddenly
pricked up my ears: 'But tracts and pamphlets are not enough,'
he was saying, 'if France is to remain alive. Products of the mind are
needed, books above all. And I am turning to you, Vercors, still
unknown and already famous . . . '

I did not catch the rest very well. My ears were buzzing. So *Le
Silence de la Mer* had got out of France, crossed the Channel, probably been reprinted in London, perhaps in America . . . And there
was I, all alone in bed, on a hilltop above the village asleep in
the dark, hearing myself addressed through the prison-walls by the
representative of General de Gaulle! . . . I did not know that Claude
Bellanger had given a copy to Yvon Morandat who had taken it
with him one moonlit night on the plane which, all lights exting-
uished, had come from England to fetch him; nor that the person
who had ordered the volume to be reprinted in London was the
chief of Free France. Neither did I know that my story had already
been republished in Algeria, in Senegal, in Australia, Switzerland,
Quebec, Beirut . . . On another day, going into the garden early
in the morning, still in pyjamas, I found in the meadow a miniature booklet on bible paper, still damp with dew. It was one of
the millions dropped by the RAF all over France on certain nights,
and this one was a reprint of my tale. With a printer's error on the
title-page! The title appeared as *Les Silences de la Mer*, in the plural,
an error that was to be repeated in the New York edition. In Tunis,
the novelist Pierre Moinot, having only the English version by
Cyril Connolly at hand, re-translated it himself into French in
order to circulate it. When many years later he came upon this
counterfeit version, he let me read it out of curiosity. It was amaz-
ingly close to the original, an exploit which redounds to the honours
of the two *traduttori* who, in this instance, proved to be no *traditori*
at all . . .

But I was still quite unaware of all this to-do about my story
and our press when, after a month spent in the family circle near
Saintes, in the south-west, there suddenly descended upon us such
an abundance of material that, after beating the bushes in vain for
a year—we were now faced with a terrible bottleneck.

Roulois and Aulard presented no difficulties, but when it came
to transport, binding, storage and distribution, we were at our

wits' end. All these problems clamoured for urgent solutions. The fact was that, within less than a month, we had produced *The Poets' Honour*, the re-issue of *The Silence of the Sea* and Mauriac's *Black Notebook* under the name of Forez. And simultaneously we had received, after *The Lover of Avignon*, Léon Motchane's *Patient Thought, England* by Debu-Bridel, *The Grévin Museum* by Aragon, Edith Thomas's *Stories*, and *An Ode to France* by Charles Morgan, which had reached us from London by mysterious channels and which, in turn, was closely followed by André Gide's *Pages of a Diary* all the way from Tunis. Claude Bellanger had miraculously managed to get out of gaol, thanks to his knowledge of German, but being under close watch at his office, he preferred to hand me his memories from a prison-cell on a bench in the Luxembourg Gardens, after we had indulged for fully five minutes in a sort of preliminary spider-dance destined to make sure that he was not being followed. Until September, Pierre Massé's car had been of inestimable help to us, and more than once some venerable company chairman or managing director had ridden in it never guessing that his feet were resting on dynamite in the shape of metal-type or printed sheets. But in October our friend, ill once more, had to go to the mountains for his health, and his departure at the same stroke deprived us of his wife, who was badly missed by the stitchers. The latter soon presented us with our problem number one: however zealously a few dedicated ladies might stitch, they could no longer keep up with the printing pace, and stocks were accumulating dangerously in Yvonne's small flat.

One of Paulette Humbert's friends offered us the built-in cupboards in her flat close to Aulard's press (of which she had no knowledge, of course), but even this was not enough. Then I heard of a vacant room not far from my mother's, in an ancient house in our old Rue Servandoni. Yvonne went to have a look, was received by a fat concierge, her face ravaged by a horrible lupus, who sent her to the landlord's agent. Yvonne explained to him that she was eking out a living by a little black market in cosmetics on the side, and that she needed a discreet cache for her stock. This room, in which our outlawed literature was hidden for some months, happened to be the same or next to the same where an outlaw named Condorcet[1] as is recalled by a plaque on the front of the

[1]Famous French philosopher and mathematician.

house had hidden during the Reign of Terror in 1793. There are places where the hunted spirit dwells!

This settled the storage problem for a time, but not the stitching one. Once again it was Aulard who saved the situation. He had been looking around for a professional stitcher for some time who might fold and sew our volumes mechanically, but had not found anyone whom he could guarantee as being 'safe'. At last he ferreted out a professional home-worker who worked on his own with his wife and the aid of two small machines. At the first hint from Aulard he had answered, as Aulard himself had done: 'Why . . . here!' His name was Vasseur. He came from Lille whence, at the age of fourteen, he had been deported to Germany from 1915 to 1918. He remembered his tormentors with a vengeance, and enthusiastically agreed to help us.

Yvonne and I went to see him in his small backyard shop in Rue des Fossés Saint-Jacques. It was within a rifle-shot of Rue Tournefort, which was most convenient. The trouble was to make him believe, despite this, that his friend Aulard had merely acted as an intermediary between him and us. It was already quite risky enough that Aulard's neighbours could catch the rumble of his presses in the allegedly closed premises on one Sunday in four, sometimes even one in two. To mislead Vasseur, we would sigh in his presence: 'What a pity the staff is too big at Aulard's for us to print it there!' and we would discuss in front of him the difficulties and dangers of transporting the printed sheets 'all the way from the heart of Montrouge'. He would join in these discussions, suggest the most practical and safest route to follow, and never guessed that the deliveries reached him quite simply from the next street.

There remained the question of distribution, which was still the black spot. It was getting increasingly unsafe to walk around with a suitcase or even a parcel which could be suspected of containing arms, grenades or plastic bombs, for physical attacks and sabotage were multiplying—and at every street-corner, every underground station one risked running into an enemy check-point. I met Mathieu almost every week and he did all he could. But we had to admit that his network's help was not without some inconvenience, both for him and for us. Our transports increased his agents' risk of arrest, as well as our risk of irretrievable losses.

Eventually we decided that he should take charge only of the volumes intended for his own organization, and would put me in touch with the leaders of other groups so that I could make arrangements direct with them.

He therefore introduced me in early September, on a café terrace on Boulevard Saint-Michel, to a youngish man with very blue eyes and a toneless voice who went by the *nom de guerre* of Barrès, and who, Mathieu told me, used to be a member of the extreme right-wing and royalist *Action Française*. I had no idea that I was talking to General Guillain de Bénouville, when the latter said to me almost at once:

'May I ask you a question?'

'Of course.'

'Can you tell me who is Vercors?'

'You know very well I can't.'

'But if I tell you his name?'

'I'd be surprised . . . '

'Is it So-and-so?'

And he mentioned a journalist whom I don't want to pain by quoting his name, and whom I had never heard of at that time.

'Who?' I exclaimed and burst out laughing. He repeated the name, frowning. 'This I *can* answer,' I said. 'It's not him.'

'Are you sure?'

'Absolutely!'

Benouville turned to Mathieu.

'I guessed as much!' he said. 'It's fantastic! Mind you, he doesn't actually say, 'Vercors is me', but when people compliment him on *Le Silence de la Mer*, he replies "How kind of you!" '

'But why do people compliment him on it?' asked Mathieu, who was enjoying himself enormously.

'It all started in Switzerland,' said Barrès. 'One day, the French consul there learned, or rather was informed, that Vercors was among some French internees who were caught illegally crossing the frontier. He went to get him out, and the man they released was So-and-so. He got invited everywhere and was made much of. I believe he even gave a few lectures . . . . What cheek!'

'That's not a bad ploy,' said Mathieu. 'He stands an even chance: outside Desvignes here, nobody knows who Vercors is. If the two of them get bumped off, he can stay Vercors for keeps!'

But I was inconsiderate enough to survive. Perhaps that accounts for the fact that the newspaper *Combat*, on which the wily journalist was working with Camus, was the first daily after the war to knock the reputation of the too-resistant Vercors.

Mathieu also introduced me to Pierre Brossolette, when he was dropped by parachute on a mission in France. I had met him long before with my school-friend Etienne Dennery at a time when they roomed together at the Ecole Normale; in those days he had a long black strand of hair falling over his forehead. I remembered his big nose, but now his hair was cut short, in a crew-cut. He did not seem to recognize me. I learned from him that the French Provisional Government were thinking of offering Vercors the Commissariat of Information. 'They've already made contact,' he added. 'Contact with whom?' He smiled but would not answer. I was in no position to question him more closely. The same 'So-and-so', no doubt? I had not the slightest intention of leaving France and the Editions de Minuit, but still, suppose the rogue were to strut around there . . . No, he wouldn't dare! It would be too easy to expose the fraud.

To me, the publisher Desvignes, Brossolette transmitted the offer of a subsidy. I went to great pains to explain to him why I felt obliged to decline. I don't know if I convinced him of my reasons. In his eyes, one just *couldn't* be a Resister without being an out-and-out Gaullist. I saw him walk across Place de l'Alma and disappear under the trees of Cours-la-Reine. It was soon after this that his plane failed to take off; he tried to reach London in a sailing-boat which capsized, swam back to the shore, was denounced, arrested and tortured. Fearing that he might break down, he threw himself from the fifth floor of the building where he was being held, and jumped to his death.

Those last days of summer were crammed with glad and sad events. On September 3rd, the Allies landed in Calabria. On the 6th, Italy capitulated, her troops surrendered *en masse*, her fleet steamed into Allied ports. On the 12th, Corsica rose in arms and became the first French *département* to regain its freedom. On the 17th, the buffoon of Paris Radio, Jean-Hérold Paquis, made good his week-old promise and, with a sour smile, doffed his hat to the Americans for having managed to hold on to Salerno. The next day, the Eastern front cracked all the way from Smolensk to the Sea of

Azov, the entire German army was in full retreat. In France, however, while resisting workers and farmers blew up transformers and high-tension wires, paralysing war production in Le Creusot and the valley of Briey, a photograph in German magazines showed some of the most famous contemporary artists—Despiau, Derain, Vlaminck, to name only those who are now dead—in travelling-clothes, with luggage at their feet, and surrounded by German officers. A round-up? Alas, it was an organized tour at Hitler's invitation. We registered this fall from grace more in sorrow than in anger. It is always saddening when an artist's character falls short of his artistic achievements. All these exponents of an art which Hitler had called 'degenerate' not so long ago, then went to pay a visit to the sculptor Arno Breker, the Hitler régime's top dispenser of official art, whose brawny giants had made Paris laugh at the 1937 World Exhibition, and for which they could feel nothing but contempt. They invited him to return their courtesy and were actually going to give him a gala reception in Paris.

While they were touring the German towns like a music-hall turn, Yvonne Desvignes made a mysterious rendezvous with me in the small public garden opposite the Pont Sully and the Arsenal Museum, in which stands a ruined wall supposed to be a remnant of the Bastille. There she told me that Aragon and Elsa were in Paris on a very short and naturally secret visit, and that Aragon, whose *Musée Grévin* we had recently received, wished to see me. Eluard had arranged a meeting in a ground-floor flat on Boulevard Morland, quite close by. Since Aragon would meet us under his own name, Yvonne considered that we were in honour bound to drop the mask of our pseudonyms in return. This was contrary to all the rules, especially with a man who was himself up to his ears in underground work, hunted by all the police forces, and had such a well-known face that it constituted a permanent risk. Still, it *would* be rather unchivalrous to withhold one's name when he openly declared his own . . . We knocked on the door according to the agreed code, and Eluard opened it. Aragon was standing near an upright piano, Elsa Triolet was seated in an armchair. Eluard introduced us: 'Monsieur and Madame Desvignes.' I saw Aragon smile and I began to say: 'It would be only right for you to know . . . ' But he raised his hand: '. . . That you are Jean Bruller? We met in 1938, at Jean-Richard's.' Eluard stared at me in surprise, but my surprise was even greater than his: what a memory! That party dated back five years, and we had not exchanged ten words. But I was glad I had listened to Yvonne, since in any case . . . The immediate sequel was less happy. Before authorizing us to publish his text, Aragon wished to clear up a misunderstanding. It concerned *The Lovers of Avignon*. Was it true that Paulhan had at first rejected Elsa's story?

I set out the facts in their true light and exculpated Paulhan. But I was flabbergasted: so the literary scandalmongers, even in the Resistance movement, were busy with their idle gossip, their in-fighting, their little game of stirring up ill-feeling and feuds among writers . . . As a result, Paulhan was suspected of another misdeed: who else would have dared to pencil on the galleys a series of suggested cuts? I swore that those marks were my own doing, and that they had been prompted not by literary criticism— perish the thought of such impertinence! —but by a very vital consideration. It was impossible to run off, on any one Sunday, more than three formes of thirty-two pages, making a total of ninety-six at the outside. The story, however, contained over a hundred. Ought I, for the sake of five or six pages, to endanger the printer's safety for another Sunday? If Elsa agreed to the suggested cuts—the least essential paragraphs—that much time would be saved . . . . Was she convinced? Anyhow, she accepted my explanations and left us her piece which she had been on the point of withdrawing. Aragon confirmed his consent for his own text and even promised us another manuscript. All was well that ended well.

The following day, Mathieu informed me that he was leaving for London. We were to meet as usual in the little café near Saint-Augustin, but when I pushed the door open, I understood at once that something was amiss. Mathieu looked up and promptly lowered his head again over his newspaper. A man in a raincoat was sitting near-by, smoking and idly blowing rings while watching Mathieu. I sat down at a third table, ordered black coffee (of roasted acorns) and some notepaper. The customer got up and went inside to telephone. Mathieu calmly left his seat, passed by me without a glance, and walked slowly up the boulevard. I waited for the man's return, felt his gaze upon me as I wrote a note, sealed the envelope, drank my coffee. He rubbed his nose with an air of uncertainty. I called the waiter, paid, waited for my change and then unhurriedly walked away in the opposite direction. A little way away I stopped, turned round: I was not being followed. I retraced my steps; the man in the raincoat was still sitting there. I walked on up the boulevard. Footsteps behind caught up with me. It was Mathieu. He crossed to the opposite pavement and, each on his side of the road, we walked towards the square. He went into the Brasserie of the Military Circle, practically plumb below the swastika banner, while I walked round the block before following him into the café. He smiled. I sat down next to him and said: 'Do you think that. . . ?'

'I don't know. I don't like the smell of it. There's been a wave of arrests. My contact-man got himself pinched. If I don't put my outfit into cold storage for a while, there's the risk of seeing it dismembered once again. Besides, I've been sent for from London. If nothing goes wrong, I'll introduce you to my right-hand man who will take over in my absence. You can settle things with him. He's a grand fellow, seriously wounded in the First World War.'

Half an hour later, on the opposite pavement, he did indeed introduce us: 'Desvignes—Lebreton.' I saw before me a greying man of pale complexion who had lost the sight of one eye. He was dressed in an old herring-bone overcoat, had a self-effacing air and seemed overawed by the responsibilities that would weigh on him after Mathieu's departure. I was much surprised, therefore, to learn after he had been arrested and sent to Buchenwald, that he was in fact a great barrister and a future Master of the Order, Paul Arrighi . . . On a previous occasion, Mathieu had let me meet another of his collaborators, whom he called Charpentier: a slim handsome man in his thirties, always impeccably turned out, with the black Eden hat and rolled umbrella of a top-flight official of the *Inspection des Finances*—the cream of the civil service. His manly, resonant voice, his sharp intelligence frequently tinged with irony, added to the impression of calm energy that emanated from him. 'He's my military aide,' Mathieu had told me. 'He runs the whole armed organization in the East and in Normandy. An absolute champion. He has regular army colonels under his command, and guess his age? Only just twenty-three . . . ' That man was

Paul Arrighi's son, but this too I only learned when he, in turn, was caught and sent to Mauthausen. The father returned from deportation, the son succumbed to it.

I did not see Mathieu again before he left, so it was only after his return that he gave me the humorous account of his eventful departure. Things had begun to go wrong early in October, when he had recognized a cyclist as one of his own contacts dressed as a woman. In a sudden surge of mistrust, Mathieu gave him the slip. His instinct rarely deceived him, and this time again it had saved his life. A few days later his friend Triboulet warned him that the disguised agent had gone over to the enemy and had already got his chief arrested. A quick getaway was imperative. A rendezvous was fixed in Lyons to get him to his plane at a place called La Guillotière. Was he late for the rendezvous? Whatever the reason, Mathieu found nobody waiting in Lyons and returned to Paris where he now no longer had any contacts. This was a calamity and he had somehow to get out of it. But how? For want of any better idea, he started lounging about the neighbourhood of a certain café—the Louis XVI—where he knew that Resisters often met—too often, in fact! And indeed in less than an hour he met the whole crowd there . . . .

He might equally as well have met the Gestapo. So when I knew him to be safely in London, I heaved a sigh of relief and sometimes even caught myself wishing they would keep him there for good: accustomed as I was to the strict rules Lescure had drummed into me, I trembled for Mathieu every week for I knew that his manifold tasks led him all too frequently to indulge in hair-raising acrobatics, this playing into the hands of the traitors spontaneously generated in any clandestine struggle. This is how, despite all precautions, Jean Moulin had been trapped, the man responsible for federating the whole of the Resistance movement, the creator of the *C.N.R.*—the *Comité National de la Résistance*, the legendary 'Max'. A stricken Mathieu informed me one morning of Moulin's arrest, together with his entire general staff. Ever since the summer, the Gestapo and the Militia had been making increasingly dangerous swoops. While in the early days they had been powerless to discover anything by themselves, as time went by they collected ever more lists of names, diaries and address-books, with the result that their efficiency increased and snowballed. Mathieu's own network suffered more and more losses and I was afraid that if he returned to Paris he would be arrested on the spot.

This inevitable imprudence, which frightened me for him, was not his monopoly, though. Other people were foolhardy by nature, abhorring precautions like the newly-fledged officers from Saint-Cyr who in 1914 had charged the enemy in bearskins and white kid-gloves. Shortly before Mathieu's departure, Paulette Humbert told me that her brother Jean would like to see me. We had not met since that snow-laden December evening of two years ago, when we had warmed ourselves at the Café Weber's brazier while he talked to me of his feelings of shame and disgust. This time we met on a café terrace near Trinity Church. He had just arrived from the southern zone, and talked in a loud, unruffled voice as if we were alone on a desert island.

'I don't know what exactly you're doing, but whatever it is, I take it your work puts you in touch with the Gaullists?' he said calmly in front of the waiter who was serving us *apéritifs* in the warm July sunshine.

Respect for rank is a terrible thing: does a lieutenant in the reserve dare to admonish a general and tell him to keep his voice down? I lowered mine as I answered, in the hope that he might imitate me. But not a bit. 'Personally,' he went on, 'I am for Giraud. I've come here to make contacts. We must all join forces, even with the Communists. There'll be time to scrap again afterwards,' he added, with a good-natured laugh. He asked me to present him to some of the leading men. The waiter hovered around us, wiping the nearby tables with meticulous care. I answered in an even lower whisper and saw Humbert taking down names and addresses in a little notebook, which already bore an impressive list on which I figured. I was still paralysed by respect and military discipline. At last we left the terrace. The waiter gave me a wink of amused connivance. A fresh date was fixed for the following Thursday.

No sooner had I left him than I telephoned his sister, telling her that I must see her at once. An hour later we met outside the Métro station of the Chamber of Deputies. In the café opposite the station I told her of our talk and of my own stupid diffidence. 'But you simply *must* make him realize that his lack of caution will cause catastrophes! He obviously has not the slightest idea of the dangers he is up against in Paris, he still thinks he's in

the free zone. And first and foremost, he *must* destroy that notebook!'
I left Paris with a somewhat easier mind. Two days later I received
a note: *My brother has been taken away to a clinic. An ambulance came
for him yesterday. No risk of contagion: the prescription-pad with the
medicines marked on it is in a safe place. I'll let you know as soon as I have
more news.*

INTERMEZZO

A hare perceives a suspicious noise: he will start with fright,
give a jump or two. The noise stops: back he goes to his marjoram
and promptly forgets his fear. If he remembered his constant
alarms, he would never stop trembling and lose his taste for thyme.

To keep enjoying the taste of bread, we behaved just like the
hare. Looking back, I am astonished to recall how a rattling alarm
or a friend's disappearance could be closely followed, on the same
night, by something very much like a beano. But this dichotomy
was an absolute necessity. I have mentioned how my mind would
'split' the moment I left town. But the split could occur right
inside town too. For instance, after Chazal's transfer to Paris
(where he was later to become an exemplary judge of juvenile courts
and an outstanding reformer of antiquated methods), we would
sometimes get together with Grenier, the former medico of the 15/9
Battalion, who too had recently set up in practice in Paris. With
them I would be just Jean Bruller, while Desvignes, Vercors, the
Editions de Minuit dropped into a well of oblivion. Back in the
days of the battalion, Grenier had already seemed 'a character',
with his face of a city rat and his physique of an advanced T.B.
case, who never renounced a tumble in the hay even within firing-
range of the Germans. In civilian life, he was even more of an odd
fish. Having put up his brass plate somewhere behind the Bastille,
he recruited most of his patients among tarts and their pimps.
The first time he stood us a drink at the bar of a near-by pub called
La Marquise, he had invited a swaggering, outrageous pimp to
join us: 'Monsieur Chazal is in the Law Court business, he's a pal
of mine and may help you out some time . . . ' He also looked after
a clientele of Chinese smugglers and took us along one night to

see them play mah-jong for impressive stakes in a shady joint in an even shadier alley. Quite at home in this environment where the black market flourished, he collected his fees in the shape of turkeys, hams, legs of mutton, foie-gras and other delicacies, which he invited us to share in the indescribable chaos of his dilapidated living-cum-dining-room, crammed with medical apparatus. The first few times we arrived punctually at eight p.m., but we soon gathered that this was far too early. Grenier himself showed up, cadaverous and full of beans, at ten at the earliest, often later. Even then, there were more surprises in store.

One evening at that hour we found neither him nor his wife at home, but instead a weird old mouse called 'Aunt Lu', who kept trotting between the roast in the oven and the baby's washing hanging in front of the stove, whence there wafted the steamy odour of washing-powder and urine. Hunger blended with boredom to produce an irresistible drowsiness. At last our hostess appeared, removed neither hat nor coat but called out to us in a hurry: 'I'm just popping round to my dentist, never have time during the day;' and left us to our own devices till half past eleven. Aunt Lu was still trotting busily. It was midnight before Grenier himself turned up, looking more than ever, with his sharp bony face, like a dying man on a binge. Aunt Lu must have been a terrific *cordon bleu*, for despite the unconscionable delay her roast mutton was cooked to a turn, and we washed it down with a vintage Hermitage which a whorehouse madam had brought back from Tournon. Chazal and Grenier swapped experiences of their respective professions fit to make the ladies lose their appetite. One of these stories concerned an Auvergnat mother who had insisted on attending, with Chazal, the post-mortem on her son who had broken his neck falling from a scaffolding. She suspected the authorities of trying to diddle her by claiming that alcohol had been found in her son's stomach, and she kept poking her nose into his guts to sniff them while dabbing her eyes with her apron-hem . . . Then there was the street-walker whose pimp had asked Grenier for the address of a dentist who would make gold fillings for the thirty-two perfectly good teeth of his protégée, this being the only marketable currency at Saint-Lazare, the women's jail . . . We left the dinner-table sated for a month, but it was long after curfew. Chazal, as a member of the judiciary, had a safe-conduct, but my wife and

I had to spend the night there. The only available sleeping-place was the stained sofa on which Grenier examined his patients, facing a cracked wash-basin redolent of phlegm and disinfectant . . . In the long run, we found that this was a bit much to pay for the leg of a duck or a saddle of lamb—even in time of famine. As for Chazal, he felt increasingly perturbed by the acquaintances of our egregious doctor, whose over-permissive morality might some day overstep the bounds. So in spite of our still friendly feelings, our common memories and his cordial insistence, we let the intervals grow between our feasts and finally dropped them altogether. But apart from savouring the recollection of those Rabelaisian hours, I could not leave them unreported without misrepresenting my life in those days, which was only incompletely dedicated to the struggle for spiritual survival.

* * *

Léon Motchane, alias Thimerais, was as good as his word. He reorganized part of our distribution service by prudently restricted means: three bicycles with three ladies on them. One of them, for a certain time, was again the mysterious 'Renée' but she vanished no less mysteriously between one day and the next, probably on some assignment that kept her away from Paris. Yvonne, now released from her stitching and impudently pooh-poohing my categorical instructions (for if she got caught I should lose my right-hand man) replaced the departed Renée. 'Which Roman general was it,' she asked Debu-Bridel, 'who got his head chopped off for being victorious as a result of disobeying orders? Do you think Desvignes will go as far as that?' Happily, nobody saw anything suspicious in those three smartly dressed *Parisiennes* in spite of their armfuls of parcels in the Métro or the bulging bags on their bicycles.

Through a variety of intermediaries I had meanwhile established contact with the leaders of several networks who would distribute our books within their ranks. Bellanger, for some time already, had been handling distribution in the ranks of the *O.C.M.* I often dropped in at the Louvre, one of the headquarters of intellectual resistance, where, since Jacques Decour's death and with the chief curator's connivance, Claude Morgan was editing *Les Lettres*

Françaises. On my first visit, though by now aware of Vercors's reputation, I still had no idea of Desvignes's own renown. When I gave this name, I saw Claude Morgan jump to his feet and display such unexpected emotion and deference that I, in turn, was moved by this token of the astonishing prestige already enjoyed by the Editions de Minuit. Thanks to Morgan's efforts, our volumes would be distributed in the Communist networks. Henceforward I could hope to reach all the diverse currents and circles of the Resistance movement.

After publishing in September *The Patient Thought* and *England,* we produced in October our eleventh and twelfth volumes with the successive publication of *The Grévin Museum* and *The Lovers of Avignon.* For November we were planning to do the *Stories* by Auxois (pen-name of Edith Thomas), and the volume was already setting with Roulois and Aulard was waiting to put it to press when Pierre Dalloz brought us from Grenoble a manuscript by Yves Farge. It was a coldly ferocious document recounting the truth about the scuttling of the Fleet. This was somewhat outside the programme we had adopted in our manifesto, but nevertheless there could be no question of rejecting it.

We decided to create a parallel collection under the title of *Témoignages* ('Bearing Witness'), with a different type of cover. We were unwilling, however, to slow down the rate of publication of the volumes already in course of production and, thinking of the printer of *Les Lettres Françaises,* I broached the subject with Claude Morgan. He introduced me to the writer Georges Adam, who was already one of our own distributors. It was Adam who had found a printer for *Les Lettres Françaises,* thanks to a friend of his, Livet, who was himself the head of the underground team of compositors in the Resistance group *Front National.* He now placed his printer at our disposal or rather, to avoid an intermingling of risks, he himself watched over the printing of Yves Farge's *Toulon,* and would do so for any subsequent volumes of *Témoignages* as well. Until the Liberation I never knew, of course, the printer's name, which was Antoine Blondin. But it was a huge relief to know that in the event of anything untoward happening to Aulard, the Editions de Minuit would not find themselves without a printer.

During all those months I was having a hard time trying to finish my new novel, the one that Lescure had urged me to write in memory of my father. It was closely modelled on his adolescence, his flight from Hungary and his arrival in France, his love for the French and the murderous end which might have been his if he had not died before the war. This end had been suggested to me by one of those odious black-framed notices with which the Nazi authorities besmirched our walls.

Among the latest victims of the firing-squads, I had shuddered to see the name: Bernheim, 72 years. This would have been my father's age, and the name was also that of a close friend of his. Moreover, little by little, I learnt the horrible circumstances of that death, revealed by the indiscretions of one of the prison-warders of Les Tourelles. Following an attack on one of their compatriots, the Germans had demanded that fifty hostages be shot as a reprisal within twenty-four hours. Whom to pick? At the Préfecture de Police they had feverishly consulted their files and hit on what appeared to them a godsend: the naturalized Jews. Fearing that most of them might have flown the nest and that it might be difficult to round up fifty, they had picked three times the required number, so that eventually there were more than a hundred of them assembled in a hangar under the gendarmes' rifles. How to choose among them? 'Let's pretend we're setting them free!' said the bright cops. 'They'll jostle to get out, and the first fifty to emerge will have had it.'

Thus died old Mr Bernheim, and thus ended my hero, delivered up by the French whom he had so much loved. I progressed slowly, laboriously, partly because the subject pained me, partly because I was striving after a manner of expression that would not immediately recall *Le Silence de la Mer*. In fact, I planned to sign the story with a fourth pseudonym, out of a slightly naïve wish to add to our list of authors . . . It will presently be seen why I mention this detail.

When I had finished at last, I felt very doubtful. Was my story any good? I no longer had Pierre de Lescure's judgment to rely on. Whose opinion should I ask? Yvonne, being such an old friend, would not be a good judge. Paulhan, on the contrary, would be too good a judge: he scared me a little. As a trial shot, I submitted it to Paulette Humbert. When she praised it, I suspected she might be too lenient; at least it helped me to overcome my hesitation to show it to Paul Eluard, on whom the decision to print depended.

I was as fearful of receiving preferential treatment as I was of a rebuff: the quality of the book must be at least on a par with the
risks involved in publishing it. In the little café behind Danton's
statue I surreptitiously handed him the manuscript, pretending
it was from a tyro among my acquaintances. 'I'm just a graphic
artist and haven't the least idea if this is any good. And we mustn't
publish anything that isn't first-rate, must we? The author himself
has doubts about certain points, so here is a list of questions on
which he would like to have your advice.'

When I returned to Paris the following Thursday, I rang up
Yvonne as usual.

'You liar!' was the first thing she said to me.

'What!'

'Nice work. Come over right away.'

What *was* the matter? What had I done? She received me with
an amused, mocking smile.

'So you still pretend you're not Vercors?'

'The idea of it! Now why suddenly . . . '

'That story you gave Eluard to read, he's passed it on to me.
You aren't going to deny that it's the story of your father?'

'Of course not, but why Vercors? Is the writing anything like
his?'

'Not in the least.'

'Well, then?'

'Well, then, Eluard came here, all agog, at eleven last Tuesday
night. "I can't understand a word of what Desvignes has been
telling me. He brings me a Vercors and asks me if it's any good!
A tyro, he says! With a questionnaire! He's crazy. Just read this,
and send it to the printer at once." Since Eluard says so, I trust
him more than you. He's got a sixth sense. Come on, own up!'

It really must have been a sixth sense, to judge from the comments
Debu-Bridel reported back to us when the book came out. 'It's
pretty good,' he said, 'but so different from the first . . . People
find this disconcerting, unless "Vercors" is a collective name?'
In front of Eluard I had no option, though, but to admit the truth.
I explained to him Vercors's idea of adopting a fourth pseudonym,
after Santerre and Roland Dolée. Yvonne shared this opinion and
suggested 'Louis Bourbon' (my father's first name and my mother's
surname), which would have sounded well over this encomium on

a naturalized Jew . . . But Eluard was adamant: Vercors must sign Vercors. I had to knuckle under.

The only point that left Eluard in doubt was the title. It had been suggested to me by a line in Claudel's *Saint-Louis*, where the good king of France ponders over Frenchmen's duties:

Ce n'est pas assez de posséder le soleil si l'on n'est pas capable de le donner . . . [1]

He did not care for *Posséder le Soleil* ('Possessing the Sun'), nor did Yvonne, and together we discussed several titles, without much success. One day, however, as I was walking down Rue de Rennes once more unrolling in my mind the vision of my father's trek on foot from his native Hungary towards that distant star, that land of asylum, the France of freedom and fraternity, I passed an old man, on whose breast was also a star—but this one was yellow and humiliating . . . the star which Pétain's France would have forced on my father if he had been alive. And there at last was my title: *La Marche à l'Etoile* ('The Guiding Star').

We stressed the hint to the point of getting the volume out on December 25th, Christmas Day. This was very shortly after General Smuts in Johannesburg had made that notorious speech in which he had buried France once and for all without any hope of a resurrection. My book provoked much discussion, as *Le Silence de la Mer* had done. Some people considered that I was accusing France at a moment when she stood in more need of being defended. They argued that I should not have let my Jewish hero die at the hands of Frenchmen—even if they were Pétainists. But alas, I had not invented anything, as I have shown, and one does not save the honour of one's country by lying or hiding its shame. Montesquieu had said so before me: one must die for one's country, but never lie for it. I believe that most of my readers shared this view, for after the war many of them told me that every year they went on a pilgrimage—if not in penitence—to the Pont des Arts in order to seek there the ghost of my hero and recapture the bitter tang of his murdered love.

[1] 'Possessing the sun is not enough if one cannot give it, too . . .'

VIII

In that same month of December two manuscripts of high quality reached us. The first was the one Aragon had promised us in addition to his *Musée Grévin*. Under the pseudonym of *Le Témoin des Martyrs* ('The Martyrs' Witness') he gave us what was in fact the quivering, heart-rending martyrology of our finest patriots, those who had been tortured and murdered during the last three years. Under the title, *Le Crime contre l'Esprit* ('The Crime against the Spirit'), it would constitute the second volume of our collection *Témoignages*. The other text had come to us from Switzerland, thanks to a young attaché of the diplomatic corps at Vichy who had managed to contact us via some of our contributors. His name was François Lachenal. We lunched together. He brought me the clandestine Swiss edition of *Le Silence de la Mer*, as well as those of *L'Honneur des Poètes* and *Les Amants d'Avignon*. Clandestine, because the Swiss Government was very careful of its neutrality and did not wish to do (or authorize) anything that might displease its powerful neighbour. 'We're like a pigeon's egg in the hand of a gorilla . . . ', as the President of the Confederacy had put it in his picturesque plea in their defence. By means of the diplomatic bag, Lachenal had smuggled our volumes into Switzerland, passed them on to the Editions des Trois Collines. Defying the official ban, this publishing-house created a discreet collection under the heading *La Porte d'Ivoire* ('The Ivory Gate') which circulated under the counter. The jacket bore a thin tricolour band. The whole thing was an open secret, though, and some of the firm's directors spent a short spell in gaol, for form's sake.

By the same channel but in the opposite direction, Lachenal brought us a short novel which had been published in America. Its author was John Steinbeck, already known in France for his excellent novel *Of Mice and Men*. In his new story, *The Moon is Down*, set in a country very like Norway, this Transatlantic author, living more than three thousand miles away from our daily fears and battles, our stifled rage and fierce resolution, displayed an uncanny intuition of the Resistance fighter's psychology. A French

translation of the book had been issued in Switzerland, under the
title *Nuits sans Lune* ('Moonless Nights'), but it was an expurgated
version, garbled and incomplete: anything likely to produce a
frown on the brow of the Great Reich had been prudently toned
down or censored. Very well: the integral version should come out
in captive France!

This would be the first volume of a third collection reserved
for foreign writers, which would bear the title, *Voix d'Outre-monde*
('Voices from Another World'). We asked Yvonne Desvignes—
whose English was excellent—to make a new translation. Aulard
took two Sundays to print it (the text this time ran far beyond
ninety-six pages) and we turned this circumstance to account by
running off a larger edition. This meant multiplying the risks,
but the success justified our efforts: there was a blaze of enthusiasm
in the press (the underground press, of course). We later heard
that the Anglo-American public, at first somewhat sceptical and
reserved about the authenticity of this work of pure imagination
penned in America by an American writer, gave it its due recog-
nition only after this guarantee from martyred France.

After the Liberation we learned that the author had arrived in
France, and all of us—translator, printers, binders, distributors—
gladly got ready to welcome him. Not a single foreign writer so far
had failed to pay his first visit to us on arriving in Paris, though
they had less reason than he. We awaited a move from him. None
came. So I eventually asked for an audience at his hotel near the
Champs-Elysées, where he was staying with his secretary, and found
it difficult to obtain. We also wished to warn him off a projected
stage dramatization of his story by someone who, to our mind,
ought to have been the last person to think of such a thing—it
seemed to us immoral.

We were received by his secretary. Steinbeck, though present,
did not leave the far end of the room where he was consulting
a directory. As regards the question of the play, he had his secretary reply to us that these affairs between Frenchmen did not
interest him. As to our invitation, which we then broached, he
snapped: 'No time.' We tried to insist, explaining how much his
refusal would hurt the people who had published and distributed
his book at the risk of their lives. He merely repeated: 'No time,'
and to make it quite clear that the audience was over, he turned

his back on us and started dialling a telephone number. It inevitably seemed to us that the American writer had found the Resistance no more than just another topical literary theme and that he could not care less about those who had fought in it. This was one of our first and greatest post-war disappointments.

In January 1944, after the murder of Maurice Sarraut—the well-known newspaper-owner and public figure of the Third Republic—the eighty-year-old president of the League for the Rights of Man, Victor Basch, a philosopher and scholar of aesthetics, was dragged from his humble lodgings in Lyons by the thugs of Darnand's Milice and taken to a field outside the town, where he and his wife were stripped of their clothes and riddled with bullets. It was just at this time that Paul Reynaud's former *directeur du cabinet*, Roger Giron, gave us a very detailed and objective but scathing account of the circumstances in which the armistice had been asked for from the Nazi invaders. This, the third volume of our collection *Témoignages*, was the first serious document to circulate in France on the true responsibilities involved in this treason, and the part played in it by Pétain, Laval and their accomplices in Bordeaux. Shortly afterwards, Aragon sent us, through Claude Morgan, an admirable autobiography by Gabriel Péri, the man who had first coined '*les lendemains qui chantent*' ('our singing tomorrows')— since become a byword for the hopes we placed in the post-war world—who had been shot at Châteaubriant. I read it right through in Morgan's office at the Louvre.

It was a beautiful piece of writing but it raised a difficulty which I explained to Claude Morgan. It inevitably presented both in form and content a glorification of the Communist Party, and this was outside our rôle. The solution to this problem appeared when we cast off the text: it was rather too short to make a volume. Might we not, I suggested, couple it with another biography, that perhaps of a Resister from a quite different sphere—a Christian, for instance, like Estienne D'Orves?

Morgan approved, and so did Aragon when consulted. The question was where to find a biographer. This problem too was solved when we received a month later a text by André Rousseaux, the essayist, who from his retreat in Dieulefit had conveyed it to Eluard (via a Controller of Official Registrations in the Paris suburb of Creil . . .). This was a series of excerpts from the writings of Charles Péguy, the Catholic and nationalist Péguy whom the Vichyites were impudent enough to annex posthumously to their cause. The very pertinent choice of excerpts, lashing out against 'that awful little Thiers', against Cauchon, Trochu and all the defeatists of past French history, contained, thirty years in advance, a withering condemnation of Pétain and his collaborationist acolytes. Entitled, quite simply, *Péguy-Péri*, the volume would come out in June, and I would meanwhile prepare a foreword to stress this symbolic coupling and the spiritual unity that underlay antagonistic convictions when the motherland's soul was at stake.

Still in January, I phoned the Ministry of the Navy one Thursday to ascertain that Lebourg was still there—one could never be sure from one week to the next that a friend was not in flight or in gaol. He answered the telephone with a sort of surprise which sounded to me like embarrassment. I heard him murmur to someone near him before he said:

'Yes, do come.'

'If you're busy . . . '

'No, not at all! On the contrary, there's someone here who'll be glad to make your acquaintance.'

Ten minutes later I walked into his office. A man with thick glasses and a Catalan face turned his big Bourbon nose towards me. His eyebrows went up and we both burst out laughing: it was Jean Cassou.

'So you know each other?' asked Lebourg.

'Yes, slightly . . . ' said Cassou. 'So this is the famous Desvignes!'

'At your service,' I said. 'And now forget it, of course.'

When he had left us, I learned that he was up in Paris on 'business', having come to ensure co-operation between the National Resistance Council—the C.N.R.—to which Debu-Bridel belonged, and the Toulouse Resistance group under his own direction. He had just been released from prison, and had told Lebourg that, to occupy his long lonely days and endless nights in solitary confinement, he had composed a number of sonnets which he learned by heart for lack of anything to write with. Thirty-three of them, to be precise. 'You must give them to us!' Lebourg had said, and at that moment I had rung up. I could not have timed it better.

After the short while needed to copy them out in their final form, Cassou sent us these sonnets, still via Paulhan, with a preface by

Aragon. This was in February. Claude Morgan also gave me one
of his own works: the opening chapters of a novel about prisoners
of war, based on his own experiences when he was tormented by
the idea that France and those he loved might be tempted to sell
their souls to curry favour with the enemy. Eluard was busy with
a second volume of *L'Honneur des Poètes*, this one devoted to the poets
of all the nations that had been victimized by Hitler: Jugoslavs,
Bulgarians, Belgians, Norwegians, Russians, Dutch, Czechs . . . A
mirror of the real Europe, even to beyond the Caucasus, that Great
Europe dreamed of by the heroic fighters whose picture stared at
us from a vile poster pasted on all the hoardings and in the Métro:
twenty-three bruised and battered faces, each inside a medallion as if surrounded by an oval string of pearls, intended to show
up the ugliness of those 'dagoes' who dared to defy the big
blond Aryans. They were the disfigured faces of Manouchian and
his companions, Spanish, Hungarian, Polish, Italian, Armenian,
shot after having sacrificed their lives for the France, the Europe
dear to their hearts—a Europe united in its common heritage of
humanism from Athens, Rome, Jerusalem.

One Sunday in January when Léon Motchane had come with
Yvonne to spend a week-end at Villiers, I thought he looked
worried, absent-minded. He seized a moment while the women
were chatting round the roaring log-fire in the big fireplace to
whisper to me:
'Do you know that Mathieu's had it?'
'What? Where?'
'In the air. The plane that was taking him back has been shot
down.'
He could not tell me the source of this news but it was a reliable
one. We were overwhelmed. We both agreed that we had better
keep it from the womenfolk. But Francette? Mathieu's children?
Ought we to keep it from them? The alternative would be hard on
Léon who was going to see Francette soon in Switzerland, to which
she had been enabled to escape when the Paris pavements had
become too hot for her in her turn. As if they had overheard us,
the women were just talking of our dead friend. They were recalling
his truculence, his absent-mindedness, his wit. 'He is so alive!' said
my wife.

The atmosphere all through that winter was sad and gloom-laden. The capture of 'Max' and his death under torture seemed to have dealt a crushing blow to the entire Resistance movement—something like the death of those epic heroes Roland or Du Guesclin. The word of mouth accounts of his legendary exploits—the instructions and news he brought from London, his moonlight parachute drops, his sudden disappearances and equally unexpected returns—all this had built up a romantic image of a sort of Cagliostro or Scarlet Pimpernel, which overnight had been replaced by that of a heroic martyr. Only then did I learn his real name and who he was. It was a very ordinary name, not a bit like Roland or Cagliostro—that of the former *préfet* Jean Moulin. But for all Resistance fighters he was henceforward the symbol of that unsung heroism which lives, acts, fights, succumbs and dies in darkness.

After the news of that arrest, followed by Mathieu's departure and his plane-crash, we worked in a growing void. Claude Morgan had been obliged to abandon his office at the Louvre and was in hiding. Eluard had vanished; we learned only on his return that he had fled to the wuthering heights of the Lozère mountains, among the mental patients of Dr Bonnafé's asylum at Saint-Alban. I was strolling gloomily along one February morning lit only by a cold crisp sun, when on the little island around Diderot's statue near Saint-Germain-des-Prés, I saw a man turn round on the kerb: it was Mathieu!

I remained speechless for a moment, then cried: 'How wonderful to see you! We thought you were dead!'

It seemed to me that his eyes looked strange.

'I should have been,' he said.

What was the change in him?

'You got away by parachute?'

'Much simpler: it was just a blind.'

'The accident?'

'No, the news of my death. The plane crashed all right, but I wasn't on it. A member of parliament, poor fellow, took my place at the last minute. No denial was issued: it suited our books that they should think I was dead.'

To make himself less recognizable, he had grown a moustache and had even undergone a small operation to correct, partially at least, his slight squint. Actually this made it worse, for I had

recognized him instantly, without even noticing his moustache.
And the effect of the operation which had left him with a blood-
shot eye, made people look twice at him. Once again I began to
tremble for his safety.

'Have you been here long?'

'I've only just arrived. I was going to call you. But let's make
the most of this chance meeting and have lunch.'

We walked a little farther and he showed me into Calvet's
restaurant. We went up to the first floor. I expected there would
be just the two of us, but he was greeted by much waving of arms.
Within moments I realised that the whole of the Resistance was
foregathered there. I could hardly believe my eyes and ears.
Everyone went from table to table (a narrow-shouldered, long-
faced man came up to talk to me at length; only much later did I
recognize him as Alexandre Parodi, the delegate-general of de
Gaulle's Provisional Government); people went to telephone or
were fetched to answer an incoming call, liaison agents came and
went. I did not know if I was more amused, or appalled. Just one
indiscretion, and what a haul! The gods are said to protect childish
innocence; perhaps they also protect blind carelessness . . .

While Lecompte-Boinet was telling his odyssey to a hilarious
audience, I could not quite prevent myself from casting anxiously
around for a possible emergency exit in case of a sudden raid. As
Mathieu told it, his return journey became a farcical comedy
worthy of the Marx Brothers, despite a hazardous landing on a
moonlit field whose flare-path was marked out by the torches of a
handful of resisters, while each passenger sat ready to crack his
cyanide pill. Just as their party was preparing to leave Dorset
Square in London, a last check was made by the British: his hat
and those of all his companions bore the label of a London hatter;
he was told to find one without a tag and had to try several shops.
At last he found a nameless hat, shoved it into his bag and only
just caught the coach for the aerodrome. He did not put his head-
gear on until he was in the train in which, after the landing, he and
his companions had dispersed in different carriages. At Lyons
Mathieu left the train, only to see in the crowd three grey hats
exactly like his own, brand-new and with a black band—probably
the only nameless model they had all managed to find . . . He
turned round and espied two more. This was crazy, they would all

get caught this way! He dived into the first doorway, got lost for a moment, and at last found his way out. In the street, he made for the nearest hat-shop, asked for a brown felt hat, took the first that was offered, paid for it and promised to call back for his own in the afternoon. 'Like the other two gentlemen?' asked the salesman with a smile and an insistent look. And Mathieu perceived on the counter two grey hats with black bands . . . Through the shop-window he could see a third approaching, and decamped without further delay.

Apart from his personal adventures, Mathieu brought back some surprising news. At General de Gaulle's instigation, and with initial capital supplied by Philippe de Rothschild, the Free French had founded a publishing-firm in London for the sole purpose of extending our Editions de Minuit: they would reprint all our books as and when they reached London under the label *Les Cahiers du Silence*. Already my *Silence of the Sea* had been reprinted with an introduction by Maurice Druon, and so had Mauriac's *Cahier Noir*. A recent number of the Liberation Committee's 'bulletin of activities', published each month, gave details of these reprints and apprised me that I was now rich: almost three thousand pounds sterling in royalties! (However, after the Liberation, I got no more than a smell of these: after paying part of the sum, not without some prodding, the person in charge made off with the rest. It was as well: I should not have declined this windfall, but I felt a certain shame: a disinterested action which has meant death for so many loses some of its lustre when covered with gold.) Mathieu conveyed this cheering news pell-mell with other news which appalled us, of a new wave of arrests. But never did I see him lose his high spirits. His responsibilities by now were considerable, but even of these he always spoke jestingly.

Perhaps he was remembering the promise we had made each other as we sat in the Café Tourville one day, talking of the unexpected importance of both his network and my publishing. It was not so much a promise as a wish I had expressed: 'Above all, let's hope we never take ourselves too seriously!' Which did not mean untragically, for we were rubbing shoulders with tragedy at every turn. But we did not want to start believing that merely because events (plus a good many lucky accidents) had given us some importance this was proof of our intrinsic worth. To try not to give

gether with André Rousseaux's *Péguy*. And now, all of a sudden, we were submerged by a positive avalanche of manuscripts.

In quick succession we received *Paille noire des Etables* ('Black Straw in the Stables') by Louis Parrot, George Adam sent us his *Appel de la Liberté* ('Freedom Calls'), René Laporte his *Maquis de Malléon* ('The Maquis of Malléon'), Paulhan forwarded to us Claude Aveline's *Le Temps Mort* ('Dead Point'), *Le Puits des Miracles* ('The Miracle-Well') by André Chamson and André Sikorska's *Zone Sud* ('Southern Zone'); Simone de Beauvoir intended us to have her *Sang des Autres* ('The Blood of Others')—but for reasons that have remained mysterious I was not told of it and the manuscript never reached us. And then rolled in *Les Propos sur la Haine* ('Talking of Hatred') by Gabriel Audisio, a beautiful *Lazare* ('Lazarus') by Charles Vildrac, *El Desdichado* by François Vernet, *La Mort de César* ('Caesar's Death') by Laszlo Dormandi, *Noroît* ('North-West') by Lucien Chauvet. Thirteen manuscripts in six weeks! After our prolonged fear of starvation, were we now going to have indigestion? Admittedly we had two printers now, a good many problems had been solved, our books were circulating surreptitiously all over Paris, booksellers stocked them at the risk of their lives—José Corti in Rue de Médicis, Camille Bloch in Rue Saint Honoré, Lucien Scheler in Rue de Tournon; we had our distributors in Lyons (Maurice Noël), in Provence (Aragon), in the Centre and the South-West, thanks to Jean Cassou, Georges Sadoul, Jean Lurçat—all well-known writers or intellectuals themselves. Finance was no longer a problem; we had a subscription service handled by Pierre Labracherie and the rest was sold (at one hundred francs per copy) within the various Resistance networks. The only ones to receive free copies were the moneyless patriots who fought in the *maquis* and a small number of privileged persons figuring on our 'press list'. We even made a profit, which would be distributed in full after the war, under the control of the National Committee of Writers, to help the needy families of executed or deported printers.

All this was fine, but thirteen volumes in six weeks was more than we could manage. Two volumes a month was already a difficult feat, three was well-nigh impossible, six utterly beyond our capacity. We should have to establish an order of priorities. From now on, Paul Eluard (often accompanied by Nusch), Jean Lescure, Claude

Morgan, Lucien Scheler, George Adam, Jacques Debu-Bridel and I formed a sort of editorial board which met every week in Yvonne Desvignes's flat. She served us tea in the English manner, and to an outside viewer our meetings must have looked like some social 'five o'clock tea'; but apart from our 'shop talk', an eavesdropper would have heard mention mainly of prison, torture, deportation and death. An absent friend was never referred to without fear and trembling, and with our ears straining for footsteps on the stairs.

Some of the decisions we had to take were self-evident: François Vernet had just been deported, his manuscript had already been widely read in the southern zone, if we published him we should endanger his life. Vildrac too had circulated his *Lazarus* too freely; it would be tantamount to giving his name away to the Germans. Lachenal had already forwarded Louis Parrot's and René Laporte's texts to the *Trois Collines*; they would soon come out in Switzerland, so they could wait. Meanwhile, after publishing Aragon's *Crime against the Spirit* in February and Steinbeck's *The Moon is Down* in March, we had just brought out in April Roger Giron's *Armistice*. For May we planned *Europe* and Cassou's *Thirty-three Sonnets*; for June, Aveline's *Dead Point* and Claude Morgan's *The Mark of Man*; for July *Péguy-Péri* and the second volume of the *Forbidden Chronicles* (comprising Charles Morgan's 'Ode to France' which I had translated into French; pages from Gide's *Diary*, and those which Bellanger had written in prison on scraps of paper with a pencil-stub; Audisio's pages, also from prison: and finally Chamson's powerful and moving evocations, to which would be added the Raymond Mortimer essay saved from the flames). If possible, we should also publish in July George Adam's *Freedom Calls*. For August, September, October, we decided to keep our programme open, since important manuscripts were in the offing: from Sartre and perhaps from Giraudoux, from Jean Guéhenno and Pierre Bost almost certainly. I myself had two new texts ready—*Le Nord* and *Le Songe*—but for different kinds of scruples I hesitated to submit either of them.

Le Nord ('Compass Bearing') was a sort of philosophical essay, an attempt to establish a rationale for our reasons for resisting, independent of national or political passions and emotional impulses. What restrained me was uncertainty lest my closely reasoned demonstration contained some weak points which might be breached by opposing arguments and conclusions. In that case, publication would be a blunder, since I should merely have rendered less conclusive what I intended to be irrefutable. I passed my essay to Paulhan with the request to tell me frankly whether I had succeeded. This was badly misjudging Paulhan's particular turn of mind . . . He wrote me a charming and attentive reply which stated neither one thing nor the other and left me more muddled than before. However, one word in his letter settled the issue: he reminded me that one does not write to convince but to disquiet. Since the last thing I wanted was to disquiet readers in the Resistance movement, I shelved *Le Nord*.

Le Songe ('The Dream') presented another problem, and a much graver one. At this point I must make a confession. Even in those early days of 1944 I still naïvely wanted to preserve my confidence in Man and refused to believe that a civilized creature, even if he were a Nazi, might outstrip in cruel savagery the most brutish primitive tribes. I distrusted any kind of 'propaganda'. I remembered the sort that had been dished out in the First World War, those chopped-off hands, corpses transformed into soap, all that had been revealed as false after the victory. I did not want to fall into the same errors. So much so that even much later, after the Liberation, when the atrocities of Struthof in the Vosges were discovered and the newspapers got hold of the stories of human vivisections and deportees' skins being used for lamp-shades and bookbindings, I still wrote to Bellanger, now promoted to the directorship of *Le Parisien libéré*, with the urgent exhortation to eschew propaganda at all costs and stick to closely checked facts; otherwise nobody would believe anything any more and the Germans would come out as white as snow. In fact, there was no propaganda in these stories, and when the hells of Auschwitz and other places were discovered the following year, they left those earlier atrocities far behind.

And yet, at the end of the previous year, I had already been put wise, at least in part. A deportee, practically the only one of his kind, had managed to get out of the inferno of the Oranienburg camp. This was the concentration camp where, before the war, Ossietzky, the German Nobel Prize winner, had died. I therefore imagined that it was one of the very worst, whereas in fact it was one of the less inhuman. Consequently what I learned about it did not make me guess the horrors being perpetrated in other camps, which transcended imagination.

The deportee in question, who had so miraculously escaped, was someone I knew well. Our relationship was peculiar, and my sentiments towards him even more so. I might have had grave personal reasons for distrusting and disliking him, for he had already done me a great wrong which I had forgiven him: but his charm and youthfulness, perhaps some spark of loyalty, too, despite his irresponsible conduct, redeemed the grudges which I had forced myself to disregard and when I learned from Pierre de Lescure one day, as we strolled through the Luxembourg Gardens, that he had been arrested in Tunis where he was running a youth centre, I was both saddened and surprised. I had not guessed that he was mixed up in anything compromising, for his letters were not those of a resister, but rather expressed a certain bewildered confusion in the shadow of Pétain. His father, moreover, was a well-known figure for whom I had formerly entertained great respect but who had climbed on the victor's bandwagon in pursuit of goodness knows what blind dreams. This had not prevented his son's deportation to Germany—though only for a short time: three months later he was released.

I saw him on his return. His bewilderment had merely grown: after what he had seen he would have liked to join the Resistance, but could not bring himself to do so for fear of compromising his father who had obtained his release from the camp. Since his return he had teetered about in pathetic indecision, guilt-ridden whatever he did. He clung to me, but as soon as I lifted a finger he disappeared for weeks on end. I suggested to him one day that, to save the honour of his family name, I should help him edit a complementary volume to the shameful, truncated anthology of German poems for which his father was one of those responsible, in which, to please the Occupants, neither Heine nor Brecht nor Kaestner were included, nor any Jewish or liberal or revolutionary poet, but only the poetasters of the most virulent racist vein.

He accepted enthusiastically on the spur of the moment, and then the months passed without my seeing him again. So much so that in the end Claude Bellanger, to whom I had introduced him, took the matter in hand himself; and together with his friend Cannac—both excellent German linguists—they reinstated the

banned poets, translated and annotated their verses and assembled
them in a volume which, at Duhamel's suggestion, we entitled
Les Bannis ('The Banned') and had printed for the National Committee of Writers.

But the first time I saw him after his return from Germany
he knew nothing of my activities, though he probably guessed
their general direction. I obviously represented for him an open
window through which he could shout the monstrous truth that was
choking him, and he described to me the martyrdom of the prisoners of Oranienburg. It was not a camp of slow extermination, like
Ravensbrück, Mauthausen, Auschwitz and so many others, of
whose horrifying reality he had no more inkling than I, but the
slaughters of Oranienburg were quite sufficient to make one's
hair stand on end.

Those abominations, at least, I could no longer doubt. Nor,
now that I knew them to be true, could I bear the French to be
left in ignorance. I could only trumpet them into the sleepers' ears.
Yet still I dared not reproduce this harrowing evidence as an established fact: does not the wish to impress a listener sometimes cause
a witness to exaggerate unconsciously? This is why I related the
facts in the guise of a dream and under that title. I thought at
the time that nothing could possibly outstrip its horror, which now-
adays seems almost mild compared to those which *have* outstripped
it . . .

After finishing the story, I was gripped by anxiety: how many
mothers, how many wives had a son or a husband in a similar hell?
And possibly, probably, even certainly—to judge by myself—
still knew nothing of the abominable, almost invariably fatal con-
ditions in the camps? Who lived on hopes which, if they read my
story, would be all but dashed? Was there not a case in point quite
close to me—the young wife of my cousin Pierrot? For a year now
she had had no news of him except that brought by a member of
the Milice, who claimed to be able to forward to her husband,
through a German friend, the parcels she made up. (But Pierrot
was dead, had been shot the first day and would later be discovered
in a mass grave. The go-between was well aware of it and simply
sold the parcels.) Like her, I thought he was in a German camp;
like her I knew nothing—had till then known nothing—of the full,
horrible extent of the prisoners' sufferings. Should I tell her, now

that I did know? Should a doctor describe in advance to the wife of a man suffering from cancer the thousand deaths in store for her husband? Those wives and mothers were legion already, they would grow more numerous every day, and all of them lived on hope. I wavered for a long time, and then my courage failed me: I left *The Dream* in my drawer.

IX

Wᴵᵀʜ the coming of spring it became evident that the war was taking a different turn. The Allied air raids suddenly multiplied over France and Germany, on ports, factories, bridges, railway yards. Cologne, Hamburg, Berlin, the major German cities were bombed every night, at times, it was said, with phosphor bombs. This made me wince, but at least the German people were at last going to experience in their own flesh the calamities that the folly of their chosen leaders had brought upon the rest of the world. And whenever I heard the drone of bomber squadrons passing overhead at Villiers, I felt warring within me justice and pity, a certain horror and a grim satisfaction.

Inevitably, there were some 'mis-hits' which caused numerous victims among the French population. The French reacted well and were not taken in by Marshal Pétain's mealy-mouthed commiseration, nor by his fulminations against the 'aggressor' when he had never so much as raised a peep against the German crimes. His unpopularity spread like oil on water. Drieu La Rochelle sadly announced the demise due to circulation failure of the *Nouvelle Revue Française*, and no longer even concealed his pessimism as to the way the war would end. One evening, when the lights went up at the end of a film in a cinema on the Boulevards, I heard someone call: 'Bruller!' It was Flodobert. We were with friends, I tried to turn a deaf ear and lose myself in the crowd, but he jostled through to me, gripped my arm, dazed me with his volubility. Outside the cinema I managed to shake him off, I still had not said a word, but he turned to my wife, hung on to us and kept talking and talking. Our silence finally choked him; he said a sudden 'Well, good-night!' and walked away, his hair blowing in the wind, without even daring to hold out his hand. My heart ached. 'I cannot offend any man without suffering . . . ' But he had succumbed, just as Lescure had predicted, and been unable to stick to a harmless collaboration; he had soon had to take sides and, to justify himself in his own eyes, to burn his former gods, condemn democracy and glorify in his writings the totalitarian Nazism which he had so abhorred. And now he too realized that he had backed the wrong horse.

This awakening of the French, the new vigour of their moral fibre did not spread to the domain of the black market, which had become almost an institution. Rare were those who had resisted this contagion, and a large part of the young people had succumbed to it. One of my friends, wishing to wrest his young son from this evil traffic, had got him the offer of a job at a very decent annual salary. The boy had smiled condescendingly: the sum offered was more or less what he made in a week . . . . Fortunately another kind of youth redeemed this gangrened part. But they paid for it dearly. Two tragedies in quick succession came to my ears. One of them, worthy of Aeschylus, involved a famous actress who had demeaned herself to consorting with the Occupants; her only son, shamed and revolted, set off for London with a friend. Crazed with anguish, his mother denounced the two young people to her German lover, and the officer promised to get her son sent back to her. While she was preparing the celebrations for his return the boys were actually caught, thanks to her information, but being armed, they were shot down. It was the boy's dead body that was sent back to her. Almost in the same week, Dominique Corticchiato, a young post-graduate with a degree in English, the author already of some brilliant translations (from Walpole, Coleridge) and the son of José Corti who distributed our publications, was returning to the book-shop one day when a neighbour warned him that the Gestapo were in there, questioning his mother. Twice he wavered around the block, like a moth around a lighted candle; then, unable to resist any longer, he threw himself into the flame. He was arrested on the spot, deported and never came back.

The moral decay affected one branch of activity in particular— transport. If you left your bicycle by the kerb for a moment, even if it were padlocked, you could never be sure of finding it again. For the one who had been robbed this was like losing his legs. One day Yvonne Desvignes lent her bicycle to a girl-friend who returned the next day, quite distraught, to tell her that it had been stolen from the corridor of her block of flats. This was a terrible blow, even for our Press. But on the day after Easter the friend returned, this time with the bicycle. The thief was wont to go to confession once a year at Easter and, before being given any other penance, he had been told to restore his theft. 'These things only happen to me!' said the girl-friend. 'I must be miracle-prone!'

Mathieu was spending that same Easter Day with us at Villiers. Actually he had come to recover his hens which Francette had entrusted to us before leaving France. We had put the hens in with ours: 'You can have the eggs!' Mathieu had declared magnanimously. A piece of pure brag: although very well fed, they absolutely refused to lay until the very morning their master returned to fetch them, when they left us their first and only egg, no doubt by way of thanks.

Easter this year was full of hope and high spirits. Mathieu believed himself to be safe: his voice heard on the London radio only a few days ago must, he was sure, have convinced the Germans that he was still in England. The subject of his broadcast was the Editions de Minuit and this posed a family problem for me: if my wife listened in, she would find out at one stroke about Mathieu and me. I therefore asked her to stay away, and she did so unprotestingly, busying herself in the kitchen while I listened in my room.

So as not to give ourselves away, we had to be careful what we said in front of her, but fortunately this did not apply to our discussions about the war in general. All sorts of signs were increasingly pointing to an Allied landing taking place sooner or later. But where? Personally, I felt sure it would not be in the Pas-de-Calais, as the British troop movements on the other side of the Channel were trying—and successfully—to make the Germans believe. The massive German fortifications in that area seemed to me impregnable. Whereas a vast bridgehead might be gained at lesser cost, either by beheading Denmark through the neck of the Schleswig-Holstein isthmus, or by isolating the Cotentin peninsula by a similar operation somewhere near Granville. I inclined to favour Denmark, as being closer to the Eastern front and the vital centres of the Reich.

Meanwhile I told Mathieu about the extraordinary double hit obtained by the aerial bombardment of the marshalling yard at Vaires, some miles away from Villiers. No more *Gott mit uns* for the Germans, God was definitely letting them down: an ammunition train had been blown up by the bombs at the very moment when two troop-crammed convoys were going through. Not a single survivor. And all the shattered goods-wagons destined for

Germany had disgorged, amid disembowelled cattle, their loot of sugar, flour, cognac and innumerable cases of champagne. Next day the whole town of Vaires was dead drunk.

Those massive destructions, while filling us with optimism, complicated my weekly trips to Paris. The trains now moved at a funereal pace over makeshift lines, through a cataclysmic tangle of rails and sleepers, writhing like pythons over distorted carcasses. Often fresh bombing raids prevented the trains from getting through at all, and it was necessary to cycle as far as Chelles, some twenty kilometres from Villiers, and heave the bicycle into the luggage-van piled high with hundreds of others; pedals caught in spokes, and the cycles were extracted only by dint of much shaking and pulling, which often caused damage.

My bad kidneys made the journey troublesome at times. I remember one occasion when I was returning with Yvonne and Léon (who had rented a small house near us for the summer) when I thought I was washed up for good, for there I was paining and straining to follow them, as if they were riding hell-for-leather. In fact, though I pedalled as hard as I could with my aching back, I was making no headway and was already envisaging myself with one foot in the grave when I realized, shortly before our destination, that I had been riding the whole time with one brake caught in the buckled rim of my wheel . . . But we gladly accepted these inconveniences caused by the blows dealt to the enemy. Every week, fresh carcasses of calcined iron were scattered along the railway lines, and the travellers would count their growing number with sadistic satisfaction. The count would come to an abrupt stop when we suddenly realized we were being escorted by an Allied bomber formation ten thousand feet up. The carriage fell silent. A young girl said: 'That's what we'll look like in five minutes!' and was hushed by her scared mother. Small puffs of cloud burst up there near the planes, and sometimes one of them would detach itself from the rest, trailing a little black smoke, start to dip one wing, break up gently, and swirl downward with dreamy slowness as if it were really in no hurry to fall; and we would peer into the sky for the small white specks of parachutes. Then, with cowardly relief, we watched the planes move off towards some other target which they would shatter with their bombs, and the carriage came to life again.

Motchane was very optimistic at the end of this April (we were dining at his place with Mathieu). He foresaw the Wehrmacht's disintegration. Perhaps he had got wind of what was to become the unsuccessful 20th July attempt on Hitler's life? I myself was worried because Eluard had told me something that afternoon which was a threat to our publications: having been unable to discover anything about us (thanks to our obstinate prudence) and consequently to lay hands on us, the Germans had conceived the diabolical idea of discrediting us by an indirect attack which we could not parry: they were printing fake editions of the Midnight Press! With the purpose of spreading in our name the sort of veiled propaganda that could be imagined. What could we do against it? How could we expose the fraud?

To make me forget my worries, Mathieu told more anecdotes. He had sent one of his agents, a big fellow with a beard who was in need of a hide-out, to some friendly monks who made it their business to find a bed in private lodgings for young men on the run: tracked Resisters, escaped prisoners or crashed airmen. The agent was received, on their recommendation, by 'a perfect gentleman'. But the only bedroom in the house contained just one bed. And he had some difficulty getting to sleep in that bed, at least until he had used his fists to put his too enterprising host in place. The kindly monks had no idea that they were purveyors of young flesh to an affable connoisseur of Grecian love, who had shrewdly calculated that his victims would be hard put to decamp after curfew, and even more so to make a scene . . .

Every week we dreaded seeing the bogus Editions de Minuit books appear. But nothing happened. Until we learned one day, roaring with laughter, the very Teutonic cause of their failure to come out.

The whole run of the first volume had been duly delivered to Hachette, the official distributing agency. Eighty thousand copies in all! Lest they appear insufficiently 'clandestine', the printer's end-note bore a conspicuously phony censorship permit: No. 00002. Hachette had seized on this to demand a written order to distribute, so as to be covered. This put the Germans in a spot: a written order would put an end to their alleged 'clandestinity' and lead to indiscretions which would upset the apple-cart. But without something in writing, how could they compel Hachette to expose themselves to prosecution for illegal distribution? They never managed to find a way out of this dilemma, and at the Liberation the eighty thousand copies were still stocked in Hachette's basement . . .

Even had these books seen the light of day, they would have done us no great harm. What imbecile had been charged with this amazing production? The contents alone were laughable enough: a rehash of the prophecies of Nostradamus, full of dark hints of Britain's imminent doom, so inane that one almost wished to see them circulate. As to the cover of this rubbish, it was so outrageously ugly and so utterly unlike our own covers that the dullest layman would have smelled a rat a mile off.

This heartening blunder was soon followed by another. The British and Americans were marking time in Italy, unable to get beyond Naples. In the last days of May a huge poster appeared on the walls of Paris, showing the tip of Italy's boot, and on it a snail painted in Allied colours. The bill-sticker's paste was not yet dry when we learned of the capture of Cassino, soon followed by that of Rome. And grinning Parisians watched the bill-posters removing their handiwork with the utmost haste . . . .

June 4th. Already the broadcasts from London were multiplying their code messages, sending out twenty or thirty at a time: 'Albert's braces are too tight, twice. We repeat: Albert's braces . . . ' There was no doubt that the Resistance movement was being got ready for the big battle. But when? And where? Denmark or the Cotentin? We were seething with impatience. And when, after a last message: '*Le premier accroc coûte deux cents francs*' (The first cut costs two hundred francs), I woke on the morning of June 6th in the bright country sunshine, with the scent of freshly mown hay wafted through the open window, and heard on the radio the wonderful news so long awaited and so often delayed, my excitement was tempered with worried disappointment: why in Normandy? Why so far from the Cotentin's waist? I had no idea that the success of the landing depended on the fabulous construction, in a single night, of a vast artificial port—operation 'Mulberry'—and that Arromanches was the nearest beach-head on which it could be established. Nevertheless, I was not fully reassured until two months later when Patton's troops, forcing a break-through at Avranches after many setbacks and casualties, at last cut off the peninsula.

These worries about which I could do nothing were swelled by

others about which I *could*. We argued about them at Yvonne's
flat with Eluard, Debu-Bridel, all the others. Henceforward, the
battle was for Liberation. The whole of the Resistance forces
would be geared for this fight. All efforts must aim at striking the
enemy's war machine. The whole clandestine press would be
mobilized for this purpose, to direct the armed struggle, organize
acts of sabotage, reinforce the people's militia, coordinate the
forces of the two armed Resistance groups, the F.F.I. (*Forces Françaises de l'Intérieur*) and the F.T.P. (*Francs-Tireurs Partisans*), prepare
in detail the insurrectional strikes. In the circumstances, should
we, could we still contemplate publishing books in defence of
'spiritual purity'? Had the moment not come for us, too, to raise
the call for battle and revolt?

At Yvonne's flat the argument raged with some heat. Opinions
were divided. I gave my own: by all means let us scuttle ourselves
and let each one, individually, get into the fray. But let us not at
the last moment deflect the Midnight Press from its initial purpose
which it could not now disown, even for the best possible cause,
without weakening its original meaning. Eventually it was decided
that no more manuscripts should be accepted or sent to set, but we
would still publish those written and received before the Allied
landing, out of fairness to the authors involved. Moreover, a one-
page advertisement of our titles, boldly slipped into the latest,
perfectly official issue of the *Bibliographie de France*, the booksellers'
trade paper, had just announced them quite calmly to bookshops
all over the country . . . .

From now on we were all in a fever of excitement. In joy and
hope, but also in fear and trembling. This time the Apocalypse
was upon us. The Allies were advancing at the cost of mountains of
ruins, the Germans multiplied arrests, tortures, executions, acts of
terror. The annihilation of Mortain reminded us that we had all
planned—Yvonne, Léon, my family and I—to go there for a while
on account of its greater food facilities. Our duties, by keeping us
in Paris, had probably saved our lives. In Tulle, the Nazis had
strung up from trees and balconies ninety-nine innocent people,
termed terrorists for the occasion, to the accompaniment of dance
music. In the north a troop train was derailed at midnight, with
little harm to anyone. Sabotage or accident? The Germans did not
bother to find out: half an hour later, the entire railway personnel

at Ascq was dead. At 1 a.m. all the male population—boys, adults and old men—were dead too. Next day, the field-marshal and head of the state went to salute the victims of an American bombardment. Of the slaughtered people of Ascq, not a word. One morning, the charming, peaceful little hamlet of Oradour was encircled by the SS. division, *Das Reich*. We learned of the ensuing massacre through an eye-witness account which Georges Duhamel obtained for *Les Lettres Françaises* and which Eluard reproduced in the *Eternelle Revue*. All the inhabitants of Oradour-sur-Glane were assembled outside the village hall. The Germans first took all the men away and shot them. Then, while the houses were set on fire one by one, the women, children and old people were herded into the church, over which cans of petrol had been emptied, and burnt alive in the blazing edifice. The next day, the field-marshal and head of the state went to salute the victims of a British bombing raid. Of Oradour, not a word. Nor of Beaufort, Saint-Nizier, Liverdun, Saint-Gingolph, La Chapelle-en-Vercors.

Unfortunately our indignation, grief and anger were not caused by one side alone. One day Henriette Gröll, the painter-wife of Pierre Dalloz for whom, some time before, I had procured contacts enabling him to leave for Algiers, read me a letter from her husband; it had arrived goodness knows how, and its bitterness distressed her: *I am a field of ruins*, he wrote. Neither she nor I knew that he had gone there to demand arms for the *maquis* of the Vercors, whose founder he was with Yves Farge and Jean Prévost. All he had been able to obtain were vague promises, and he knew that without arms the mightiest *maquis* of France would be wiped out. He knew that his friends would die and that he could do nothing to prevent it, for over there he was fighting against shadows.

And indeed, after foiling a Panzer division and several mountain regiments and keeping many another fighting unit away from the battlefields of Normandy by virtue of the threat they represented in the rear, the six thousand *maquisards* of the Vercors ran out of ammunition and heavy arms. They searched the sky for planes that would drop the anxiously-awaited containers over the plateau. Ah! there they were at last! . . . But 'they' were a fleet of German gliders which disgorged a whole army of SS. From forest to forest, from cave to cave, our fighters were hounded by enemy forces far superior in numbers and equipment. Jean Prévost—'Captain Goderville'—came and went, holding the Germans at bay for a long time. At night, in the cavern which was his command post, he discussed philosophy and literature with his friends and worked on an exhaustive study of Baudelaire; in the morning he resumed the fight. In the end, being almost alone, he had to break out. He knew the country like the back of his hand. He was actually within sight of Sassenage, where Pierre Dalloz had his house, when a German patrol suddenly appeared in the ravine which he was following. He was shot down on the spot. Infuriated by this prolonged resistance, the Germans wreaked vengeance for their casualties by burning down the villages and finishing off the wounded.

Amid the turmoil and bloodshed of so many gigantic events in this war which rocked the universe and its oceans, the disastrous abandonment of the Vercors illustrated the extent to which politics and rivalries had already infiltrated the camp of Fighting France; the forces of the exterior already resented those of the interior, sentiments were no longer pure, hope mingled with doubt, trust with suspicion, and as Liberation drew near, everything that during the past four years had seemed so limpid began to get cloudy and blurred like curdling milk. The Resistance which Jean Moulin had so painstakingly unified—a unity still symbolized by our volume *Péguy-Péri* published at the end of June—split again into rival political factions, already preparing the ground for their future access to power, even shooting it out amongst themselves at times.

As with the groups, so it was with individuals. While Patton's army advanced along the Loire and might perhaps outflank Paris, new clandestine papers suddenly began to mushroom. Everyone discovered that he had always been a resister at heart, was determined to have his own 'war news bulletin'. *En avant* ('Forward') launched its first issue in June, *L'Honneur de la police* ('The Pride of the Police Force') in July, *La France de demain* ('The France of Tomorrow') opened with a long disquisition on . . . the causes of the defeat of France. *Délivrance* ('Deliverance') came out in August, the *Official Gazette of the F.F.I.* appeared in Paris on the eve of the insurrection, *La Revue noire* ('The Black Review')—edited by the quondam author of a luxurious album devoted to Pétain—actually came out a few weeks *after* Liberation . . . These were the famous 'September resisters' . . . I was defeated on my own home-ground.

I should have liked the Editions de Minuit to close down at the Liberation, its very name—the Midnight Press—imposed this obligation. Besides, we were not professionals, we had no capital: if we did not raise funds, we should soon be paralysed; and if we did, the business would not take long to slip from our hands . . . But the opposite view carried the day. At least I wanted Vercors to preserve his incognito; but it was explained to me that he had no right to, that there would be need of him.

Need: I sensed the threatening degradation implied in that word. Once again we should have 'need' of another, each one would 'need' his neighbour for this or that, to be upheld, defended, to climb on the back of a third party. Whereas during those four years all we had had to give one another was loyalty and faith, with death perhaps at the end of the road. Nothing else, nothing more. Our common misfortune had stripped us naked, all we knew of one another was a face, the sound of a voice, rarely a name (which must be forgotten), mostly a false identity so short-lived and change-able that it was no more than a sign, a reference mark. In this loneliness and nakedness the underground fighter saw a good part of his own self dissolve: the part which society had fashioned and used for its own advantage. All that remained to him in its pure state, the only residue, was whatever inner nobility he possessed.

Whereas now, when our struggle and our anonymity would soon be over, when each would once more represent a social factor to be reckoned with, a help or a hindrance, and while professional intriguers would slip in with all their paraphernalia of high office, decorations, promises, promotions and veiled threats; now that we should once more be daily witnesses of the ambitions of one, the frailty of another, the calculation indulged in by all, I was forced to recognize, already with a hint of poignant nostalgia, how happy we had been . . . Bereavement, misery, rage, tears, anguish for friends, and yet happiness. Should I be ashamed to admit it? In our common distress, but also in our common determination, our fervour, our innermost exaltation, the knowledge that these feelings we shared were pure and selfless had stirred deep within us some-thing ample and alive, hidden but winged, and what else could we call this sentiment but happiness? It was the only true happiness in the world, I discovered: to feel the beat of a noble heart in those one loves. The rest is mere illusion.

Our reward for all we had done was this happiness. And I knew that henceforward any other kind would seem to me insipid. Success, honours? I knew what they were worth and that they were primarily a trap in which nobility risked its neck. One Thursday in July, Debu-Bridel had said to me: 'Since you know Vercors, tell me something I've been asked about: is he a suitable candidate for the French Academy?' I don't know which made me laugh more: having to answer, with those two eighty-page stories to my credit: 'No, honestly, I don't think so!' (and Debu stared in surprise at seeing me laugh) or the realization that people were already busy with their little games, and that forty elderly gentlemen were getting worried at not being 'in the swim'. Not that I despise the Academy, but at a time like that it seemed such a ludicrous pre-occupation! Shortly after Liberation, Georges Duhamel welcomed me at our first meeting with the words: 'Ah, Vercors! How you interest me! Like you, I found sudden fame after the last war, and like you, it was due to a single book. Make the most of it, believe me! Never again will fame be as pure as it is at this moment. Later you'll have to fight to keep it.' As I had not the least desire to fight for it, I was forewarned of what to expect, and what indeed came about just as my elder had foreseen.

Under a sunny, almost constantly blue summer sky, the Allies were advancing on Paris. Increasingly, our lives were permeated by violence. In June the Milice had murdered Jean Zay, a pre-war Minister of Education; a week later it was the turn of the hateful Minister of Propaganda, the sinister Philippe Henriot, with his enormous projecting ears and his insinuating voice, who was shot dead in his bed in the middle of Paris by a Resistance commando; another week, and the Milice's vengeance was turned against Georges Mandel, whom the Germans handed over to his killers. Another week or so, and Hitler narrowly escaped the attempt on his life plotted by his generals. Rommel committed suicide, Stulp-nagel was hanged. In quick succession, we learned that Benjamin Crémieux had died 'of extreme exhaustion' at Buchenwald, and that Saint-Exupéry had disappeared somewhere in the sky between Provence and Algeria. The Germans were driven out of Rennes, Orléans, Alençon . . . Never had there been such a peculiar atmos-phere at our weekly meetings; it was something like the last days at

school before breaking-up, when you already feel half on holiday
and the last lessons, the last homework don't really count any more.
We were busy publishing our final volumes, the second number of
Forbidden Chronicles, Dans la Prison ('In Prison') by Guéhenno, the
writings of Pierre Bost, George Adam without being sure that the
last two would have time to appear or be distributed before the
Occupant's departure . . . .

But the Allies were marking time along the river Avre. One
Thursday in August, at Yvonne's, we were waiting for Debu-Bridel
and worrying about his being late. The atmosphere was bad:
arrests had snowballed frighteningly during the last few weeks;
for the first time I felt the net tightening around us, and we strained
our ears more and more for noises on the staircase. Any day I
expected to hear that Mathieu had been arrested, his freedom
henceforward was a sheer miracle. And still Debu did not arrive!
And this just when news had come of the deportation to Germany
of one of the leaders of his network, Tristan *alias* Pierre-Henri
Teitgen, whose father Henri and brother Paul had already been
deported. Trainloads of Jews and Resisters multiplied in proportion
to the arrests. On returning to Villiers the week before, one of
these trains had overtaken ours, a succession of cattle-trucks
curiously followed by an old third-class carriage, its windows
criss-crossed with rough iron bars. Through them I had caught
sight of a pair of magnificent but fear-strained eyes, staring at me
out of a very young, poignantly beautiful face. A little farther on
a man had extended his two hands through the bars, and they
waved to us like the wings of a trapped bird, in a sort of frantic
farewell. At the station in Lagny we found the train again, at a halt.
Following some attempt to escape or pass on a message, a dozen
Jews were made to get off the train, strip, and race naked under a
volley of lashing whips. When our train moved off, I could have
thought it empty, so heavy with humiliated distress was the silence
in my packed compartment.

When I reached Villiers, I learned that one of the village boys,
who had operated a clandestine radio though I never knew it,
had been shot dead while trying to escape through a window, a few
steps away from our house; the Gestapo's direction-finding cars
were busily spotting the secret transmitters; groups of resistance
fighters were being tracked down and shot by firing-squads on the

plateau, in the forest. I had prepared an emergency exit for myself, though without much confidence, in anticipation of receiving a visit from these gentlemen. And during all this time the Allies were pinned down before Verneuil, where they appeared to have run into trouble; if they did not arrive soon, we should have had it. It would have been best to join the real *maquis*, but since it had been decided that we should carry on with the books in course of production, there could be no question of it. And there we were waiting for Debu-Bridel with mounting anxiety; we did not admit it of course, but the conversation languished, the silences lasted and lasted . . . The door-bell rang. Was it Lebourg, or . . . ? One of us went to open. A sigh: it was he all right.

He apologized. He had cycled over to see his family near Dreux and had lingered a little before coming back. But he brought us fantastic news, he said: he had met *nobody* on his way back to Paris. Did we grasp the fact? Not one German soldier. As he neared the front, he had expected at any moment to have to turn into a side-road to avoid the troops, lorries, artillery, supplies, which he feared he might find all over the main road. But no! He had been able to ride along it unimpeded all the way. Not a soul. A complete vacuum. Behind the thin battle-line there was no German Army any more.

We could hardly believe him. What did it mean? If it were true, then the Allies could arrive any day now. It did in fact take them some weeks more which, after this surge of hope, seemed to us interminable. Their air raids assumed gigantic proportions. Constantly kept informed by the group *Résistance-Fer*—the railwaymen of all ranks, from the lowliest lampman to the engineer-in-chief— the British and Americans were systematically bombing convoys, reinforcements, supplies. Throughout a whole night, the uninterrupted explosions set the sky over La Villette alight with an inferno of fireworks. The blaze was so terrific that, though I felt no conscious fear in face of this rather remote danger, I had nevertheless been unable to prevent my knees from shaking convulsively.

Next day, there was a sharp alarm: far from giving up, the Gestapo were frantically busy. Early in the morning, four men and a woman barged into Blondin's printing-works. By chance, he happened to be away. They searched his office, the works, unearthed from a drawer some rubber stamps which had been used for faking ration-cards and, pleased with their find, left again after affixing seals on the doors. But they had failed to discover either the type of the *Lettres Françaises* or the thousands of sheets of *Freedom Calls* by George Adam, our last volume . . . For the review, this merely involved some delay in publication: it was entirely re-set elsewhere, and was on public sale at the barricades during the week of the uprising. With regard to the book, the matter was more ticklish, since we had to recover the printed sheets to get them to the binder. So one of the final activities of the Midnight Press was to organize a 'burglary' in the premises under seal. The operation was successful and the book was distributed on the day after General Leclerc's troops entered liberated Paris.

The acts of sabotage multiplied, the Resistance everywhere was blowing up bridges, factories, transformers. In three weeks *Résistance-Fer* alone destroyed more locomotives than Allied bombs in three months. In my village, all the able-bodied men were obliged to take it in turns to guard the high-tension pylons against possible attacks. The difficulty was—and the Germans were no more able to resolve it than they could resolve the problem of the bogus Editions de Minuit—that the pylons had to be defended with our bare hands, since it was of course strictly forbidden for the population to carry arms. All we were allowed was a club, whereas the saboteurs were armed with sub-machine-guns. So everything was settled *en famille*: the men on watch brought a rope with them, and the Resisters tied them up, after which the pylon could be blown up without their having to pay for their passivity with deportation. I did not even have to be bound, since nobody came during my hours on duty. The butcher was not so lucky, and preferred to disappear for a while. This deprived us of meat: ever since the night when I permitted him to slaughter an ox clandestinely in the barn where my old Ford was sleeping, he had let us have some meat. We had watched him arrive at dusk by way of the barred wicket-gate between our garden and the park of the château, dragging the wretched beast with the help of his aides. We had sent the boys to bed and heard, until midnight, an awful racket of muffled blows coming from the barn. The next morning, there was not a trace of the murder left.

Each night now I heard the drone of a light plane in the sky above our house, followed by the din of an aerial dog-fight. Soon we knew that it was a British Mosquito on its daily hunt for prey over Voisins, two miles away as the crow flies, where an aerodrome

was used by the German air force. And every night he shot down
a plane or two.

One evening, when the fight above had just broken out, I heard
the siren-like scream which a plane makes when it dives down on
you, while a dramatic glow illuminated my shutter-slats. A second
later came the explosion. I leaped to the window, a swirl of flames
rose just beyond the trees, while the ammunition continued to
explode intermittently amid the blaze. I did not know whether it
was a German or a British plane (next day they discovered the
charred remains of twenty high-ranking Nazi officers), I remained
transfixed at my window for quite a while, and then, well what?
Any rescue attempt was impossible, the plane was now burning
soundlessly, I went back to bed and, aided by the silence, even fell
asleep in the end.

But another silence had long kept me awake: the awful silence
in my heart. It had throbbed a little, perhaps, but not really very
much. And I was horrified to recognize its slow degradation, its
passive acceptance of what, till recently, would have kept it awake
for a week: those fierce battles, those millions of dead, those wholesale destructions in which the heritage of centuries was engulfed
together with irreplaceable things of beauty. And more than ever
I loathed the Nazis, the Germans, for what they had made of us,
for this moral decay in which the noblest elements of the best were
constantly corrupted. For I was obliged to recognize that we were
now in the grip of feelings which I had been wont to abhor: hatred,
and the urge to kill and avenge, and the satisfaction of seeing the
enemy suffer, and this icy indifference towards the too-numerous
dead.

Of course I hoped that these contemptible feelings would fade
after the Nazis' defeat, but we were already too far gone for the
horrors around us to appal us to the same degree. This cooling
of the heart is the curse of old age, which is no longer capable of
feeling anything with intensity. I knew that in this sense the Nazis
would remain victorious, even after their defeat and disappearance:
because of them, mankind would find that it had aged, even
including its youth. In this ambience of unfeeling old men, how
could a youthful heart awake? The mind of a child can feed only
on the milk offered it by adults, and we should see a young generation
of indifferent sceptics grow up in our image, older at eighteen than

we had been at forty, and blaming us for their desiccation; how could we make them understand the true cause of this evil and point out the real culprits, twenty years after the Nazi reality had died and dissolved? They would not listen to us, and all we could do would be to avert our heads so as not to see ourselves in their eyes.

Events now followed in a headlong rush. The Allies landed at Hyères, and Brosset in his jeep was the first to enter Toulon, his ardour carrying some still-hesitant forces with him. Now he was pushing along the Rhône valley and claimed that from now on all he ever saw of the Germans was their back view. Pétain and all his clique had fled to Sigmaringen. Before running away, the broadcasting buffoon Jean-Hérold Paquis had spouted for the last time, with obstinate rage which he took for elegance, his catch-phrase: 'England, like Carthage, will be destroyed', and then shut up for good. The ceaseless air raids round the capital had made it impossible to get there by train. The telephone and telegraph were cut, the wires dangled between the uprooted poles in inextricable tangles. Motor-cars filled with Germans, streaked along the roads on their eastward flight; it was their turn now to carry protective mattresses and prams on their roofs; the families were being evacuated. Often a *feldgrau* sat on the mudguard, with a tommy-gun in his fist and a scared look in his eyes, for the *maquisards* were everywhere.

There was nothing for it but to try to get to Paris on my bicycle. This was risky because I was supposed to have handed it in, and the penalty for disobeying the requisitioning order was prison. Like most people, I had taken good care not to obey, but to ride it to Paris was asking for trouble. Thereupon Léon Motchane turned up one morning, all alone at the wheel of a black Citroën. He was naturally close-mouthed about the origin of his *Ausweis*, but I suspected that this might not be unconnected with the attempt on Hitler's life (might not one of the conspirators, feeling himself a little too compromised, have been anxious to be helped into Switzerland?). Léon intended to be back within forty-eight hours, would take the same road, pick me up in passing and then bring Yvonne back to their cottage near by: no point in the women staying in the capital when the critical moment came.

So I should not be seeing my family again before the Liberation. But I wasn't going to have them learn from the press and radio about my doings. To be sure, the machine of the Nazi repression was still functioning like a robot, like the broom of the sorcerer's apprentice, with a bovine obstinacy. But if I was unlucky enough to receive a visit here from the Gestapo on the eve of our liberation, my last-minute revelations would hardly worsen my case . . . So I simply gave my books to my wife and my mother to read, without any further explanation: *Le Silence de la Mer* to the former, who would recognize our home, and to the latter *La Marche à l'Etoile*, with its portrait of my father. I had the feeling that an ever so slightly injured surprise paralysed my wife a little; but while I was bending over my drawing-table, working on my *Hamlet* plates, I heard soft footsteps gently approaching and felt my temple brushed by a tender, tremulous kiss from my mother, who was too moved to speak. And she withdrew again just as softly, while I enclosed this unspoken reward in my heart.

Why did Motchane, on his way back from Switzerland, decide to reverse his programme? I no longer remember, but the fact remains that he passed through Villiers as promised but did not take me with him: he preferred to fetch Yvonne from Paris first, drive her back here and then leave again with me. On the face of it, this merely altered the order of events by two hours, but in actual fact it was to spoil everything for me. I waited in vain for him to return with Yvonne. The afternoon wore on, so did the night, the next day. Had he, had they both, been arrested on the way? The truth was less alarming: Léon had managed to return to Paris but had been unable to leave again, all the gates being guarded. But this I did not know and could not find out, since all communications with Paris were cut.

So there was nothing for it but to take the bicycle and try my luck. During the night, however, there was an incessant rumbling all around us: hundreds of tanks and lorries were moving along the road to Meaux. In the morning another noise mingled with it: the rumble of distant gunfire. How was I to pass through the re-treating columns without getting 'nicked'? I must wait for a lull. But there was no lull, the rumbling along the main road increased hourly. No doubt about it, this was the army in full retreat. Would Paris be outflanked and fall without a fight, like a ripe fruit? I had no idea that in the meantime the insurrection had broken out in Paris. I only learned it from the BBC that evening. What a blow! I must, I must get back! I simply *had* to see this! But my attempt next day to follow side-roads in order to avoid the troops failed at the first cross-roads: I came bang up against the Germans and had barely time to turn back. There was nothing I could do but return to Villiers and champ at the bit.

In the afternoon, the German tanks stopped in the village for a few hours, then trundled on again and took up positions on the other bank of the Morin, opposite the bridge. If they meant to resist, we should be in their line of fire. Fortunately, in anticipation of my departure and a possible struggle for the possession of the village, I had had a trench dug in our garden to serve as a family shelter, by the old grave-digger who was one-eyed, lame, simple-minded and always merry. However, we never needed to make use of it: the next morning the tanks had gone.

The cars which were now racing through the village were crammed with officers. This wasn't even a rout, it was a stampede! The faces were set, the eyes stared straight ahead so as not to see the mocking smiles that escorted them. One day, two days . . . Tuning in to the BBC I heard the pealing of bells: all the bells of London were celebrating the Liberation of Paris! Was it possible? I could not bring myself to rejoice, it seemed so strange to me. And indeed it had been a false report: soon the BBC had to climb down, the insurrection was still going on. There had been negotiations, a cease-fire for a couple of hours; but the Germans were still there, and there was a rumour that Paris was mined, that everything would be blown up. Could I have overcome my inveterate pessimism? For I found this news hard to believe: it would require a whole army of sappers to blow up an agglomeration this size. The bridges, perhaps? So long as there was fighting going on and troops still on the left bank, von Choltitz could not destroy the bridges behind them. Probably, it was just blackmail.[1]

All the next day and the following one I naturally remained

[1]If the authors of *Is Paris Burning?* are to be believed, the officer in charge of blowing up the bridges was called Ebrennac. He probably walked straight out of my *Silence of the Sea!* This name of Gascon Huguenot origin, which was my own invention entirely, cannot be very common in Germany . . . Actually, the bridges were never mined: protection units of the Highways Department went to check them every hour.

glued to the radio. The rumble of the convoys on the road, of the nearest cannon, never stopped for a moment. Towards the end of the third day there were pauses, stretches of prolonged calm, and that evening our charwoman brought us a newspaper. It was entitled *Front National*. It was being sold on the barricades, she said, a villager had just brought a batch of them back from Paris on his bicycle . . . What! So he could get through? Then what was I doing here? If I could, I would have kicked my own backside for not having tried, tried and tried again until I succeeded in my attempt to pass through the army columns. It was late now, night had almost fallen, but tomorrow first thing . . .

The next day it was all over: Paris was really liberated. The insurrection was victorious, the bells this time rang out for good. All the bells of Paris. I listened to them relayed by the BBC with, now and then, a muffled burst of rifle fire—there were still pockets of resistance, and Milice snipers on the roofs. My joy was intense and profound, or rather my excitement was: true joy was another vanished feeling, like the exultation, the rapture which uplifts your whole body in a frenzy of delight: that form of joy, of elation, would never more inhabit my heart, it was dead for good, killed by the Nazis. There remained a grave, powerful emotion, the happiness of hearing those bells in full peal. But also, simultaneously, a grief, an irremediable regret: it was too late, the insurrection had been fought and won without me.

I should never know those fabulous hours, the chains shaken off in a popular rejoicing, the sandwich devoured with gusto on the barricade, the pride of imposing one's will on the surprised oppressor, the werewolf suddenly turned into a hare frantically scurrying to escape, panicking, falling from trap to trap. I should never know the Paris which had arisen from the past to live again its most thrilling pages, the arrival of Leclerc's tanks before the City Hall, the crowd and its delirious welcome. The Paris I should find would be a Paris after the act of love, a little languid and all passion spent. . . . Was there even any urgency for me to go there? I no longer knew, I hesitated, the desire gone out of me. I should hate to be part of what was going to happen there now, that vanity fair on the market-place which I had foreseen and feared. Whatever had been said to the contrary, no one had 'need' of me any longer. How many of those out there, in the hustle of resurgent life, sincerely desired my presence? How many wanted me to return, how many didn't care either way, how many considered me already as a possible, unwanted rival? In the revival of political battles, the come-back of political parties, of tendencies and ideologies, how many would deny me thrice before the cock crowed? I seemed to feel the fraternal happiness of those four years fading, abandoning me . . . Have no illusions, my friend: when the play is over, the curtain falls on the stage. What would you do there? Better to imitate Candide and go and cultivate your garden.

But the sky above the garden was like a vast drum beating a tattoo. Planes streaked across it in all directions, they were fighting up there and bullets, splinters hit the roof-tiles. I forbade the children to go out. The cannon thundered, shells passed whining overhead and pelted the hill opposite. Time passed, we must have lunch, we passed the plates amid this concert of caterwauling, but the boys, seeing us calm, did not worry. If the danger came closer, there would be time to take them down to the trench.

All at once, silence struck our ears like a shell-burst. The gunfire had suddenly stopped. Every moment we expected it to start up again, but no, quiet had really been restored. Then, at some distance the sudden din of dive-bombing. Curiosity drove us outside, and from the terrace, with our elbows on the low wall (or at least that part of it which the twins had not yet managed to demolish) we watched from afar the utter destruction of a German military convoy on the road to Meaux which was visible along the crest of the hill facing us; its lorries were brought to a standstill between the poplars and, one after the other, burst into flames. This smelt more like a rout than a retreat under a sky so blue, so calm, above the meadows . . . The contrast was startling; the mêlée of trucks and planes up there looked from a distance, behind the little blobs of trees lined up in an orderly, horizontal row, like a toy, a children's game. Yet there must be casualties, dead and wounded, there must be screams no doubt, bloodshed and suffering. But the imagination boggled, and once again I was astonished at my absence of pity. Would it return some day? A little later, it seemed to us that we could catch sounds and movement coming from the village below. We saw a neighbour coming up the hill with great strides, waving to us. As soon as she was within hailing distance, she shouted to us breathlessly: 'They're here!'—'Who?'—'The Americans!'

We did not believe her at first. We thought they were still so far away! But now, all along the footpaths, like so many processions of ants, men, women and children came walking, all heading for the main road to the West. We too followed one of these processions, walking across fields, meadows, orchards, ploughed land . . . Still nothing. Suppose it were a hoax? There was the main road, perfectly empty. But at the crossroads an enormous truck had stopped. A huge fellow in battledress climbed down from it. He was a Negro, covered with dust. I was pleased that our first liberator from the Nazis should be a Negro. He asked some questions, his way no doubt, but could not manage to make himself understood. He scrambled back into his truck and left in a great clatter.

For the time being, 'the Americans' were reduced to a score of men behind a battery dispersed at the four corners of a field on the other side of the road. In front, behind, to the right, to the left, there was nothing. They looked to me rather isolated, but this did not seem to bother them in the least. They were chatting among themselves, allowing people to come close with obvious indifference, handing out chewing-gum to the kids without so much as giving them a glance, as if it were a habit that had become automatic. Peculiar little cars equipped with aerials, low on wheels which seemed to me no bigger than dinner-plates, half toy, half tractor, went from one gun to another; we later learned that they were called jeeps.

In the evening the jeeps paraded by hundreds through the festive village in a mist of dust and merriment. But I saw with consternation the feast turning into a big scrounge: some soldiers had thrown tins of food and now a crowd of cadgers flocked round them: women, children, some men too, held out their hands, begged, carried off their booty, came back for more. I turned away, a little sickened.

I should have to go to Paris one of these days. I made up my mind and took my bicycle. I was no longer a youngster, so I decided to leave at 8 a.m. to be sure of arriving before noon. I pedalled at an easy pace. I expected some difficulties, perhaps there would be American lines to get through. But the road was deserted and I didn't meet a living soul. By nine I was already half way there. Was I, with no effort at all, managing more than fifteen miles per hour? I was rather pleased with this performance, but found it surprising . . . At ten o'clock I was riding through the Bois de Vincennes. In Rue de Charenton I had to wheel my bicycle past a barricade that was still intact (the only one I was to see). It was not quite half past ten when I reached Rue Servandoni. My buttocks ached a bit but otherwise I felt fine. I telephoned Yvonne Desvignes and Motchane answered.

'You at last! Why, you're awaited like the Messiah! Don't you listen to the radio?'

Apparently, since yesterday, the radio had been sending out repeated urgent calls for Vercors. I realized that in those four years I had grown so used to listening to London and ostracizing Paris Radio that I had kept it up automatically . . . Léon Motchane told me that I should go that very morning to the National Writers' Committee's first session in freedom: they were meeting in one of the former offices of *Paris-Soir*, now taken over by *Les Lettres Françaises*. This would be my first personal appearance; so far Yvonne Desvignes had always represented me. I got there a little before the meeting so as to talk to Claude Morgan, the secretary. I wanted to explain to him my reluctance to become a member of this committee; my double identity Desvignes-Vercors made me unwilling to join, for I wanted to preserve an independence of mind which, as a member of a group less literary than political, I should necessarily lose.

He raised an outcry. On the contrary, Vercors *must* become a member, and take part. His absence would puzzle people and lead to awkward misinterpretations. I gave in (and once again I was wrong: for I was to be led, through *esprit de corps*, to give my consent to all sorts of things that were not to my liking and to end up, worse luck, as the Committee's window-dress president and eventual scapegoat). Morgan thanked me and sent for Claude Roy to interview me for *Front National*. When he learned who I was, he goggled under his ginger mop, and stared at me as if I were an apparition. His first question was: 'What impression does it make to find oneself overnight a "great French writer"?' Should I tell him: 'None at all?' Oh, how I should have liked to feel just a little 'intoxicated'! But something had evidently given way inside me, and I couldn't manage it. Moreover, I had seen too often how ephemeral celebrity could be, how quickly it could fade with the circumstances that had produced it: in two years from now I should be forgotten. Friends came in, Jean Tardieu, Lucien Scheler, who knew me only as Desvignes. They were warmly cordial to Vercors. In came Debu-Bridel, now the director of the newspaper *Front National*. He flung himself on me: 'This time don't laugh, Vercors! You'll be in the Academy!' Indeed I did not laugh: if he went on like this in public, he would make me ridiculous. The room filled up, the writers arrived one after the other. Duhamel confided to me his 'How you interest me! . . . ' Mauriac congratulated me in his toneless voice on *La Marche à l'Etoile*, which he said he preferred to *Le Silence de la Mer*. Sartre, Camus shook my hand absent-mindedly; this saddened me a little, for I had hoped for their friendship. Paulhan paid me one of his ambiguous compliments which both amuse and disturb: didn't it hide some wicked little sting? Queneau, Vailland, Blanzat, to all of whom Debu introduced me in superlative style, gave me a vague smile but did not exchange two words with me. What was I doing here? I felt I had few friends in that room and was being made to feel that I did not really belong to the fraternity—a view which the passing years did little to change.

On the other hand, I was presented with a bundle of letters all addressed to me. Newspapers and periodicals insistently requested that I should figure in their first issue. Certain signatories, Resisters of the eleventh hour who had not always been above reproach, referred to our pre-war relations which I did not recall as having been so cordial . . . 'There'll be need of you . . . ' My fears were quickly borne out: I was to serve, above all, as a surety, a guarantor, even as a whitewasher for those in need of 'clearance'. Nothing of this was calculated to assuage my longing for anonymity . . .

When I telephoned my brother-in-law, he made a date for a drink and informed me of the presence in Paris, with the Allied troops, of my old friend, Etienne Dennery (the future ambassador, later director of the *Bibliothèque Nationale*) and his elder brother, Jacques. He had been unable to get hold of Etienne but I found Jacques with him in uniform on the sunny terrace of the Deux-Magots. We embraced each other. 'I know you've done great things,' Jacques said, 'they told me so in London, but I've no idea what they were. What *did* you do?' I saw my brother-in-law open his eyes but he said nothing. The manner in which he was going to learn about it tickled me a little. I answered: 'The Editions de Minuit', and anticipated the next question, like an inevitable ritual.

It came. Jacques jumped in his chair: 'No fooling? That was you? Then you'll be able to tell me who Vercors is?' I smilingly pointed to myself, without saying a word. He did not grasp it at once, and then he trumpeted, 'You're Vercors!' so loudly that I anxiously turned round: was he mad to bellow my name like that, on a café terrace full of people, where certain ears . . . . And then I laughed aloud at my foolishness: for a second I had forgotten that I was no longer in danger of being denounced to the Gestapo. What a deliverance! I savoured this brand-new safety. I also savoured Jacques's pleasure and his excitement: 'Listen, you're not going to tell me you're de Gaulle as well, are you?'

My brother-in-law had not said a word. Later, when he had made enquiries, he was to tell me: 'This is the first time that I see a selfless act receive its reward.'

A message reached me from Yvonne: de Gaulle had invited me to dinner. I dropped in to see her at Léon's flat, behind the church of Sainte-Clotilde, just opposite the Ministry of War in Rue Saint-Dominique where the General was at present residing. Before leaving them, I was given no end of advice, they both catechized me. Yvonne dusted my shoes, brushed my jacket, straightened my tie: I must put up a good show for the sake of our future publishing . . . Ah well, the great adventure was over, I was crossing the line now into ordinary times.

On the pavement, as I was about to step into the dark, empty little square, it suddenly seemed to me immense. I crossed it like a seafaring navigator about to reach the brightly lit harbour after an endless night. Those welcoming lights gladden his heart, yet he does not forget that behind them lurks the only-just-awakening city with all that lies in wait for him: the dusty offices, the smelly, tortuous streets, his own loneliness in the throng. What will he find there after so long a sleep? What defections? What hopes? And as he comes alongside, his hesitant step trembles a little.